FALL OF THE FLYING DRAGON
South Vietnamese Air Force 1973–75

Albert Grandolini

HARPIA
PUBLISHING+

This book is dedicated to my late friend Gilbert. Your always unremitting, incisive analyses and your refusal to be content with accepted, pre-conceived ideas has taught me how to comprehend history and helped me to explore new paths.

Consulting and inspiration by Kerstin Berger
Artworks and drawings by Tom Cooper and Ugo Crisponi
Map by Tom Cooper
Editorial by Thomas Newdick
Layout by Norbert Novak, www.media-n.at, Vienna

Printed at Grasl Druck & Neue Medien, Austria

ISBN 978-0-9825539-7-8

Harpia Publishing, L.L.C. is a member of

FALL OF THE FLYING DRAGON, South Vietnamese Air Force 1973–75

Albert Grandolini

Không Quân Việt Nam

Contents

Preface: In a crimson sky 6

Introduction 9

Acknowledgements 11

Abbreviations 12

Chapter 1: A brief history of the VNAF 15

Chapter 2: Final build-up 33

Chapter 3: The enemy 65

Chapter 4: The pretence of peace 69

Chapter 5: Fighting the poor man's war 95

Chapter 6: Beginning of the end 117

Chapter 7: Abandoning the north 131

Chapter 8: Target Saigon 159

Chapter 9: Last week of war 177

Chapter 10: The great escape 191

Chapter 11: Postscript 215

Appendix I: VNAF order of battle, February 1975 223

Appendix II: VNAF squadron activations 231

Appendix III: VNAF aircraft 1953–1975 233

Appendix IV: Artworks 235

Bibliography 245

Index 249

Preface: In a crimson sky

Dusk, 26 April 1975, and Capt Hung of the 435th Transport Squadron was falling half asleep in his chair in the unit's Operations Room at Tan Son Nhut Air Base. Hung had already flown two attack sorties in the course of the day and was now trying to relax and recuperate from the accumulated stress. For tonight's missions, he was placed in the number three slot on the planned flights board. Suddenly, he was ordered to take the next sortie. Capt Hung protested in vain, guessing why the other two pilots on the schedule had been dropped off. But an order is an order. Hung plotted the route to the intended target, the Thu Duc Reserve Officer School that had recently been evacuated and was now occupied by the enemy. At the start of the North Vietnamese invasion, Hung had been hauling cargo loads, but in these last weeks he had been increasingly involved in bombing missions.

After the catastrophic debacle suffered by South Vietnamese forces in the northern part of the country, the Communist forces had converged towards Saigon. Consequently, the duration of the missions became increasingly brief, as the front lines now extended no more than 60km (37 miles) from the capital. Capt Hung pored over a 1:500,000 tactical map and carefully noted the exact coordinates of the target that would be feed into the BOBS (Beacon-Only Bombing System) calculator. He also plotted the latest Intelligence indications concerning the locations of enemy anti-aircraft emplacements in the area. His navigator informed him that the flight to the target area would not take more than five to seven minutes; then the BOBS would take over for the radar bombardment procedure.

Hung made for the cargo compartment to check his load: some 24 370kg (750lb) bombs installed on six pallets.

After taking off, Hung turned 180 degrees and then climbed to altitude and contacted the Bien Hoa BOBS station – one of two remaining –and waited for his instructions. His controller then locked his aircraft on his radarscope, and then activated the homing beacon.

'Herky 27, turn right, heading zero nine zero. Climb to 22,000ft [6,706m].'

Hung now had to concentrate on flying steadily and exactly on the indicated route. The ground controller plotted his heading, altitude and speed, which were entered into the computer. This calculated the heading to the target, the optimum release point for the designated area to be covered by the bombs, and the type of ammunition with the correct ballistics. The chosen release altitude depended on weather and anti-aircraft threats and usually varied from 15,000 to 22,000ft (4,572 to 6,706m). The C-130A now began turning towards the aimed point and Hung levelled his flight, exactly on the indicated heading. The pilot would now hold the correct course and not deviate by more than one degree. If he was to fly left of the intended course, a continuous 'A' tone in the Morse alphabet would be heard in his headset; if he strayed to right, he would hear a continuous 'N' tone. If the aircraft was to fly away from the target, the pitch would become louder, and the tone would be accelerated. With Hung flying directly towards the release point, the pitch would slow down. The system also warned the pilot if he had over-flown the target without releasing after 10 seconds; this would force him to initiate a new bomb run.

That night, Capt Hung was exhausted. It took him three tries, each of 15 minutes, before he was on the correct track.

'OK, Herky 27. Lead in. On course, do not acknowledge?'

'Attention to the countdown.'

Hung entered two clicks on the button over the yoke to thank the controller. The BOBS computer now began the 10-second countdown. In the cargo compartment, the loadmasters and armourers were ready. A first warning, and the rear ramp was lowered. Ten seconds later, the armourers released the pins that retained the pallets. Capt Hung pushed through to full throttle and grabbed the wheel. The aircraft nosed over while the bombs separated from their pallets and plunged earthwards. They would fall on the targeted area, measuring 100m (328ft) wide by 300m (984ft) in length. Hung could see the flashes from the corner of his eyes, but did not hear the explosions from this altitude.

In the cold night sky, Hung relaxed a little. Surely he had been designated for the sortie because he was considered one of the best pilots in night flying. But were all these efforts still worth it? After decades of war, he now witnessed what appeared to be his country's final agony. Many around him considered the situation hopeless and they began to plan their escape with their families. Over a week earlier the Americans had begun to evacuate their citizens, as well as some South Vietnamese, using C-130 and C-141 transport aircraft. Some high-ranking officials and their relatives had made use of these outbound flights. They were more and more cases of defections and misdemeanours that ignited a chain reaction leading to the current debacle. In the view of many, incompetent and corrupt officials ought to be trialled. Despite this, in the last three weeks the last remaining intact units of the armed forces had stiffened their resistance, and had fought heroically against a much superior enemy, as at Xuan Loc. Still, the politicians seemed remote from the reality, and were unable to nominate a new government after the resign of President Nguyen Van Thieu. They hoped, unrealistically, to negotiate a settlement with the enemy and even to constitute some sort form of 'coalition government' with the Communists.

Every time Hung dropped bombs, he had doubts as to whether any had hit the target – even with the help of the BOBS system. He was increasingly preoccupied with the fighting now taking place directly within Saigon's populated suburbs. How many civilians were also the victims of his bombardments? The suffering of civilians had meanwhile become the terrible law of war. Hung had no doubts that the Communists must be stopped, although the Americans had already decided to abandon his countrymen. But at what price? As a devout Buddhist, he wondered when and how all this suffering would come to an end. He asked his wife to go to temple to pray to Buddha and for the wandering souls. He tried to impose on himself a vegetarian food regime by way of repentance. Hung was not a coward. He always confronted the enemy. He satisfied himself with the idea that his missions at least helped gain time to allow a maximum of people out of the country, should they so wish. But perhaps it was time to consider his own position and the future of his loved ones.

Hung continued to fly offensive sorties for the next two days, with targets moving ever closer to Saigon. When dispatched to bomb a target at Phu Lam, a densely populated area, his Hercules was loaded with 48 125kg (276lb) bombs. The BOBS operator

A VNAF C-130A of the 435th Transport Squadron, 53rd Tactical Wing at Tan Son Nhut. In addition to transport operations, the South Vietnamese Hercules were also engaged in bombing missions during the final weeks of the war. The Hercules was so successful in this role that it was dubbed 'BC-130'. (Pham Quang Khiem Collection)

ordered him to make a single pass, along a north-south axis. Usually, when loaded with such a quantity of bombs, the pilot could make of to three passes. But the instructions in this case were clear. Still, Hung could not help but think about the number of civilian casualties that would be caused by this attack. Until the last moment, he remained perturbed and tried to reassure himself that Intelligence had surely detected a target worthy of destruction. Hung was sombre and did not speak to his co-pilot.

At the last moment, for the first time in his life, Hung decided to disobey an order. The co-pilot seemed to read his mind and tacitly approved. Hung then announced a transponder failure and an abort. The pilots flew their aircraft safely back to Tan Son Nhut Air Base.

The same night, enemy artillery batteries positioned in the area that Hung had been ordered to bomb heavily shelled Tan Son Nhut. The Americans suspended the fixed-wing air bridge and were forced into a chaotic helicopter evacuation. Many of the people that could have been extracted from the air base were now stranded. Perhaps if he had bombed the enemy guns as ordered, the evacuation operations could have gained a few more precious hours. That might have allowed more refugees and aircraft to be evacuated.

For years, Hung would be haunted by the decision he made that night.

Introduction

After a blitzkrieg-style offensive, the fall of Saigon into North Vietnamese hands on 30 April 1975 occurred so suddenly that it stunned many military observers. The failure of the massive South Vietnamese armed forces – with more than a million men – to stop the Communist advance appeared to indicate that the institution was a costly hollow body, badly led and poorly motivated. The performance of the Vietnamese Air Force (VNAF) was the subject of even greater disappointment. With over 2,000 aircraft in its arsenal, including 400 fighter jets, it ranked among the most powerful in the world. Indeed, the VNAF was considered the cornerstone of South Vietnam's defence strategy, its main asset against an enemy with far lesser capabilities in this field.

Many of these critical observations were valid, and revealed the flawed military organisation of the South Vietnamese. Furthermore, it was combined US and South Vietnamese air power that had played a critical role in derailing the previous two major North Vietnamese offensives of 1968 and 1972. The departing Americans had seemingly made great efforts to hand over responsibility for air power to the VNAF. Its failure in 1975 therefore tended to be interpreted along the lines that a sophisticated tool such an air force could not easily be handed over to a third-ranking player.

However, these criticisms do not fully explain why the fall of the VNAF happened in the way that it did. And critics have tended to overlook the courage and dedication of most of the VNAF airmen who valiantly fought until the bitter end.

For years, the myth of VNAF incompetence coloured most historical records. Furthermore, most Western historians tended to conclude their studies at the date of the US departure from Southeast Asia, at the beginning of 1973. It is true that archival records beyond that date tend to be rare and difficult to exploit. The US maintained only a skeleton Defense Attaché Office (DAO) to overlook the dwindling aid that was supporting South Vietnam. The DAO provides a precious source of information on this closing stage of the conflict for anyone willing to investigate.

The downfall of the VNAF was in fact interrelated to the wider context of the end of the Vietnam War, as well as the manner in which Washington managed its gradual withdrawal from the area. From these particular points of view, one must comprehend why the VNAF was organised as it was, why it grew as an institution, how it was developed within the framework of the so-called 'Vietnamization' policy, and how it was adapted to the challenges of facing the new North Vietnamese strategy of conventional war.

For an historian, perhaps the most difficult requirement is to avoid the natural tendency to view events through the prism of their own cultural background. Most Western readers have become accustomed to see the Vietnam War from the bias of the American point of view. Since the end of the conflict, however, the 'other side' – the Communist-ruled North Vietnam – has produced hundreds of books and studies, presenting their own points of view and analyses. Unfortunately, most of these works have remained confined to Vietnam, mainly due to language and political barriers. Correlating these sources against Western publications represents a fresh approach to historical research. It is an approach that sheds light on many aspects of the final phase of VNAF operations.

However, while both the Americans and the North Vietnamese are now able to present their own sides of the story, the same is not the case for the South Vietnamese. There is no official historical record for this 'lost' nation. The memory of non-communist Vietnam is carefully erased within today Socialist Republic of Vietnam, and only limited historical records – compiled without official support and in an 'underground' fashion – have been retained by the Vietnamese Diaspora living in exile. Grouped in associations, former VNAF airmen had to struggle to establish a new life in the United States, Europe or Australia. For a long time, they tended to forget their difficult past and instead work hard to secure their future and that of their families. It is only now that some of them are bringing their own experiences from the war to light, some in order to reveal their own perspectives of history, and others to honour their fallen comrades.

Albert Grandolini
August 2011

Acknowledgements

It was many years ago that the idea of writing a book documenting the final chapter of the air war in Vietnam came to my mind. Such a book would recount the fall of Saigon, an event that I personally experienced. However, the difficulty of finding reliable sources, as well as the efforts to locate the actors involved in these events made the project a challenging undertaking. Many former VNAF personnel who survived the ordeal were too busy rebuilding their lives in a foreign land, than to remember a painful past that had seen their defeat. Plenty of patience and a careful approach were required to piece together the numerous fragments of the past – a past that has also been not infrequently distorted.

During all these years, I managed to assemble various new documents that emerged from declassified US files, memoirs written by former South Vietnamese officers, and even from the Communist side. Some of the former South Vietnamese pilots I interviewed wanted to set the record straight by providing their own viewpoint of the war. The associations of former VNAF officers, often organised along chronological lines in respect to order of graduation, and in both France and the United States, have been of great help, providing valuable contacts and sources of information.

In recent years, the development of the internet has led to the creation of VNAF social sites such as Quan Su Khong Viet Nam (VNAF History) and Can Thep (Iron Wings), created by a group of former senior and junior VNAF officers. These are proved to be excellent sources, since the individuals behind them are almost exclusively former VNAF personnel. Also of use was the VNAF MANM website run by the enthusiasts of the VNAF Model Aircraft Club. Few foreign writers know of these organisations' existence, or have ever used them for their research.

Former American or French advisers who served with the VNAF also came to my aid, together with a number of other aviation enthusiasts, who provided documents and photographs, and brought new, fresh approaches to my studies.

To all of those who helped, I wish to offer my sincere thanks.

Specifically, I wish to express my deepest appreciation to Anthony J. Tambini, Cao Tan Loc, Chau Huu Loc, Dang Huy Lang, Do Khac Mai, Gerard Gacoin, Ha Minh Tay, Ho Dac Du, Ha Mai Viet, Huynh Sanh Thong, Huynh Ba Phuc, Huynh Thu Thoai, Jacques Lebourg, Jean Delmas, Jean Dunoyer, Jean Pierre Hoehn, Ken Conboy, Le Quang Thuan, Le Xuan Lan, Leif Hellström, Lennart Lundh, Lon Nordeen, Mai Van Hai, Marc Rostaing, Merle C. Olmsted, Michel Cavenel, Michel Fournier, Mike O'Connor, Nguyen Tien Van, Nguyen Xuan Giac, Nicholas J. Waters III, Norman E. Taylor, Pham Long Suu, Pham Quang Khiem, Phillipe Picollet, Robert C. Mikesk, Roger Cottet, Roger Routin, Stephane Legoff, Ted Koppel, Terry Love, Timothy Keer, Timothy Pham, Tran Tan Tiep, Ung Buu Hoang Nguyen, Victor Flintham, Vo Ngoc Cac and Vu Dinh. I also extend my thanks to those other individuals who did not wish to be named in order to protect their families.

Abbreviations

AA	anti-aircraft
AAA	anti-aircraft artillery
AAM	air-to-air missile
AB	Air Base
AdA	Armée de l'Air (French Air Force)
AFB	Air Force Base
AFRES	(United States) Air Force Reserve
An	Antonov (the design bureau led by Oleg Antonov)
ADS	Air Defence Sector
ALC	Air Logistic Command of the VNAF
ALCC	Airlift Control Centre of the VNAF
ALO	air liaison officer
APC	armoured personnel carrier
ARVN	Army of the Republic of Vietnam, the South Vietnamese Army
ASCC	Air Standardisation Coordinating Committee (US, UK, Australian and New Zealand committee for standardisation of designations for foreign [primarily Soviet] armament; its standardisation codenames are usually known as 'NATO designations')
ATC	Air Training Centre of the VNAF
Brig Gen	brigadier general (military commissioned officer rank)
BOBS	Beacon Only Bombing System
CAP	combat air patrol
Capt	captain (military commissioned officer rank)
CAS	close air support
CBU	Cluster Bomb Unit
CIA	Central Intelligence Agency of the United States
C-in-C	commander in chief
c/n	construction number
CO	commanding officer
COIN	counter-insurgent or counter-insurgency
CRP	control and reporting post
Col	colonel (military commissioned officer rank)
DAO	Defense Attaché Office, the US organisation that controlled military aid to South Vietnam after 1973
DASC	direct air support centre
DMZ	Demilitarized Zone that marked the border between South and North Vietnam along the 17th Parallel
ECM	electronic countermeasures
ELINT	electronic intelligence
FAC	forward air control
FAE	fuel-air explosive (type of weapon)
FFAR	Folding Fin Aircraft Rocket
FLIR	forward-looking infra-red
GCI	ground control interception

Gen	general (military commissioned officer rank)
GOC	general officer commanding
GP	general-purpose (bomb)
HALO	high-altitude, low-opening (computer-aided parachute drops)
HEAT	high-explosive, anti-tank
ICCS	International Commission for Control and Supervision created in 1973
Il	Ilyushin (the design bureau founded by Sergey Vladimirovich Ilyushin)
IR	infra-red
JGS	Joint General Staff of the ARVN
KIA	killed in action
LORAN	long-range navigation system
Lt	lieutenant (military commissioned officer rank)
Lt Col	lieutenant colonel (military commissioned officer rank)
1st Lt	first lieutenant (military commissioned officer rank)
2nd Lt	second lieutenant (lowest military commissioned officer rank)
MACV	Military Assistance Command Vietnam, the US military command in Vietnam before 1973
Maj	major (military commissioned officer rank)
Maj Gen	major general (military commissioned officer rank)
medevac	medical evacuation
MiG	Mikoyan i Gurevich (the design bureau led by Artem Ivanovich Mikoyan and Mikhail Iosifovich Gurevich, also known as OKB-155 or MMZ 'Zenit')
MR	Military Region of the ARVN
OCU	Operational Conversion Unit
OUT	Operational Training Unit
PAVN	People's Army of Vietnam, the North Vietnamese Army
RHAWS	radar homing and warning system
RHWR	radar homing and warning receiver
RoCAF	Republic of China Air Force
RPV	remotely piloted vehicle
SA-2	ASCC codename for S-75, Soviet SAM system
SA-3	ASCC codename for S-125, Soviet SAM system
SA-7	ASCC codename for 9K32 Strela-2, Soviet man-portable air defence system
SAM	surface-to-air missile
SAR	search and rescue
VPAF	Vietnam People's Air Force
STOL	short take-off and landing
TACAN	Tactical Air Navigation
TACS	tactical air control system
TACC	tactical air control centre
TEWS	Tactical Electronic Warfare Squadron of the USAF
USAF	United States Air Force
USMC	United States Marine Corps (includes Marine aviation)
USN	United States Navy (includes US Naval Aviation)
VNAF	Vietnamese Air Force, the South Vietnamese Air Force

Chapter 1

A BRIEF HISTORY OF THE VNAF

The roots of the VNAF date back to the late 1940s when the French granted limited autonomy to the State of Vietnam within the French Union Organisation. The purpose was in fact to mobilise the non-Communist side in a widening civil war, with the aim of supporting the French expeditionary forces in the fight against the Viet Minh insurgents. After protracted political negotiations, Emperor Bao Dai, then in exile in Hong Kong, was accepted as head of a new government in June 1948. At the time, it was hoped to achieve full independence in the foreseeable future. The new state would meanwhile raise its own armed forces. However, the French saw these as merely an auxiliary to their own forces, something little different from the locally raised colonial troops that they traditionally employed. From the start, the ambiguity of this policy had an adverse effect on any Vietnamese military developments. Struggling to achieve full independence and recognition, Vietnam's armed forces had throughout their history to contend with far more powerful 'patrons' – first French then American. As a result, they tended to be seen as little more than an overlooked 'auxiliary' service.

Right from the outset, the Vietnamese sought to create an air force, as a powerful symbol of modernity and independence. This was exacerbated by the fact that the new Vietnamese Army Commander in Chief, Gen Nguyen Van Hinh, had served with the French Air Force during World War II and in Indochina. However, he was not the first Vietnamese to serve as a military aviator.

As early as December 1911, Do Huu Vi became one of the first Asian aviators when he received his wings in France, with Military Flight Certificate number 78. Barely a year later he served with the Escadrille Coloniale in Morocco. The outbreak of World War I saw him recalled to France where he flew numerous observation and bombing missions before being shot down in 1915. Discharged from flying, he was reintegrated in the infantry but killed on 9 July 1916 during a battle in the Dompierre Fort sector.

Many other Vietnamese were to follow between the World Wars, even though the French only trained them as mechanics to serve with the locally based squadrons. Nevertheless, a few of them obtained private civilian pilot licences with the local flying club, including Emperor Bao Dai, as well as Le Van Hoach, a future vice-president of the country. Several were to serve with distinction with the Armée de l'Air during World War II: Nguyen Van Hinh, who badly resented the French defeat of 1940, became an accomplished Douglas B-26 Marauder pilot and later flew Amiot A.A.C. 1s (French-built Junkers Ju 52/3ms) of Groupe de Transport II/62, based in Vietnam.

On 8 March 1949, Emperor Bao Dai issued a decree for the establishment of an air unit. The French, who found the idea 'fanciful', immediately vetoed the project. After heated exchanges, Paris resented and gave its accord, in principle at least – although

Vietnam's first ever pilot was Do Huu Vi, a graduate of the prestigious Saint Cyr officer school in 1904. He later joined the nascent French military aviation branch and was part of the first generation of French-trained military pilots. He served in Indochina, Morocco and France, where he was killed in July 1916.
(Albert Grandolini Collection)

the affair would drag on for another three years. Only a VIP Flight was established in 1949, and this was staffed by French military personnel and contracted civilian pilots.

Only the worsening political and military situation in Vietnam, combined with increasing pressure from Washington, finally forced the French to consider establishing units manned by the Vietnamese. The Americans established the Military Aid and Advisory Group (MAAG) to assist both the French and the Vietnamese. Lacking manpower and financial resources to wage a costly war, the French reluctantly expanded the Vietnamese military, and Gen Hinh took the opportunity to return with his idea of creating an air force. The first step in this direction was the establishment of an aviation school equipped with Morane-Saulnier M.S.500 Criquets (French-built Fieseler Fi 156 Storchs) at Nha Trang, on 8 May 1952. The same type was used to equip the 1st

Among the first Vietnamese pilots was Emperor Bao Dai, who acquired a private flying certificate and owned two aircraft, a French-built Morane-Saulnier M.S.343, illustrated here, and a de Havilland Tiger Moth. Ironically, the Viet Minh captured both after 1945 and efforts were made to return them to airworthiness in a first attempt to create a Communist Vietnamese air arm.
(Ung Buu Hoang Nguyen)

Nguyen Van Hinh was one of the two Vietnamese that served with the French Air Force during World War II. He is seen here, standing second from left, together with his crew of a French B-26 Marauder from Groupe de Bombardement 1/32 in 1944.
(SHAA)

and the 2nd Observation Groups, while the 1st Liaison Squadron flew M.S.500s, Beech D18s and Republic RC.3 Seabees. All of these units were established between May 1952 and March 1953.

To fly these aircraft, the Training Centre at Nha Trang graduated 75 carefully selected pilots between 1952 and 1955, while 50 others were trained in Marrakech, in French Morocco, and 77 more at Aulnat in France. Future transport pilots were subsequently trained at Avord, while fighter pilots were introduced to the jet syllabus alongside their French comrades, flying the Lockheed T-33 and de Havilland Vampire. Around a dozen Vietnamese completed staff and engineer courses at Salon-de-Provence during the same timeframe – often graduating at the top of their classes.

Despite the good qualities displayed by the Vietnamese pilots, the French remained reluctant to expand the role played by the nascent air force. The operational readiness of the two observation units also left much to be desired. Nevertheless, they soon began flying visual reconnaissance and artillery spotting missions in support of Army units in the southern and central part of the country – in the course of which pilots also sometimes dropped hand grenades – generating up to 100 sorties a month from January 1954 onwards. Gen Hinh's push for the establishment of combat units equipped with US-made aircraft was flatly denied by the local AdA commander, Gen Lechère. Instead, the French proposed the establishment of 'light attack squadrons' flying various modified training aircraft. The French meanwhile pushed for the acquisition of their own transport aircraft, like the Dassault M.D.315 Flamant, of which the first 20 out of an eventual 39 reached Vietnam in late January 1954. The Flamants entered service with the 1st Combat and Liaison Group at Nha Trang, reaching full operational status already by June of the following year.

Following the French defeat at Dien Bien Phu and the Geneva Conference, France was forced to withdraw its troops from Indochina and grant full independence to its

Established in 1949, the VIP Flight had the task of transportation of the government of the new State of Vietnam. The Flight was staffed exclusively by detached French military personnel and French civilian pilots. The Imperial coat of arms is seen here adorning the nose of the Flight's Consolidated C-87. (Jacques Lebourg)

former colonies of Cambodia, Laos and Vietnam. In the case of Vietnam, the country was 'temporarily' divided in two parts along the 17th Parallel for two years, pending elections that were to lead to a final decision on the form of its government. Meanwhile, the Communists regrouped in the northern part of the country, while the Nationalists held the southern part where over a million refugees from the North attempted to find a new home. From the very start, the agreement planted the seeds for the permanent division of the nation, and established the basis for a future conflict.

American support

All the personnel and equipment of the fledgling air arm found themselves in South Vietnam, but first faced a lengthy period of reorganisation and many upheavals, as men and their families were distributed around the country. Political infighting raged

These M.S.500s from the 1st Observation and Combat Support Squadron are departing for another mission from an advanced airfield in 1953. The French-built version of the German Fi 156 also equipped the Air Training Centre. (SHAA)

Gen Nguyen Van Hinh can be considered as the 'father' of the VNAF. It was under his leadership that the Vietnamese armed forces finally acquired an air arm branch, despite French reluctance. Gen Hinh is seen here, second from left in the back row, among high-ranking French officers. In the background are the two Vietnamese RC.3 Seabees that equipped a liaison squadron alongside Beech C-45s and M.S.500s.
(SHAA)

An M.S.500 of 1 Groupe Aérien d'Observation et d'Accompagnement au Combat (GAOAC), or 1st Observation and Combat Support Squadron, in flight over central Vietnam. This first combat-capable Vietnamese aviation unit was mainly used for artillery spotting and visual reconnaissance. However, its aggressive pilots often also prosecuted attack missions by dropping mortar rounds over enemy positions.
(Jacques Lebourg)

The first VNAF combat aircraft were the M.D.315s of the 1st Combat and Liaison Group at Nha Trang. Some of these are seen here during the base handover ceremony from the French to the South Vietnamese on 7 July 1955. Note the new national markings that replaced the former roundel.
(Jacques Lebourg)

The 1st Fighter Squadron was established in June 1956 at Bien Hoa with former French F8F Bearcats. They were engaged against Viet Cong guerrillas from 1958.
(Jacques Lebourg)

in the capital of the new nation, Saigon, as well. Eventually, backed by the US, staunch Vietnamese nationalists had forced Emperor Bao Dai to resign and had proclaimed a Republic. The new president severed all links with France and instead increasingly relied on the US to support his regime against numerous opposition groups. Reflecting these developments, the Vietnamese Air Force (VNAF) was officially established on 31 January 1955, becoming a fully independent branch of the military under the command of Lt Col Tran Van Ho, and adopting new national markings, strongly influenced by those of the United States.

This new, somewhat 'cosmetic' change apart, for the time being the training and support of the VNAF continued to be jointly overseen by both French and US advisory missions, the work of which was coordinated by the Training Relation and Instruction Mission (TRIM), commanded by a French officer until 1956, at when time the French handed over no fewer than 86 aircraft and the airfields at Nha Trang, Da Nang (Tourane), Bien Hoa and Tan Son Nhut. Additionally, the US provided 32 Douglas C-47 Skytrains, which entered service with the 1st and 2nd Transport Squadrons, in 1955 and 1956, respectively, while the French finally handed over 49 Grumman F8F Bearcats (including 21 that were used as a source of spares) for the 1st Fighter Squadron. In summary, during the second half of the 1950s, the VNAF was expanded to include one

The VNAF transport force had been expanded to two C-47 squadrons by 1958. For a decade these two units bore the brunt of air transport tasks. These Skytrains were seen at Tan Son Nhut in the mid-1960s.
(Robert C. Mikesh Collection)

fighter, two transport, two observation and one liaison squadron, a helicopter flight and a training establishment, and it also operated a logistical depot and radar units.

Throughout this expansion period the number of trained personnel, and in particular pilots, also grew to fulfil changing requirements. The number of pilots grew from 80 in 1955, to 86 transport, 54 observation, eight helicopter, and 15 fighter pilots only a year later. By 1957 the VNAF already had 108 transport, 74 observation, eight helicopter and 29 fighter pilots.[1]

First blood

It was in the midst of this reorganisation that the VNAF launched its first offensive operations. Even if 'peace' had officially been restored, various armed factions opposed the new South Vietnamese government. The most serious threat came from the religious sects of Hoa Hao and Cao Dai, as well as the criminal Binh Xuyen gang. These organisations had all set up paramilitary units that had to one degree or another cooperated with the French against the Viet Minh. They now refused to be disarmed and openly rebelled against Saigon from their fiefs in the Mekong Delta area.

Throughout early 1955, AdA C-47s with hastily applied VNAF markings and flown by French pilots dropped paratroopers in the course of Operation Hoang Dieu, while MD.315s flew attack sorties deploying 50kg anti-personnel bombs and machine guns. During 1956, the 1st Fighter Squadron saw limited action against various sect bands, as well as some unruly aboriginal tribes who rebelled in the Central Highlands area.[2]

In December 1955, M.D.315s were used to escort C-47s dropping supplies to the besieged outposts at Cai Cai and Thong Binh, and also supported the final Army of the Republic of South Vietnam (ARVN) drive against rebels holding the town of Cai Vuong in January 1956, in the course of which nearly the entire VNAF was mobilised for combat operations.

Meanwhile, internecine fighting between various Nationalist factions was leaving ever deeper scars within the armed forces and opened the way to future military med-

The new President Ngo Dinh Diem had abolished the monarchy and was opposed by various political factions from the outset. The VNAF was therefore deployed to suppress the religious sects of Hoa Hao and Cao Dai in the Mekong Delta area throughout 1955. The President is seen here with the pilots of the 1st Combat and Liaison Group, who had been engaged in attack missions during the course of these operations.
(Jacques Lebourg)

The transport units were initially placed under the control of the 1st Transport Group that later became the 33rd Wing. The unit was originally placed under the command of a rising star of the VNAF, Maj Nguyen Cao Ky. He is seen here (left) in a still from a colour 8mm movie, after returning from a training sortie in 1958.
(Gerard Gacoin)

dling into political issues. One of the victims of repeated purges was no less a figure than Gen Nguyen Van Hinh, the father of the VNAF, forced to resign after being accused of preparing a coup. He was exiled to France, but joined the AdA and pursued a brilliant career that culminated in appointment as the head of the Material Command, where he supervised the introduction of nuclear weapons. The situation in the country worsened follow the cancellation of the elections that had been agreed upon by the Geneva Accords, after which several dormant Communist cells slowly initiated an armed struggle against the government. By 1959 they began to receive weapons and personnel reinforcements from North Vietnam. Most of these arrived along the newly opened logistic corridor via Laos and Cambodia, which became known as the 'Ho Chi Minh Trail'. The Viet Cong forces quickly expanded their zones of control and before long operated in battalion-sized units.

As the VNAF's Bearcats meanwhile began to show signs of age, the air arm launched a search for a replacement. Corresponding negotiations with the US did not proceed far since the Americans argued that the Geneva Accords forbade the delivery of 'any new weapon system' – a specious argument, considering that both Washington and Saigon had rejected the Accords. Instead, in September 1960, the VNAF began receiving the first of an eventual 329 Douglas AD Skyraider piston-engined fighter-bombers that it was to acquire over the next 10 years.[3]

Starting in 1960, the VNAF replaced its remaining F8Fs with AD-6 Skyraiders. The type was to serve up to 1975, equipping at least six squadrons. All of these brightly coloured machines belonged to the 1st Fighter Squadron, each fuselage band indicating a distinct flight.
(Robert C. Mikesh Collection)

At the end of their career in the early 1960s, the surviving Bearcats had been stripped of their original night blue camouflage scheme and were left in natural metal overall. This particular machine was one of the rare F8F-1P photo-reconnaissance variants then in service. The aircraft has the insignia of the 1st Fighter Squadron painted on its engine cowling.
(VNAF)

Star of the VNAF

The deteriorating military situation led the US to step up its provision of aid. In regards to the VNAF, this effort resulted in the establishment of a second helicopter, third observation, and a second fighter squadron, as well as a reconnaissance flight, made possible through the introduction to service of North American T-28B/D Trojans, RT-28s, RC-47s, and Sikorsky UH-34 Choctaw helicopters. Overall, by 1962 the air force counted 5,700 men and some 140 aircraft, reaching a size at which it had to adapt the designation system of its units, replacing the single-digit identification numbers with a three-digit system.

Despite its growth, the VNAF remained unable to provide the required amount of air support for the ARVN and it was in this context that US President John F. Kennedy decided to deploy US aircraft to South Vietnam, initiating Operation Farm Gate. Curiously enough, the involved aircraft wore South Vietnamese markings and were officially part of the VNAF until July 1963, when the Farm Gate detachment was reorganised as the 1st Air Commando Squadron of the US Air Force (USAF).

Between 1962 and 1964, the VNAF was again involved in several coup attempts. On 26 February 1962, two A-1Hs bombed the Presidential Palace in Saigon in an attempt

A rare colour view of a Skyraider of the 'Satan's Flight' from the 1st Fighter Squadron at Bien Hoa. The unit was later renamed as the 514th Fighter Squadron. (Pham Quang Khiem Collection)

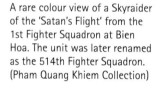

The VNAF and the other branches of the armed forces were involved in a series of coup attempts seeking the removal of President Ngo Dinh Diem in November 1963. In fact, the sight of the VNAF over Saigon at that time became commonplace, with aircraft being used to back one faction against another. These two A-1Hs from the 514th Fighter Squadron were seen at low level over the city in order to deter a coup carried out against the then current ruler, Gen Nguyen Khanh, on 19 February 1965. (Robert W. Kelley)

A second squadron of Skyraiders, the 518th, was created at Bien Hoa in 1963. This A-1H from the unit is seen returning from a strike sortie. (Le Xuan Lam)

against the life of President Ngo Dinh Diem. One aircraft was shot down by anti-aircraft fire while the other managed to flee to Cambodia. On 1 November 1963, a group of generals launched a coup against Diem after learning that he had opened secret negotiations with Hanoi. Four A-1Hs and two T-28Ds bombed the Presidential Palace and the dictator was subsequently removed by the ARVN units.

The overthrow of Diem only resulted in the spread of political instability, as one coup followed another. Nevertheless, this political misery had one positive effect upon the VNAF, in so far that Col Nguyen Cao Ky – a brave and charismatic pilot from North Vietnam, who had developed into one of the most dynamic young officers – was appointed its new C-in-C. Ky was not only a member of the council of generals who ruled the country, but quickly boosted morale by personally leading attacks on the Viet Cong and flying clandestine agent-dropping missions over North Vietnam. However, outside of the air force, Ky soon caused much controversy and friction as his outspoken comments repeatedly created a furore in Saigon and Washington. Although Ky was later to relinquish his post to become prime minister, he retained the honorific rank of vice air marshal.

During early 1964 the VNAF was again reorganised and expanded, adding four new squadrons, and having introducing a wing structure. Bien Hoa thus came under the control of the 23rd Tactical Wing, Tan Son Nhut under the 33rd Tactical Wing, Da Nang under the 41st Tactical Wing, Pleiku under the 62nd Tactical Wing and Binh Thuy under the 74th Tactical Wing.

After the overthrow of President Ngo Dinh Diem, Gen Nguyen Cao Ky rose to prominence by becoming the commander of the VNAF. He belonged to a group of young and aggressive officers, dubbed the 'Young Turks', and provided some stability after a series of coups and counter-coups. By mid-1965 he had resigned from his post to become prime minister, but continued to oversee the VNAF. He later served as vice-president between 1967 and 1971. (USAF)

Another Skyraider squadron raised in the early 1960s was the 520th, based at Binh Thuy. The unit operated mainly in the Mekong Delta. The unit's aircraft were distinguished by their coloured tails denoting different flights: yellow with blue stars, blue with white stars or red with white stars. The practice was maintained when the squadron converted to the A-37B.
(USAF)

Americanisation

Following the Gulf of Tonkin incident in August 1964, the US opened a campaign of 'reprisal' air strikes against North Vietnam, which led to an escalation process that would culminate in a massive deployment of American air, ground and naval forces in South Vietnam. For all practical purposes, the air war over South Vietnam became very much a US-controlled affair as well, the VNAF being seen only as an adjunct within the ever increasing tempo of operations. While the service had to adapt to new working methods developed by the Americans, the US and the South Vietnamese maintained distinct command structures and had clearly defined tasks: the US forces were fighting a 'big battalion war' against the North Vietnamese Army, while the ARVN was concerned with 'pacification' of the Viet Cong guerrillas. While pleasing many South Vietnamese politicians, this resulted in deep mistrust between the allies, a poor US perception of the local requirements and the South Vietnamese military not benefitting from the American military expertise.

As the war continued to expand, the VNAF replaced its T-28s with additional A-1s, no fewer than six squadrons of which became operational by 1966. Keen to become

Viet Cong sappers infiltrated Bien Hoa Air Base on the night of 1 November 1964, targeting the USAF's newly deployed Martin B-57B bombers, with five destroyed and 13 others damaged. VNAF aircraft were hit as well, with three A-1Hs destroyed and three – including this example from the 514th Fighter Squadron – badly damaged.
(USAF)

An A-1H from the 514th Fighter Squadron en route to a target. The aircraft has a mixed load of 250lb bombs and 2.75in (70mm) rocket pods.
(Leif Hellström Collection)

An A-1H from the 522nd Fighter Squadron of the 83rd Special Operation Group is departing for a mission. The Skyraider had been repainted in this very specific camouflage scheme of green and dark maroon-earth. In fact, it was the first of a pattern-type camouflage to appear on a VNAF aircraft. The national insignia was removed and instead was replaced by the Group's insignia with the inscription 'Than Phong', or 'Divine Wind'.
(Don Griffin)

involved in the aerial campaign against North Vietnam, the air force insisted on deliveries of jet aircraft, and – following a short period in which Vietnamese crews flew Martin B-57s of the USAF's 8th and 13th Bomb Squadrons from Da Nang – in 1967 the VNAF received the first batch of Northrop F-5B and F-5C Freedom Fighter jets. The aircraft in question were the former mounts of the USAF's 10th Fighter Commando Squadron and these re-equipped the 522nd Fighter Squadron of the VNAF, which was staffed by the most experienced Vietnamese pilots. Over the following two years, this unit was reinforced through the delivery of additional F-5As and even RF-5As, eventually operating 35 aircraft.

Vietnamisation

Public outrage forced a change of US strategic posture across Southeast Asia, following the Tet Offensive launched by the Communists in early 1968. This saw a shift from offensive operations against North Vietnam to a situation of stalemate and the gradual withdrawal of US forces. In turn, the US administration decided to expand the South Vietnamese military while hoping to reach a political agreement with Hanoi.

The new situation resulted in the emergence of a diametrically opposite role for the VNAF as compared to earlier times, and a new period of rapid expansion. In 1968 the air force grew in strength to 19,000 officers and airmen and 420 aircraft organised in 20 squadrons. By the summer of 1968, several of these – the first was the 524th Fighter Squadron – began to operate the first of 60 Cessna A-37B Dragonflies that were deliv-

Cessna O-1s quickly replaced the M.S.500s inherited from the French. They provided the core of eight observation squadrons throughout the war. This O-1E from the 118th Observation Squadron at Pleiku was photographed over the typical terrain of the Central Highlands area where it usually operated. (USAF)

ered that year. After no fewer than 162 pilots had qualified on the type (112 formerly flew A-1s, and 50 used to fly Cessna O-1 observation aircraft) a total of three units became operational on A-37Bs by the end of 1969.[4]

While this force fought well during the Tet Offensive, flying no fewer than 7,213 sorties (compared to 16,833 sorties flown by the USAF, excluding those undertaken by Boeing B-52 Stratofortress bombers), some questions remained open.[5] Did this process of 'Vietnamisation' of the VNAF really meet the genuine requirements of supporting the South Vietnamese Army, bearing in mind the operational constraints existing at the time?

Namely, expecting US air power to remain in the area and bolster the VNAF in the case of a new invasion from the North, and facing the relatively limited availability of manpower to bring their ambitious plans to successful fruition, the American advisers foremost expanded the transport and close air support capabilities of the air force, while doing almost nothing to render it capable of attacking targets in North Vietnam. Many South Vietnamese commanders perceived this as Washington deliberately curtailing the development of the VNAF out of fear that it could launch an independent campaign against North Vietnam when the US administration suspended its own attacks. Unsurprisingly, a number of officers advocated the development of a much smaller but far better equipped air force that could operate in a less permissive air defence environment than that currently encountered in South Vietnam.[6]

It was only in 1966, in imitation of the USAF, that the VNAF began to standardise the camouflage applied to its aircraft. This A-1H from the 520th Fighter Squadron at Binh Thuy has been freshly repainted. (VNAF)

The introduction of the disruptive camouflage pattern aimed to make aircraft less conspicuous to the enemy. However, many VNAF aircraft continued to carry colourful and oversized wing or squadron insignia, as on these A-1Hs from the 518th Fighter Squadron. (USAF)

On the contrary, the Americans continued to insist on expansion. Correspondingly, between the Tet Offensive in 1968 and early 1972, the VNAF grew in size to 42,000 men and 1,397 aircraft, organized in 44 flying squadrons. It was during this period that the VNAF received its first fixed-wing gunships in the form of 16 Douglas AC-47 'Spooky' aircraft that entered service with the 817th Attack Squadron. In September 1971, the 819th Attack Squadron was established to operate 24 Fairchild AC-119G 'Shadow' gunships. The transport fleet was reinforced as well, foremost through provision of 72 C-123Ks, used to equip the newly established 421st, 423rd and 425th Transport Squadrons.

Characteristically, the helicopter force experienced the most massive expansion, growing from five squadrons equipped with H-34s in 1970, to no fewer than 19 squadrons equipped with Bell UH-1Hs (each including 20 troop transports, three command and control helicopters and eight gunships) and one squadron (the 241st) equipped with Boeing Vertol CH-47A Chinook heavy-lift helicopters, by the end of 1971. A second Chinook squadron was to follow in early 1972. Over 1,100 South Vietnamese helicopter pilots were trained during this phase.[7]

Needless to say, such massive expansion within a short period of time diluted the core of experienced aircrews among the newly established units. Time and again the VNAF experienced periods of disruption and a significant reduction in operational efficiency, maintenance and flying-hour management. The major problem within the combat units was how to both distribute and retain the most experienced pilots in order to maintain a credible level of readiness, as expressed in a report prepared by the Chief of the USAF Advisory Group in 1970, Brig Gen Kendall Young. Young stated that the USAF advisers flying with the VNAF were full of praise for the skill and courage of the

Another example of a camouflaged aircraft with a brightly coloured unit marking was this damaged A-1H of the 524th Fighter Squadron. It carried the typical fuselage recognition marking of the 62nd Tactical Wing. (USAF)

Loaded with six napalm bombs, an A-1H of the 516th Fighter Squadron at Da Nang awaits its next mission. The blue band with white stars was the recognition marking for combat aircraft of the locally based 41st Tactical Wing. (MAP)

Transport assets were bolstered in 1968 with the establishment of the 413th Transport Squadron. The unit was equipped with second-hand C-119Gs, a type that served faithfully until the end in 1975. (Pham Quang Khiem Collection)

Vietnamese pilots – some of whom had over 4,000 combat missions under their belts – and that it was of the utmost importance to preserve this 'very professional group' that was 'amazing at delivering ordnance accurately, better than USAF units', so as to diffuse their experience to the younger generation.

In order to improve and centralise the VNAF supply and repair capabilities, an Air Logistics Command (ALC) was established at Bien Hoa in early 1971. The ALC was to provide depot-level maintenance and logistic support for the entire VNAF structure, thereby reducing supply and maintenance requirements at the individual bases. Maintenance training programmes were established in South Vietnam, using Vietnamese instructors trained in the US in addition to American training teams. Here also, the lack of experienced technicians was felt acutely but the widespread posting of young graduate cadets to US units for 'on the job' training alleviated some of the burden.

The VNAF massively expanded its helicopter force, built around the UH-1H. The first 'Hueys' were delivered in 1969 and subsequent deliveries allowed the creation of no fewer than 25 squadrons. This machine belonged to the 217th Helicopter Squadron at Soc Trang. (USAF)

Nevertheless, progress was steady. Of the 7,215 strike sorties flown by the USAF and VNAF over South Vietnam in February 1970, 40.8 per cent were flown by the latter, despite the fact that it operated only 24.6 per cent of the aircraft.[8] One of the major reasons for such intensive flying by the Vietnamese was that their low-performance aircraft could carry less ordnance than those flown by the Americans. Despite the VNAF successfully operating less-sophisticated aircraft in the face of heavy concen-

The VNAF finally set up its first true jet squadron in April 1967 when 17 F-5Cs and 2 F-5Bs were turned over from the USAF and served to re-equip the 522nd Fighter Squadron. The chequered black and yellow fuselage band was the recognition marking for the combat aircraft of the 23rd Tactical Wing of Bien Hoa. (Jean Pierre Hoehn Collection)

trations of enemy anti-aircraft artillery, and despite the fact that the fighting in Laos in 1971 had shown that whenever the South Vietnamese launched a major offensive, the North Vietnamese would counter with forces in full corps strength, supported by tanks and anti-aircraft artillery, and with the nature of the war switching increasingly towards conventional fighting, the Americans still did not consider the VNAF able to offer the highly sophisticated support that US air power provided when there was a major engagement. On the contrary, they expected the VNAF to be able to handle most of the CAS requirements only in the Military Region (MR) IV (4th Corps), in the southern part of South Vietnam. They were expected to require major US assistance almost anywhere else, but particularly so in the MR 1 (1st Corps) area in northern South Vietnam. In essence, the American advisers did not expect even this major expansion of the VNAF that they had implemented to 'function'.

The North Vietnamese provided more than a 'perfect' opportunity to test this concept. On 30 March 1972, they deployed 200,000 troops supported by 400 tanks, and covered by a powerful and sophisticated air defence system, across the Demilitarized Zone (DMZ) that separated the country along the 17th Parallel, in order to invade South Vietnam. Although revealed in good time by intelligence, the scope of this offensive took the Americans by surprise. Within two months the Communist forces drove the South Vietnamese from the DMZ up to the gates of Hue, the ancient capital city of

The North Vietnamese used a great number of tanks during the Easter Offensive launched in spring 1972. The VNAF pilots proved especially successful as tank hunters in their slower A-37s and A-1s. Capt Tran The Vinh of the 518th Fighter Squadron, credited with 21 tanks destroyed, was the best-known South Vietnamese 'tank ace'. He was sadly killed on 9 April 1972 when his Skyraider was shot down during an armour-hunting mission near Dong Ha.
(VNAF)

The first group of VNAF-trained F-5 pilots is seen here at Bien Hoa just after their return from conversion training in the US. This handpicked group represented an elite with considerable combat experience and formed the core of the newly created 522nd Fighter Squadron. Here they pose beside a USAF 10th Air Commando Squadron F-5C that would later be transferred to South Vietnam.
(Pham Quang Khiem Collection)

the country, and had conquered the northwest part of the Central Highlands. A third push, directly against Saigon, was stopped at An Loc, where the besieged ARVN garrison fought tenaciously. The US reacted to the invasion by tremendously bolstering US air power in Southeast Asia and 'resuming' the bombardment of North Vietnam.[9] US and VNAF operations broke the back of the Communist invasion, and in autumn 1972 the South Vietnamese launched their counteroffensive, lifting the siege of An Loc and recapturing Quanq Tri.

Peace negotiations resumed in Paris but soon became bogged down, the US proposing a ceasefire that would 'freeze' the front lines, pulling out its own troops and aerial assets and implementing a new political process that would lead to elections in South Vietnam in which the Viet Cong could participate. Unsurprisingly, Saigon rejected these conditions since they implied that North Vietnam could continue maintaining its massive troop presence in the country while all US forces would withdraw. President Nguyen Van Thieu demanded all North Vietnamese forces withdraw and the 17th Parallel to be recognised as the international border. Hanoi then left the negotiation table, prompting the Nixon administration to order the Linebacker II campaign, in December 1972, including massive attacks by B-52 bombers against Hanoi and other major cities in North Vietnam. Simultaneously, Nixon put Thieu under immense pressure, warning him that if he refused to sign a ceasefire, the US would sign it alone and cut off all military and economic aid to South Vietnam. In exchange, the US administration promised to tremendously bolster the VNAF – because air power had played such a decisive role in blunting the Communist invasion.

Thieu had no reason to distrust Nixon. In fact, even at the height of fighting in the summer of 1972 the expansion of the VNAF continued unabated, thanks to Project Enhance. In view of the very promising results of current operations, Washington promised to further accelerate this process through Project Enhance Plus, the purpose of which was to increase the size of the VNAF to 2,000 aircraft operated by 66 squadrons.

Although even the most optimistic observers expressed their doubts that this new 'surge' within the VNAF could be sustained over any period of time (it was known that the air force could only have 70 per cent of the required personnel), such promises reassured the government in Saigon. After all, the South Vietnamese considered the surplus equipment a 'war reserve' in case of a new war with the North. Furthermore, in a series of letters to Thieu, Nixon promised a massive influx of contracted US civilian personnel to help the VNAF support such a large force, and issued guarantees of US military intervention in the case of 'blatant violation of the ceasefire'.

Cornered, yet with such promises in mind, Thieu abided and signed the Paris Peace Agreement on 27 January 1973 on the terms that so favoured the Communist side.

1   Grandolini, 'Criquet sur le Mékong, l'histoire de l'aviation militaire en Indochine', *Fana de l'Aviation* magazine, February 1991.

2   Grandolini, 'Indochinese Fighting Cats: Grumman's Superb Bearcat in Vietnam', *Air Enthusiast* magazine, Volume 70/July 1997.

3   It was initially envisaged to deliver second-hand Douglas AD-4s to the VNAF. The type was in the process of being phased out of service and a sufficient number of airframes were available. However, the Americans and the South Vietnamese eventually concluded that it would be difficult to logistically sustain the AD-4. Instead, the US Navy accepted to hand over some of its own AD-6s.

4   VNAF Improvement and Modernization Programme, HQ PACAF, 5 February 1970 Report, Project CHECO, p58.

5   The Vietnamese Air Force, 1951–1975, An analysis of its role in combat and fourteen hours at Koh Tang. USAF Southeast Asia Monograph Series, Volume III, Monographs 4 and 5, p33.

6   Indeed, the C-in-C VNAF, Lt Gen Tran Van Minh, advocated the acquisition of the Douglas A-4 Skyhawk, at the time his US advisors insisted on continuous replacement of remaining A-1s through A-37Bs and the establishment of two additional F-5A squadrons. Also, there was no positive answer from the US side when – during the Midway Conference of 8 June 1969 – the South Vietnamese requested deliveries of McDonnell F-4 Phantoms and Lockheed C-130s. See VNAF Improvement and Modernization Programme, HQ PACAF, 5 February 1970 Report, Project CHECO, p10 and p17.

7   VNAF Improvement and Modernization Programme, HQ PACAF, 5 February 1970 Report, Project CHECO, p76. Notably, at least for some time, the Americans had envisaged to provide CH-53As to the VNAF instead of CH-47As.

8   The VNAF played a substantial role in the air operations over Cambodia after March 1970, supporting the US and South Vietnamese offensives against the Communist logistic sanctuaries there. During 1971, the VNAF reached a new milestone when it flew more combat sorties in Vietnam than the US air arms combined, some 63 per cent of all such missions. It constituted a 69.8 per cent increase if compared to the previous year. Gene Gurney, *Vietnam; The war in the air*, Sidgwick and Jackson Limited, 1985, p207.

9   In March 1972, the USAF had only 83 fighters (60 F-4s and 23 A-37s) and five AC-119Ks left in South Vietnam, with 192 additional fighters (161 F-4s, 16 F-105Gs and 15 A-1s), 62 bombers (52 B-52s and 10 B-57Gs) as well as 23 gunships (13 AC-130s and 10 AC-119Ks), in Thailand. President Nixon ordered a rush reinforcement into the area. The USAF then quickly deployed an additional 180 F-4s, 72 A-7Ds, 54 F-111As, 12 F-105Gs, and 161 B-52s. The US Navy increased the number of aircraft carriers from two to six, with over 400 combat aircraft, operating off the coasts of Vietnam. The USMC also returned to Vietnam, deploying three squadrons of Phantoms at Da Nang and two of A-4Fs at Bien Hoa. The air group deployed at Da Nang later moved to Nam Phong, Thailand, and was reinforced by a squadron of A-6As.

Chapter 2

FINAL BUILD-UP

When the ceasefire finally came into effect, the VNAF was able – at least temporarily – to make pause for reorganisation, and to prepare a thorough assessment of its recent operations. From an overall point of view, the VNAF had performed unexpectedly well for such a young and fast-expanding service. However, alongside for a number of positive developments and strong points, there were also a number of weaknesses. Throughout the Communist Easter Offensive, the VNAF had flown 41.6 per cent of the close air support and attack sorties inside South Vietnam – some 20,000 sorties, with an average of 150 sorties per day, with surges of over of 500 per day in case of emergency.[1]

However, many missions in the areas well defended by enemy heavy anti-aircraft artillery were left to the USAF or the US Navy. On numerous occasions, the VNAF pilots proved their determination by pressing attacks despite serious AAA opposition. For example, VNAF A-1s and AC-47s repeatedly attacked North Vietnamese forces during the Kontum Battle, while the A-37 squadrons acquitted themselves well at An Loc and Dong Ha. In fact, the slower VNAF types often proved more accurate in their attacks than the higher-performance US aircraft. One highlight among VNAF performances was its very high rate in killing enemy tanks. Of the 530 tanks claimed as

One of the main points in the South Vietnamese acceptance of the Peace Accords was the significant expansion of the VNAF in order to compensate for the withdrawal of US air power. The Americans then urgently rushed in additional aircraft from their own stocks. Washington also sought help from its allies in obtaining additional F-5As to fulfil the promise. This F-5A is being offloaded from a USAF C-5A, after having been shipped direct from Iran. (USAF)

destroyed by allied air forces between March 30 and June 9, some 300 were attributed to the VNAF.

The South Vietnamese propaganda machine therefore began to portray several of its 'tank-killing aces'. The best known of these was Capt Tran The Vinh of the 518th Fighter Squadron who was credited with 21 tanks destroyed before he was shot down and killed near Dong Ha 9 April 1972.

These positive points could not mask more worrying facts. The VNAF had not been able to operate continuously over high-risk areas and played next to no role in the vital interdiction campaign against the North Vietnamese logistic lines, notably along the famous Ho Chi Minh Trails in Laos and Cambodia. Night operations were also a long-lasting problem that had not been addressed. Now, with the massive arrival of new equipment before the ceasefire date, the VNAF had the choice of integrating this immediately by raising new, understaffed units or placing the equipment in reserve. Against American advice, the South Vietnamese opted for the first option and stead-fastly pursued this goal despite considerable opposition from high-level USAF planners. The move attested the importance the South Vietnamese placed on air power, as well as their determination and confidence in initiating such undertaking. In fact, the leaders in Saigon had no illusions about the prospects of peace and exerted extra efforts toward building the strongest possible air order of battle in the shortest time. The VNAF embraced the logic of immediate transition training with the newly delivered aircraft, and to make as much use of the presence of US advisors before they were forced to depart the country.

Expanding the attack force

For years the VNAF tried to acquire more modern equipment, but to no avail. Since the early 1960s the propeller-driven A-1 Skyraider remained one of the main aircraft equipping the fighter squadrons. The 522nd Fighter Squadron remained the sole unit to fly the F-5. By the time of the ceasefire, the VNAF had received 31 F-5A/Cs, 10 RF-5As and

A flight of F-5As from the 63rd Wing is heading towards their target with a mixed load of 500lb bombs and napalm. (USAF)

eight F-5Bs. From that total it now deployed some 20 F-5A/Cs, seven F-5Bs and eight RF-5As, including five F-5As received under Project Enhance. Although the A-37B was intended to supplement, and eventually replace the Skyraider, only three squadrons operated the type. While the Dragonfly had shared the burden of combat missions in 1972, it was now clear that it lacked the performance, notably in terms of speed, required to survive in the new threat environment. Nevertheless, two additional A-37 squadrons were established within Project Enhance: the 532nd at Phu Cat in October, and the 534th at Phan Rang in November 1972.

Maj Nguyen Van Thi remembered the circumstances of the creation of the 532nd Fighter Squadron:

'I was then flying the A-37B at Binh Thuy when I was ordered to command a newly raised squadron that would be based at Phan Rang. My first task was to reconnoitre the new installations. I flew there with Maj Tran Man Khoi who was waiting to command another A-37B unit that would be set up there a few months later, the 548th Fighter Squadron. I flew back a little disconsolate to quit the mild climate of the Mekong Delta for this very hot spot that was Phan Rang, even if the base was on the seaside. At Binh Thuy, the headquarters had gathered a group of senior pilots and experienced captains coming from the other A-37 squadrons to serve as a cadre for the newly raised units. They would serve as instructors and flight commanders for the newly graduated pilots that would constitute the core of the new squadrons. I found old friends, some belonging to the Class of 1958 and who had flown the Skyraider at Binh Thuy. When we moved to Phan Rang, I brought along Nghia Dai, Le Vang, Vu Phi Ho and Duong Quoc Lam who were posted to the key staff positions; some of them came from the 516th Squadron at Da Nang. There was also Hieu Thanh Binh, a graduate from the ARVN Thu Duc Reserve Officer School and Ho Vang Dang, a taciturn Eurasian but a real tiger in the cockpit!

'The squadron parking area was between those of the 524th and the future 548th Squadrons. We were all down to underwear due to the heat while helping to clean off the buildings and arrange the Operations Room. It was there that we chose a name and a logo for our unit. Initially the name of Bear was retained, but it soon

A group of 538th Fighter Squadron pilots pose in front of an F-5A parked inside a hardened aircraft shelter. In addition to air defence missions, the main task of the squadron was close air support operations in support of ARVN units within Military Region I.
(Vu Dinh Collection)

Some F-5As had been received between and after delivery, the aircraft were initially stored on parking slots awaiting assembly and delivery to the newly created squadrons. However, it was several months before all the airframes would be operational.
(USAF)

evolved into Buffalo. Finally we settled on Golden Buffalo, a courageous animal at the service of the people. We submitted the insignia to the headquarters that soon homologated it.

'By early December 1972, after a hectic period of organisation and training, we launched our first sorties in the areas of Thai Duong, Thien Loi and Gau Den. I remembered that during a mission we were taken on charge by an O-1 FAC from the 114th Observation Squadron.

'Hearing our radio call sign, he expressed doubts; 'Who are you Golden Buffalo? I don't want amateurs. I need a very precise strike for the designated target, which is very close to friendly positions.'

In addition to aircraft delivered by Iran and South Korea, the USAF also handed over its own F-5As, seen here in protected revetments at Bien Hoa in December 1972. The airframes probably came from the 425th Tactical Fighter Training Squadron at Williams AFB, Arizona. This was the training unit for foreign pilots converting to the type.
(USAF)

Northrop-contracted personnel working for the Defence Attaché Office (DAO) reassembled the delivered airframes in a specially established pool at Bien Hoa. The aircraft were test-flown by USAF and VNAF pilots before their allocation to the newly raised squadrons.
(USAF)

"Don't worry, I'm a rooky', came as a reply! In fact, the FAC pilot happened to be Capt Huong who just had been transferred from the 116th Squadron and someone I personally knew. 'OK, go ahead Golden Buffalo!'[2]

Now, with Project Enhance Plus, the VNAF expected to see its fighter force expanded and modernised. Since the implementation of the 'Vietnamization' policy, the fighter force modernisation became a point of contention between the South Vietnamese and the Americans. The scheme was inscribed within the modernisation plan of the Republic of Vietnam Armed Forces known as the Consolidated RVNAF Improvement and Modernization Program, or CRIMP. The plan was regularly reviewed and updated according to local needs as well as the evolution of US policy. A few months after its implementation, during the Honolulu Conference that took place in July 1968, a Plan 6 CRIMP was reviewed, in which it was envisaged that 36 McDonnell Douglas

In addition to the F-5As, the VNAF also received a small number of F-5Bs that proved essential for the conversion of new F-5 pilots. This ex-USAF aircraft is seen at Bien Hoa after being reassembled but has not yet received South Vietnamese markings.
(USAF)

This USAF pilot had just conveyed a freshly reassembled F-5A to Da Nang. The aircraft still has American markings but was soon handed over to the VNAF and helped establish the 538th Squadron, the third F-5 unit.
(USAF)

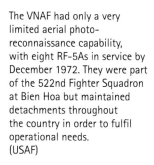

The newly raised F-5 squadrons were immediately pressed into combat operations. The newly posted pilots continued their 'on the job training' by being introduced gradually into the operational missions. This F-5B then accompanied a group of F-5As during a strike sortie. (Pham Quang Khiem Collection)

The VNAF had only a very limited aerial photo-reconnaissance capability, with eight RF-5As in service by December 1972. They were part of the 522nd Fighter Squadron at Bien Hoa but maintained detachments throughout the country in order to fulfil operational needs. (USAF)

F-4D Phantom IIs and 127 Vought A-7 Corsair IIs would fulfill future VNAF requirements. The scheme was hotly debated, with no sign of being fulfilled in the near future. The VNAF returned to the question in a series of meetings between 1969 and the end of 1971. At one point, the Nixon administration agreed on principle that the VNAF would receive four squadrons of older F-4Cs.

Once again, the VNAF would be disappointed by the US response. Instead of Phantoms and Corsairs, the service had to contend with additional A-37s, F-5As and even obsolete A-1s. The core of the fighter force would now be the F-5A, destined to be replaced in the near future by the improved F-5E. In addition, all these F-5As were second-hand aircraft and most of were not even readily available in the US. In fact, Washington was forced to scrounge from allied air forces in order to obtain the required airframes.

South Korea, a strong supporter of South Vietnam that had deployed an expeditionary force of nearly 50,000 soldiers throughout the conflict, was the first to respond to Washington's plea by delivering 36 F-5As. The Shah of Iran was also willing to help Saigon and dispatched some 32 F-5As that had been refurbished before delivery, as well as an important stock of spare parts. Taiwan also dispatched 48 of its own F-5As, alongside 17 J85 engines.

From USAF stocks came nine F-5As; these aircraft had mainly been used to train foreign pilots, including those of VNAF, on the type. Except the aircraft delivered by

For several months there were more aircraft available than trained personnel to man them. These ex-Iranian F-5As were stored at Bien Hoa awaiting a squadron's assignment.
(USAF)

The 538th Fighter Squadron became operational in early 1973 and immediately took over the air alert task at Da Nang. This flight of F-5As was preparing to depart for an air combat patrol along the border with North Vietnam. Note the variety of camouflages of the aircraft.
(VNAF)

An F-5A of the 538th Fighter Squadron departs Da Nang for an air-to-air training sortie. It is seen here in the usual configuration for the task, with a ventral external fuel tank and two AIM-9E Sidewinder missiles.
(Pham Quang Khiem Collection)

the United States, the other machines were considered as loaned. When the new F-5Es arrived, they were to be returned to their owners. Both the former South Korean and Taiwanese aircraft were supposed to be returned to their owners by 31 July 1974.

The new F-5E was without doubt an improvement over the F-5A, with slightly superior performance, and, for the first time, airborne radar that would give it a true all-

Expansion of the F-5 force proceeded relatively smoothly. This was due in no small part to a core of very experienced pilots posted to key staff positions in the newly raised squadrons, some with the incredible tally of 7,000 to 10,000 hours of combat time. A group of these instructors poses here at Bien Hoa.
(Thanh Thuyen)

weather interception capability. On the other hand, the jet still lacked the advanced electronic countermeasures equipment that would allow it to operate in a high-risk environment.

In meantime, Enhance Plus also provided an additional 90 A-37Bs that permitted the establishment of the 546th Squadron at Binh Thuy, the 548th Squadron at Phan Rang and the 550th Squadron at Da Nang. The last 28 USAF A-1s still present in Southeast Asia were also handed over to the VNAF; these served to bolster the three squadrons that still flew the 70 remaining Skyraiders. They were later all upgraded with BOBS compatibility for all-weather bombing.

Overall, if the VNAF fighter force excelled in close air support, it rarely operated by night. The VNAF had no night strike effort, despite the fact that its fighter pilots were night- and all-weather-qualified, and that the service had a night-training continuation programme.

There were a number of reasons for this. First, the VNAF had no overall night air-targeting capability. Since there was little in the way of pre-planned night targeting, there was no requirement for pre-planned night air strikes. Usually, nocturnal targets were engaged during hamlet attacks or troops in contact situations, and these were usually covered by fixed-wing gunships. Second, rules of engagement specified that FACs control the delivery of ordnance by fighters. However, VNAF observation aircraft were not equipped for instrument or night operations. Consequently, the VNAF fighter squadrons were fully committed to daytime sorties, leaving the night strikes to the better-equipped US units. However, with the Americans now gone, the VNAF was forced to develop its own night-attack capabilities. From 1973 on, the fighter squadrons maintained armed alert flights to respond to emergencies and began to develop a night-attack programme. However, these efforts never reached the level previously offered by the USAF.

Complementing the fighter squadrons was a third fixed-wing gunship squadron that was added in December 1972. Some 22 AC-119K 'Stingers' were received to equip the newly created 821st Attack Squadron, which would bolster the 817th Squadron on the AC-47D and the 819th Squadron on the AC-119G. A special USAF training team helped to accelerate the transition by beginning to cross-train VNAF AC-119G and C-119G aircrews and maintainers on the new gunship version.

The A-37B was destined to be the primary attack type following its introduction to service in March 1969. Project Enhance and Enhance Plus expanded the A-37 force from three to eight squadrons. A mix of experienced officers and young, recently graduated pilots staffed the new units. Some O-1 FAC pilots also converted to the type to become attack pilots. Here, pilots attend a transfer ceremony for former USAF A-37Bs.
(USAF)

One of the newly delivered A-37Bs is reassembled at Nha Trang. In the background is an AC-47D from the 817th Attack Squadron. Despite the new threats that the South Vietnamese airmen had to face, including modern anti-aircraft systems that necessitated high-performance aircraft, the US continued to deliver weapons systems optimised for low-threat-level anti-guerrilla operations.
(John Massey)

A VNAF pilot returns from a mission aboard his F-5C. This aircraft was inherited from the USAF's 10th Air Commando Squadron that had carried out combat trials of the aircraft until 1967.
(USAF)

It was hoped that these three fixed-wing gunship squadrons would be sufficient for interdiction operations against enemy logistic corridors, at least in the less well-defended areas. However, they were deemed too vulnerable to operate over most of the Laotian part of the Ho Chi Minh Trail. For the same reason, it was decided to terminate Project Credible Chase. This programme, which received high-level interest and support in late 1971 and early 1972, had envisaged equipping the VNAF with five squadrons each of 32 short take-off and landing 'mini-gunships'. Several South Vietnamese pilots had even been sent to the US to test the Fairchild AU-23A Peacemaker and Helio AU-24A Stallion, with a marked preference for the former.[3]

Some 90 additional A-37Bs were handed over to the VNAF at the end of 1972 under Project Enhance Plus. This airframe is seen being loaded for reassembly. The refuelling probe on the nose would be removed, since the VNAF did not have a tanker force.
(USAF)

The assembly of newly delivered A-37Bs at Binh Thuy at the end of 1972. The aircraft was likely assigned to the newly created 546th Fighter Squadron. They shared ramp space with aircraft of the 526th Fighter Squadron, which already operated from the base, and wore the characteristic unit markings of white stars on the wingtip external tanks. (Pham Quang Khiem Collection)

Among the newly raised units was the 534th Fighter Squadron, which stood up at Phan Rang in November 1972. Some of the unit's pilots pose here for a group photo in front of the squadron's operation room. The 'Golden Buffaloes' soon became renowned for their willingness to take the most difficult missions in support of ARVN forces in Military Region II. (Nguyen Van Thi)

This A-1H from the 514th Fighter Squadron was departing Bien Hoa for an attack sortie with a typical load of 10 500lb bombs. The Skyraiders still equipped three VNAF squadrons from 1973 on. (USAF)

In addition to the single-seat A-1H/J, the VNAF also operated two-seat A-1E/G models. This A-1E from the 518th Fighter Squadron is seen returning from a strike sortie. (USAF)

The AC-47D was the first fixed-wing gunship put into service by the VNAF in 1969. It still equipped the 817th Attack Squadron in 1973 but its vulnerability to increasing enemy anti-aircraft fire restricted its missions to the less well defended areas. (USAF)

The VNAF's fixed-wing gunship force was enhanced with the introduction of the AC-119G to service with the 819th Attack Squadron in 1971. Even though the aircraft offered an improvement over the AC-47D, its weapon system did not allow it to operate effectively over the most defended enemy areas. (USAF)

Rationalisation of the transport force

Throughout the North Vietnamese offensive in 1972 the VNAF also continued to expand its transport force. On the eve of this campaign, the service maintained one squadron of C-47s, one of C-119Gs and three of C-123Ks. All these units performed well in view of the difficult circumstances. The transports were engaged in re-supplying encircled ARVN positions, notably at Kontum and An Loc, despite heavy AAA. Several C-123s and C-119s were shot down or destroyed on the ground by enemy artillery, and 15 others were damaged.

From May 1972, the VNAF also joined USAF Lockheed C-130 Hercules in high-altitude, low-opening (HALO) parachute drops in order to reduce its losses. Ten beacon-transponders were installed on some C-119s and C-123s to fulfil these missions, in conjunction with two mobile AN/MSQ-77 ground surveillance radars that had been transferred to VNAF control.

In addition to participating on combat missions, the VNAF Airlift Control Centre (ALCC) that commanded all the transport assets had to supervise the creation of three additional squadrons operating de Havilland Canada C-7 Caribous. The 427th Trans-

The VNAF finally acquired a more potent night interdiction gunship when 22 AC-119Ks were transferred from the USAF to form the 821st Attack Squadron. The 45-day transition training took place at Tan Son Nhut from December 1972. However, contrary to the USAF model, the VNAF aircraft saw some of its most sophisticated sensors removed before delivery, including the Texas Instruments AN/AAD-4 FLIR.
(Pham Quang Khiem Collection)

The AC-119K offered a greater punch compared to the AC-119G. In addition to the four 7.62mm (0.3in) Miniguns, it had two 20mm M61A1 'Gatling' cannon. It was hoped that the 821st Attack Squadron would be sufficient for interdiction operations against enemy logistic corridors. However, AC-119Ks were deemed too vulnerable to operate over most of the Laotian part of the Ho Chi Minh Trail.
(Pham Quang Khiem Collection)

port Squadron was declared operational in March, followed by the 429th in July, and finally by the 431st in August. To ease transition to the type, the USAF's 483rd Wing set up a special training detachment with eight C-7s. A total of 56 Caribous were eventually handed over to the South Vietnamese.

The then commander of the 427th Squadron, Lt Col Pham Van Can, remembered the formative months of his unit:

'When the headquarters decided to set up new squadrons on the C-7 Caribou, selected experienced C-47 pilots from the 415th and 417th Transport Squadrons were gathered for conversion training and to serve as instructors for the rest of the crews. After a short conversion at Phan Rang and Cam Ranh Bay Bases with the departing USAF squadrons, I was chosen to command our first C-7 unit, the 427th Transport Squadron. I had as deputy an experienced pilot, Maj Nguyen Ba Dam, with Maj Tran Van Minh and Ha Van Hoa as Operations and Training Officers, respectively. Maj Nguyen Van Kim was in charge of the Security.

'After flying the venerable C-47s for years, the STOL C-7 was a completely new aircraft to fly. I found it very responsive, full of power and its modern cockpit very comfortable. It was a real Mercedes of the air! Its most noticeable feature was the ability to land on very short runways of only around 300m [984ft] of length. It had a practical payload of three tons or 27 soldiers.

'Our first assignment was the base of Phu Cat. At this time we were in need of additional aircraft to continue the training. We were then ordered to go to Cam Ranh to pick up airframes just released by the Americans. I went there with Maj Cung Thang An and Nguyen Viet Xuong. After signing the forms, I shook hands and said goodbye to the USAF colonel who received us. I said that we would make a low pass in formation over the base by way of thanking him. I felt that he was uneasy because he surely knew that we were not yet officially cleared for formation flying on the Caribou. Aboard each of the aircraft were four US mechanics who came along with us as instructors and who also expressed doubts about our idea. After taking off, in very close formation, we made the low pass anyway before flying up north, still maintaining our formation. While overflying the Nha Trang Harbour, I looked back into the cargo compartment, waiting to see recriminating faces. Instead, the American mechanics smiled at me while still looking out to see how we were able to maintain perfect wing-to-wing flying. They praised our flying skill when we landed. In fact, I had no doubt about the flying, which was done by very experienced wingmen.

'Soon after, the three squadrons of C-7s were regrouped at Tan Son Nhut. Finally, it was decided to move one of them to Da Nang. I went to the ALCC and volunteered my squadron to be posted there. Some of the officers asked me to think twice about the idea, for many of us preferred to stay at Tan Son Nhut, having a chance to live comfortably in Saigon. But personally I hated the formality of the life there, for there were too many high-ranking officers around. I preferred to be away from the headquarters, believing that when you are far away from the sun, it burns less!

'I found an ally in the person of Col Nguyen Hong Tuyen who headed the Instruction Detachment at Phu Cat. There, he had taken particular care of us, finding for the squadron two Dodge trucks as well as a van. Now, thanks to contacts with people at Da Nang, he helped me a lot when I prepared the redeployment. He came with me for my first introduction to the base. I was then warmly received by the 1st Air

Division Commander, Brig Gen Nguyen Duc Khanh, and the commander of the 41st Wing, Col Thai Ba De and his deputy, Lt Col Nguyen Van Vuong. Tuyen also introduced me to others with responsibility in Military Region I. We then landed at the command post of the 1st ARVN Division that we were supporting and were greeted by its commander.

'One of my top priorities was to fully qualify all my pilots, for many of them had just graduated from US air schools. I imposed a very strict flight schedule, day and night, poor weather, combining training and operational sorties. I also fully took into account our operational area and wanted to open as many airfields and remote airstrips as possible to our operations, notably in the mountains west of Da Nang with the isolated Ranger outposts. I wanted my pilots to be familiar with these locations as soon as possible.

'The most delicate airstrips to fly into, down into narrow valleys or surrounded by high cliffs, were those of Nhon Co, Gia Nghia, Ha Thanh and Ba To. For each of these missions, we carried two crews per aircraft; the first one flew on the way in; the other on the way out. Several of our aircraft were damaged by enemy AAA or targeted by artillery when we landed but, fortunately, we lost none of our aircraft.

'I remember one of these missions when I had to land on the bank of a river. The Rangers quickly emerged from their positions and helped us with trepidation to offload the aircraft. Suddenly, enemy artillery rounds began to land among us. They brought in three of their wounded when I pushed into full throttle for the take-off. The rounds exploded in our path as I went airborne and I quickly left the valley by flying at treetop level to evade AA fire. I often think about our courageous Rangers, some of them not having seen their families for more than three years.

'In another mood, I remembered a sortie on a small airstrip near a village in the Quang Ngai Province. While I was on the ground, I was approached respectfully by an old peasant. The man then asked me if he could touch the aircraft. He at first passed his hands cautiously but when reassured, began to punch the fuselage surface; no, it is not made of paper! I then offered him to climb inside the cargo compartment. With his feet, he began to kick the floor; no, it is not made of bamboo! For all these isolated villages and outposts, we were the life line with the exterior world.

'One of my pilots, who now lives in Australia and who would later transition to the C-130, thanks me for having trained him so rigorously in STOL operations. He later told me that it surely saved his live on several occasions. That led me to recall

The first C-7 unit to be established was the 427th Transport Squadron. The first group of qualified instructors poses here with the unit's commander, Lt Col Pham Van Can at third from right, at Phu Cat, which was the squadron first assignment before its move to Da Nang.
(Pham Van Can)

A view of the Phan Rang parking area in early 1973 shows a mix of aircraft from two of the three VNAF Caribou squadrons that stood up there before being posted to their assigned parent units. The C-7As from the 427th Transport Squadron of the 41st Wing at Da Nang wore the 'Y' tail code, and the 431st Transport Squadrons of the 33rd Wing at Tan Son Nhut wore 'G' tail codes.
(Robert D. Young)

These C-47s of the 415th Transport Squadron were seen at Tan Son Nhut before the disbandment of the unit. However, due to the poor readiness of the C-130As, many of them were retained in service with the 314th Transport Squadron, a VIP transportation unit. The aircraft had their bellies painted in black for flare-dropping missions.
(Pham Quang Khiem Collection)

how, as a young, graduated pilot, I was taken on charge by Maj Ha Hau Sinh himself. He was then considered the best transport pilot in the VNAF, with over 10,000 flight hours, and was already a living legend. He took our group of youngsters, one after another, day after day, for a rigorous training programme, sometimes not even taking time for lunch. I learned much from him. Sadly, he died in a Communist prison camp after 1975.[4]

Despite the increasing size of the transport fleet it appeared that it was still insufficient to meet the ARVN needs. The VNAF was unable to sustain the various air bridges without the help of USAF C-130s. In order to rationalise and modernise the transport fleet, the VNAF made the request to standardise its equipment on the Hercules. In fact, Saigon had requested the delivery of C-130s as early as 1960. In the first instance, the Americans, once again, had turned down the request. But the decision to finally deliver the Hercules was taken by the Secretary of State himself, Henry Kissinger, during a visit he made to Saigon on 20 October 1972. Project Enhance Plus now included the provision of 32 C-130As to the VNAF. The plan was to replace all C-123s, C-119s and C-47s with the new aircraft.[5]

All the aircraft came from various units of the Air National Guard or the USAF Reserve. The Hercules were ferried across the Pacific from 29 October to 6 November 1972. A conversion class began immediately on 27 November, under a team of 46 USAF instructors. A first group of eight VNAF crews was soon qualified and then served as instructors to speed up the training on the C-130. The training proceeded smoothly and quickly, the American instructors being impressed by the level of experience of most of the VNAF pilots. By 24 February 1973 some 32 crews had been fully qualified and served to establish the 435th and 437th Squadrons at Tan Son Nhut.

The lack of mechanics for VNAF transport aircraft was temporarily compensated during this period of build-up by an additional 188 USAF technicians for the C-130As and 163 technicians for the AC-119Ks. The C-130A was initially intended to replace all the other transports, except the C-7s. The VNAF was now required to turn over its remaining Providers, and both the 423rd and 425th Transport Squadrons were to be deactivated by the end of April 1973. However, in order to ease the transition to the Hercules, the 421st Transport Squadron continued to operate its C-123Ks for another

The VNAF had a versatile tactical transport when it introduced to service the C-123K at the end of 1970. However, it saw only brief service, destined to be replaced by the more powerful C-130A in 1973. This Provider of the 423rd Transport Squadron is seen in a protected revetment at Tan Son Nhut in 1972.
(USAF via Jean Pierre Hoehn)

The Paris Peace Accords stipulated prisoner exchanges at the implementation of the ceasefire in January 1973. Both sides agreed to release prisoners at designated locations under international supervision. These North Vietnamese prisoners were to be loaded onto C-123Ks of the 423rd Transport Squadron at Tan Son Nhut for transit to their release point.
(USAF)

The Provider was gradually phased out before being completely retired from service by mid-1973. This C-123K of the 425th Transport Squadron is seen embarking military passengers for a liaison mission. Note the newly delivered C-7A in the background.
(John Massey)

A first group of eight VNAF pilots was qualified on the C-130A after a brief conversion course in November 1972 and served as instructors to speed up the training of the rest of the crews. The commander of the 435th Transport Squadron, Lt Colonel Ngo Xuan Nhut, second from left, posed here with the USAF instructors at Tan Son Nhut3.   (Ngo Xuan Nhut)

Some 32 C-130As were transferred to the VNAF from the USAF inventory. The aircraft came from various units, including those of the Air National Guard and USAF Reserve. Some airframes were already worn out and required a complete overhaul, but time and budgetary constraints prevented this. These newly delivered Hercules have already received their VNAF markings but were waiting to be posted to a specific squadron. Note that one of the aircraft has an overall light grey paint scheme instead of the usual 'Southeast Asia' camouflage.   (Pham Quang Khiem Collection)

This C-119G of the 413th Transport Squadron was seen at Tan Son Nhut before the disbandment of the unit in 1973. However, many of its aircraft were retained and transferred to the 720th Squadron, a unit that was initially destined for maritime reconnaissance missions. (USAF)

six months. In fact, the two Hercules squadrons continued to suffer from the poor logistics support that hampered their initial operations. But things were improving, and by June 1973 the VNAF could deploy an average of 16 C-130As per day, a figure that continued to improve, with a reliability rate of over 75 per cent of the fleet by the end of the year. By the end of 1973 the VNAF had given up its last Providers, these being distributed to others allied air forces; eight to Cambodia, seven to Laos, eight to Thailand, and the remainder to South Korea and Philippines.

The VNAF also fielded a special transport unit for government use and VIP movements. This was the 314th Transport Squadron based at Tan Son Nhut. In October 1973 the squadron operated one Douglas DC-6, four VC-47s, two U-17s and four UH-1Hs.

By March 1973 the VNAF transport squadrons were hauling a monthly average of 1,700 tons of supplies and 4,400 passengers, which represented 80 per cent of the usual ARVN requirements. It was clear that in case of emergency, the ground forces could not expect the same level of airlift support experienced during the 1972 campaign. However, the transport fleet was unsuspectingly reinforced – with another squadron of Flying Boxcars.

The beginning – and the end – of the maritime patrol force

During 1972, the headquarters in Saigon decided to establish a maritime reconnaissance unit in order to assume responsibility for the long-established Operation Market Garden, the air surveillance of enemy sea infiltrations. In previous years, US Navy Lockheed P-2 Neptune and Lockheed P-3 Orion squadrons had carried out this task. But instead of equipping the VNAF with a well-proven and specially designed maritime patrol aircraft, such as second-hand Neptunes or Grumman S-2 Trackers, it was decided to deliver a specially developed version of the C-119.

Known as the RC-119L, the aircraft was intended to receive special sensing equipment, including radar and night observation devices. The 720th Reconnaissance Squadron was created in December 1972 in order to operate the new platform; its ranks were filled by 52 C-123K crewmembers that had been suitably retrained. Some 13 C-119Gs were taken on charge and dubbed 'RC-119Gs' pending their modification for their new role. The Fairchild Aircraft Service Division of Crestview, Florida, retained another airframe in the US for system development and integration. A contract signed on

The Market Garden missions, the coastal patrolling of the coasts of South Vietnam, would be taken over by the RC-119Ls which were intended to receive special sensing equipment. However, due to budgetary constraints, the scheme was dropped and the aircraft was used only in its initial transport role. This unmodified C-119G of the 720th Squadron was seen at Tan Son Nhut in early 1973. (Wayne Mutza)

14 March 1973 requested that the modified prototype would be completed by the summer and that the remaining kits would be readied for installation by the end of the year.

However, the lack of funds to continue the scheme finally led to the cancellation of the contract. The 720th Squadron continued to operate its unmodified aircraft, but strictly in a transport role. The VNAF was unable to fly the crucial role of air-sea surveillance.

Enlargement of the helicopter fleet

Since 1969 the VNAF helicopter fleet had been greatly expanded in order to introduce the ARVN to airmobile operations as conducted by the US Army. When the Communists launched their offensive in 1972 the VNAF fielded 13 helicopter squadrons manned by 1,400 pilots. While the Vietnam War experienced a considerable development in airmobile tactics to counter the guerrilla attacks, the recently changing nature of the conflict led many to question the wisdom in continuing that policy for the young VNAF.

At the eve of the North Vietnamese invasion, the VNAF had 628 UH-1Hs on inventory but losses had been heavy during the campaign, with 63 'Hueys' shot down and 391 others damaged. Suddenly, facing an increasingly sophisticated enemy air defence, the helicopter force appeared very vulnerable.

Furthermore, the performance of the VNAF helicopter force had been the subject of much criticism. The recently created squadrons were mainly staffed by young and inexperienced pilots thrown immediately into the battle. Just after their graduation from Fort Wolters, Texas, and Fort Rucker, Alabama, they were attached to US Army helicopter units in Vietnam for three months of 'on the job' combat training, before their posting to a newly raised Vietnamese squadron. Unsurprisingly, on many occasions – notably during the An Loc Battle – the ARVN complained that VNAF helicopters failed to press into areas defended by AA fire or would not land to pick up wounded in drop zones covered by enemy artillery.

The VNAF oversaw a tremendous expansion of its helicopter force between 1970 and 1973, with the UH-1H replacing all the UH-34s by early 1971. The number of 'Huey' squadrons consequently rose to 19, manned by over 1,600 pilots. These VNAF mechanics are installing rotor blades on a newly accepted example. (USAF)

However, it would be fair to observe that US Army pilots often showed similar reluctance to fly such hazardous missions. Besides, after disciplinarian actions were taken against VNAF pilots judged to have failed in the line of duty, the situation improved markedly and most South Vietnamese pilots began showing great courage despite heavy losses. For example, on 11 June 1972, 21 UH-1Hs landed within the besieged An Loc and picked up 200 wounded soldiers, even though three helicopters were shot

With the influx of additional helicopters during Project Enhance and Enhance Plus, it was decided to bring the strength of each 'Huey' squadron from 31 to 38 machines. These 'Hueys' belonged to the 215th Helicopter Squadron. (USAF)

down in the process (in the course of the same battle, the 237th Squadron lost no fewer than 10 of its Chinooks).[6] Just two days later the US Army mimicked this manoeuvre and flew a similar operation in An Loc.

Suffice to say, during the 1972 campaign, the VNAF flew 53.5 per cent of overall helicopter sorties. Nevertheless, for the remainder of the war, the morale of the helicopter crews was always considered 'fragile'. Many judged that they lacked adequate equipment to fly their missions, notably to counter the SA-7 surface-to-air missile threat. Infra-red suppression kits, mounted at the end of the engine exhaust, and funnelling the hot air upwards towards the wash of the blades to dilute the heat, began to be shipped to Vietnam in August 1972. Of course, priority was given to US Army 'Hueys': those of the VNAF had to wait.[7]

The lack of a true gunship to protect the transport helicopters, or to hunt enemy tanks, was the most evident problem. As early as July 1968, during discussions for Plan 6 of the CRIMP, it was envisaged that the VNAF would receive at least a squadron of Bell AH-1G Cobra. However, a corresponding measure was never financed.

The new table of organisation for each UH-1H squadron from 1973 included 23 troop transports and three command and control aircraft. This 'Huey' was taking off from Bien Hoa for a re-supply mission. (USAF)

Some 300 additional UH-1Hs were delivered in 1972, in the course of Project Enhance, enabling the VNAF to raise the number of 'Huey' squadrons to 19 and to replace all the losses suffered during that year. Most of these machines came from departing US Army Aviation units.[8]

Eventually, Project Enhance Plus brought no fewer than 286 UH-1Hs and 23 CH-47As to South Vietnam, increasing the total number of helicopters in inventory to 929 as of February 1973. Surplus helicopters were used to establish six additional squadrons as well as eight flights for medevac operations – the latter were subsequently reorganised within a group-sized squadron. Eventually, no fewer than 109 UH-1Hs were effectively assigned to the task of battlefield medical evacuation.[9]

Nevertheless, a scheme to acquire 48 UH-1Ns for long-range search and rescue operations was never fulfilled. To man all these helicopters, no fewer than 420 additional helicopter pilots had graduated by summer 1972. Furthermore, it was decided to bring the strength of each 'Huey' squadron to 38 machines.

The new table of organisation for each UH-1H squadron now comprised 12 gunships, three command and control aircraft and 23 troop transports. The gunships also received 19-tube rocket launchers for 2.75in (70mm) FFAR rockets, instead of the usual seven-tube launchers, at a delivery rate of 200 pods per month beginning in November 1973.

Despite plans to acquire AH-1Gs, this was never financed and the VNAF had to contend with armed UH-1Hs for helicopter attack missions. The crew of this gunship display the standard armament configuration of two Miniguns and two seven-round rocket pods.
(Tran Kim Hai)

In order to increase the firepower of the 'Huey' gunships, new 19-tube rocket launchers for 2.75in (70mm) FFAR rockets were taken into service in place of the usual seven-tube launchers.
(Grant Mackie Collection)

In order to cope with the growing SA-7 threat, the 'Hueys' were modified from late 1972 with infra-red suppression kits. These VNAF mechanics are seen installing the kits on UH-1Hs at Tan Son Nhut.
(Roger Routin)

Two additional Chinook squadrons were created at the end of 1972, bringing their number to four. The purpose was to allocate one unit of heavy left helicopters to each of the four ARVN Military Regions. This CH-47A of the 241st Helicopter Squadron is seen on a re-supply mission.
(Boeing Vertol)

Some 23 additional CH-47As had been handed over to the VNAF by departing US Army Aviation units under Project Enhance Plus. This brought the VNAF Chinook fleet to 72 machines equipping four squadrons. These airframes are seen stored at Tan Son Nhut awaiting inspection and repair before being returned to operational service. (USAF)

A training programme for night operations was launched to alleviate deficiencies in this field. The 'Huey' units began flying night gunship sorties on a regular basis, notably in Military Region IV of the Mekong Delta area. This last zone would also see the allocation of an additional 22 gunships to work in cooperation with Navy patrols boats in the numerous waterways. It was subsequently decided to create two new Chinook squadrons as well. This would allow one squadron of CH-47s to be assigned to each Military Region. In October 1972, some 90 'Huey' pilots were sent to the US to train on the new machine. On their return they established the 247th Squadron at Da Nang and the 249th Squadron at Binh Thuy. Even if the figures seemed impressive, the VNAF helicopter force must be compared with the availability of over 5,000 American machines at the height of the US involvement in Vietnam.

Observation and reconnaissance shortfalls

One of the most significant shortfalls of the VNAF concerned the observation and reconnaissance roles. The VNAF maintained eight observation squadrons, the last

The Cessna U-17 supplemented the ubiquitous O-1. A total of 56 were on strength by July 1973, including these examples from the 116th Observation Squadron at Bien Hoa. Based on the civilian Cessna Model 185, the aircraft was also used for liaison and medical evacuation missions.
(USAF)

Sixteen U-17s were modified for psychological warfare. They were supplemented in this role by some modified C-47s and de Havilland Canada U-6 Beavers.
(USAF)

one raised in August 1972, equipped with O-1s and U-17s, and these performed visual reconnaissance and forward air control (FAC) tasks. During the 1972 operations the VNAF FACs generally performed poorly over their areas of operation. This was the result of various different factors. First, the FAC aircraft proved to be very vulnerable to heavy anti-aircraft defences. In order to survive in these high-threat areas, the VNAF was forced to operate at higher altitude or even avoid entering zones covered by SAMs and heavy AAA. All too often, the VNAF relinquished these missions to USAF FACs, usually flying North American OV-10 Broncos. In the most dangerous sectors the Americans also operated 'Fast FACs', flying specially equipped F-4s.

The VNAF possessed no such assets. Occasionally, the South Vietnamese used the A-37B in the FAC role in high-threat areas but the aircraft lacked suitable communications equipment. The other problem was a product of the VNAF FAC training programme itself. Contrary to USAF or USMC practice, in which experienced pilots were posted for the task, most of them coming from the fighter community, the VNAF assigned young and inexperienced pilots to the FAC mission.[10] These crews were selected as observation pilots as soon as they completed their primary flight training. Furthermore, the best cadets were sent to the US for advanced training to become transport or fighter pilots. Needless to say, the observation squadrons were at the bottom of the VNAF social system. Measures were taken on a regular basis to assess the problem, but the continued expansion of the observation force simply diluted the most experienced pilots within the squadrons. It is also fair to state that on numerous occasions VNAF FACs performed well, taking charge of air strikes not only performed by South Vietnamese fighter-bombers but also those of allied air forces.

The VNAF maintained eight observation squadrons, the last of these established in August 1972, and their Cessna O-1s and U-17s performed visual reconnaissance and FAC tasks. The mainstay of the FAC force was the obsolescent O-1, with 173 on inventory by July 1973. This O-1E belonged to the 114th Observation Squadron based at Bien Hoa.
(USAF)

In order to modernise the FAC fleet, 35 Cessna O-2As were delivered under Project Enhance Plus. They supplemented the aircraft of the 110th Observation Squadron at Da Nang and the 118th Squadron at Pleiku. Their higher performance allowed them to operate in the rugged areas of the Annamite Mountains chain.
(Pham Quang Khiem Collection)

The first unit to re-equip with the O-2A was the 110th Observation Squadron at Da Nang, followed by the 118th Squadron. Pilots of that latter unit pose here for a group photo in 1973.
(Can Thep Collection)

In order to modernise the FAC fleet some 35 Cessna O-2As were delivered under Project Enhance Plus. These supplemented the aircraft of the 110th Observation Squadron at Da Nang and the 118th Squadron at Pleiku. By July 1973, the VNAF had some 256 FAC aircraft in its inventory, including 35 O-2s, 56 U-17s and 165 O-1s. Sixteen U-17s were modified for psychological warfare, equipped for leaflet dropping and fitted with loudspeakers. In order to replace FAC pilots moving on to A-37 squadrons, some observers were trained as O-1 pilots in 1973.

Other reconnaissance assets were limited to a few RF-5As, attached to the 522nd Fighter Squadron. Of the eight available in December 1973, two were totally unserviceable, leaving only six in service. Although the small number of operational RF-5As represented a significant limitation, the most serious shortcoming continued to result from the deficiencies of its KS-92A camera. A proposed solution foresaw its replacement with the KA-95 camera, but was deemed too onerous and was never funded. The VNAF then requested the less expensive KA-77 at the end of 1973, but budgetary constraints also forced the cancellation of this scheme.[11]

Another squadron was equipped with an assortment of aircraft intended for photographic, radio interception and psychological warfare operations. The 716th Squadron based at Tan San Nhut operated a fleet of 17 de Havilland Canada U-6 Beavers, including eight equipped for radio-interception or leaflet drops and loudspeaker broadcast-

ing. Also on strength were five RC-47Ds, two EC-47Ds and two C-47Ds. The RC-47Ds were fitted with improved infra-red systems that could locate enemy heat sources. These aircraft were usually used for photographic reconnaissance in Military Regions III and IV. There were also seven RC-47Ds that had been modified in January 1972 to carry Palletized Airborne Relay (PAR) sets. The VNAF received 20 of these sets, and other airframes were later modified to relay signals from the Igloo White seismic and acoustic sensors back to the PAR terminal at Tan Son Nhut. Here, the information was analysed by ARVN personnel. However, the programme was cancelled at the end of 1972 due to the fact that the VNAF lacked any high-speed sensor implant platforms, and the aircraft were returned to their former photo-reconnaissance configuration.[12]

The EC-47Ds could plot the location of a 10-Watt radio transmitter within one degree at a range of 25 nautical miles. This aircraft was supplemented by a few modified RU-6 Beavers. However, improving the VNAF's electronic warfare capability was an urgent priority. The USAF then decided to hand over its remaining EC-47s in theatre, including more advanced versions such as the EC-47Q/P with more sophisticated AN/ALR-34 equipment for the ELINT mission and even a limited jamming capability.

The process took place slowly, for it needed time to properly train the South Vietnamese. The first VNAF pilots and navigators began their training in August 1972, and at the same time ARVN radio and electronic operators also began their training with the USAF's 360th Tactical Electronic Warfare Squadron at Tan Son Nhut. In April 1973 the conversion course ended when the 306th TEWS was deactivated and turned over its aircraft to South Vietnam. The VNAF then assumed the role by activating the 718th Reconnaissance Squadron. At that time the USAF still retained another EC-47 squadron in Da Nang, the 362nd TEWS. Both squadrons operated side by side until late 1973 when sufficient numbers of VNAF crews were available to take over the American aircraft. By then the 718th Reconnaissance Squadron was the largest in the VNAF, with almost 500 members and 36 EC-47s. In reality, the squadron operated as two detachments, one at Tan San Nhut (aircraft tail code starting with 'W') covering the southern part of the country, and one at Da Nang (aircraft tail code starting with 'T') for north. Both the 716th and 718th Squadrons worked directly for the ARVN military intelligence agency, the G-7 bureau of central headquarters. The squadron flew daily missions, averaging five to 11 hours in duration. The crews were submitted to tight security controls, including passing 'lie detector' polygraph tests.

From the outset, it appeared that the numerous types of aircraft in service in the different roles of transport, gunship, reconnaissance, electronic warfare and maritime patrol would pose problems in regard to standardisation and maintenance. The USAF

The VNAF maintained only a very limited ELINT capability. Initially, this consisted of a few EC-47Ds and modified RU-6s that were used to intercept enemy radio communications and plot their locations. This poor but rare view shows an RU-6 of the 716th Squadron based at Tan San Nhut. (VNAF)

An EC-47D of the 716th Squadron departs for another radio intercept mission. The EC-47D operated alongside some RC-47Ds equipped for photo-reconnaissance and with improved IR systems that could locate enemy heat sources. (Dave Menard via Jean Pierre Hoehn)

Project Enhance Plus was to hand over to the South Vietnamese the remaining USAF EC-47s in theatre, including more advanced EC-47Q/P versions. Some 36 aircraft were transferred to establish the 718th Reconnaissance Squadron under the command of Lt Col Nguyen Huu Bach. The 'Sky Dragons' operated in two detachments, comprising one at Tan San Nhut and one at Da Nang.
(Dave Menard via Jean Pierre Hoehn)

Advisory Group of the VNAF and the Material Division of the Pentagon, strongly supported by Lockheed, pushed for a single platform to undertake all these tasks. The scheme called for the replacement of all the older types with specialised versions of the Hercules. This would include 32 C-130s, 36 AC-130s, four RC-130s, six EC-130s and 12 specially developed MR-130s.[13]

The project was swiftly cancelled as a result of several factors. First, it was rightly estimated that the VNAF could not properly operate the aircraft immediately and would need years of training to adequately maintain them. Second, the US was not willing to lightly cede highly sophisticated systems such as the AC-130 or EC-130 to a foreign country. And finally, there was no budget to finance the programme. In reality, the whole process of Projects Enhance and Enhance Plus represented little more than the handover to the VNAF of dozens of second-hand or obsolete aircraft.

Restructuring the training organisation

The huge VNAF expansion effort necessitated a parallel training effort in order to maintain and sustain the expanded front-line force. The service had grown from 47 squadrons in mid-1972 to 63 a year later, while the numbers of personnel had risen from 47,000 to 63,000, including 3,500 pilots.

The tremendous expansion of the South Vietnamese armed forces put a great strain on personnel recruitment. All services tried to attract the best-educated young men and women to fill technical and officer posts. However, the VNAF proudly considered itself as an elite force, and its high morale attracted many candidates. Regular efforts were made to popularise the air force, as in the case of this group of university students visiting an air base.
(Can Thep Collection)

The Air Training Command was fully mobilised to fulfil the needs of an expanding VNAF. Here, aspirant pilots begin the stringent selection process, based on that in use with the USAF, by conducting a coordination exercise, part of a series of psychometric tests. (USAF)

Since the mid-1960s, the limited VNAF training system had been reshuffled and now focused only on primary flying training, as well as limited technical training on some specialities. Advanced training had been transferred to schools in the US. The process was accelerated between 1970 and 1972, and graduated cadets were sent back to Vietnam where they were associated with US units for 'on the job' training in order to gain experience. In the longer term, it was ultimately necessary for the VNAF to become autonomous in its training effort. The Nha Trang Training Centre was expanded accordingly and was now home to six specialised schools, including the Air Training Centre (ATC) pilot school and the English Language School. In May 1972 a communications school and a second electronics school were added at Bien Hoa.

By mid-1971 some 5,500 South Vietnamese instructors had been graduated in US schools and returned to their country, with 1,330 others still in training in the United States.[14]

The USAF also provided advisory and instructional teams at each VNAF base to assist wherever possible. With the implementation of the ceasefire, these teams were deactivated and partially replaced by US civilian contractors. By early 1973, the ATC was able to conduct over 170 in-country formal courses annually, with a production capacity of over 19,000 personnel. It was hoped that this would suffice for the time being, and would help the Vietnamese to become at least self-sufficient in training tasks in the foreseeable future. One of the most pressing problems was the fact that the newly graduated personnel still lacked experience in their specialities. It made a great difference in a squadron to have mechanics with 10 to 15 years of experience behind them, rather than newly qualified personnel fresh from schools. Experienced technicians and mid-level managers could only be obtained through time – a commodity the VNAF could not afford.

Undergraduate pilot training began in the T-41D of the 918th Training Squadron at Nha Trang. The trainer, based on a strengthened Cessna Model 172, was capable of aerobatic flight and supplemented then replaced the Cessna U-17 in use with the ATC.
(Pham Quang Khiem Collection)

The ATC curriculum was reorganised in 1972. The undergraduate pilot training began on the Cessna T-41D Mescalero and U-17 of the 918th Squadron at Nha Trang, with 180 flight hours. It was envisaged that the Pazmany PL-2 would replace both types. This light trainer was then being marketed to several Asian air forces for local licence production. The VNAF's main matériel depot at Bien Hoa assembled and test flew one example. However, budgetary constraints led to the abandonment of the scheme.

The basic flight training continued with another 180 hours on Cessna T-37Cs at Phan Rang. Twenty-four T-37Cs had been received under Project Enhance Plus and duly equipped the newly created 920th Squadron.

However, the ATC clearly could still not meet all VNAF requirements, both in terms of numbers of graduated pilots and advanced training. At one time it was envisaged that the ATC would raise a third squadron on Northrop T-38 Talons for advanced training. This would have allowed all training requirements to be managed locally, and would also have allowed training of allied air force students from Cambodia and Laos. In the event, the scheme was never implemented, again due to budgetary problems. Instead, advanced training continued to be carried out in the US. Even after the cease-fire, the VNAF continued to run a parallel training programme, encompassing both primary and basic training cycles, with cadets sent directly to the US in order to keep pace with the required number of pilots.

It was envisaged that the Pazmany PL-2, which would be assembled locally under license, would replace the T-41D. However, only a single aircraft was assembled and test-flown by Maj Le Xuan Lang. Budgetary constraints led to the cancellation of a promising project that could have provided the foundation for a local aviation industry.
(Pham Quang Khiem Collection)

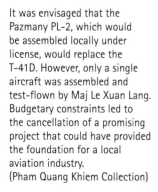

The VNAF renounced basic and advanced training in the early 1960s when the tasks were handed over to USAF schools in the United States. However, with the aim of attaining self-sufficiency, it was decided to resume the former training syllabus at the end of 1972. Some 24 T-37Cs were duly received under Project Enhance Plus. The basic training syllabus comprised 180 hours dispensed at Phan Rang. Cadet Tran Trung Quan poses here in front of one of the aircraft of the 920th Squadron.
(Tran Trung Quan)

With a backlog of 500 qualified cadets awaiting flight training, 256 were still required to be sent to the US in 1973. The figure dropped to 152 in 1974 but again rose to 215 for early 1975.[15]

These young candidates first went to Randolph AFB, Texas, for primary flight training on T-41s, and then to Keesler AFB, Mississippi, for basic training on T-28A/Bs, or to Sheppard AFB on T-37s. Advanced training also took place at Sheppard, on T-38s. Conversion courses, as provided for the F-5 or A-37, followed at Williams AFB and at Shaw AFB in South Carolina. Multi-engine and helicopter training continued to taken place in the US, even though a helicopter course was initiated in 1974 at Phan Rang on the UH-1H.

Despite efforts towards self-sufficiency in training the VNAF was still obliged to run a parallel training programme, with cadets sent to the US in order to maintain the required number of pilots. Stateside training encompassed both primary and basic cycles, at Randolph AFB and at Keesler AFB, respectively. Here, cadets of the 1st Flight, Class 72-05, pose with their US instructors in front of a T-28B at Keesler.
(Nguyen Van Chuyen)

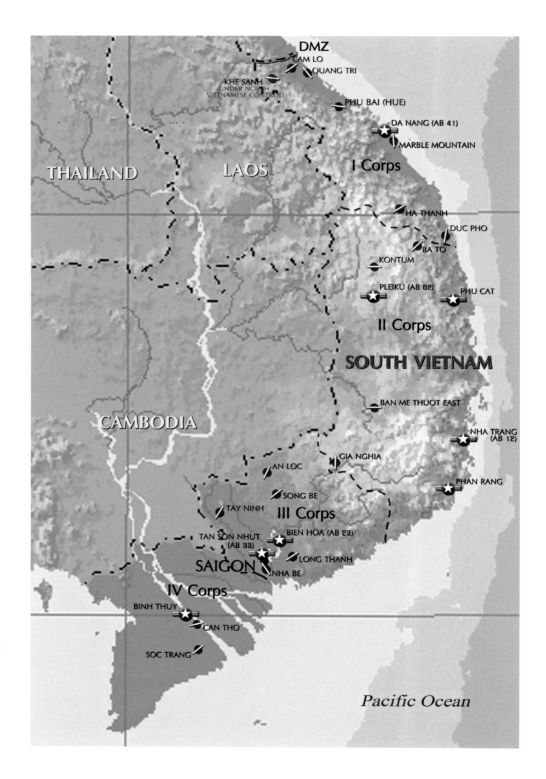

Map showing air bases (marked with the roundel of the VNAF) and other main airfields and airstrips in South Vietnam as in use from 1973–1975. Note that the airstrip in Khe Sanh was already occuppied by the Communists.

Projects Enhance and Enhance Plus

In terms of equipment deliveries, the final expansion phase of the VNAF took place over a remarkably short timeframe. Shipments under Enhance Plus were made by sea and air. The first US cargo aircraft arrived at Tan Son Nhut AB on 23 October 1972, and the last shipment arrived at Newport, near Saigon, on 12 December. Nearly 5,000 short tons of materiel arrived by air and 100,000 short tons by sea.

One of the reasons for the rapid build-up were the constraining conditions imposed by the Paris Peace Accord, which stipulated that no military equipment deliveries were authorised after the ceasefire came into effect. Only a replacement programme on a 'one for one' basis was permitted to each belligerent, in order to replace losses and normal attrition. In just seven weeks, therefore, the South Vietnamese hurriedly took charge of 618 additional aircraft. This included 236 fighters comprising 116 F-5As, 90 A-37Bs and 28 A-1s. The transport fleet was augmented by 39 additional aircraft, including 32 C-130As and four C-7As, in addition to 23 EC-47s and 22 AC-119Ks. Some 35 O-2As were pressed into service with the observation squadrons, as well as 24 T-37Cs with the ATC.

The helicopter force was augmented by 23 CH-47As and 307 UH-1Hs. This additional equipment allowed the creation of 13 further squadrons: two on the CH-47, three with A-37s, two with C-130s and five with F-5s.

Correspondingly, as of 25 January 1973 the VNAF had on strength a total of 2,075 aircraft, including 164 aircraft stored as a reserve. These were served by 61,700 personnel within an overall nominal strength of 65,000, making the VNAF one of the largest air forces in the world.

In order to man this force, the VNAF High Command developed a pilot redistribution scheme. No fewer than 144 pilots and crewmembers were taken from two C-123K squadrons slated for deactivation and assigned to the C-130A. The cockpits of the F-5 were filled by 59 A-37 pilots, increasing the total of F-5 pilots available in July 1973 to 157. The resulting shortfall in the A-37 squadrons was filled by excess C-123, C-119 and C-47 transport pilots, plus some conversion of fliers that had previously served on A-1s and O-1s. Eventually, no fewer than 49 FAC pilots were trained on the A-37B. By July 1973, the VNAF thus had some 274 A-37 pilots on strength, and 38 O-1 pilots were in the process of converting to the O-2.[16]

At the turn of 1973, the VNAF decision to opt for an all-out expansion process and drive towards self-sufficiency was showing very promising results. To the amazement of many US observers, the service had simultaneously absorbed an incredible increase in a very short space of time and meantime continued to wage combat operations. There were still many shortcomings in the fields of operations and maintenance, but there was no indication of the collapse in operational capability that some had predicted.

It seemed that the withdrawal of the US advisors had forced the South Vietnamese to act decisively to address a deteriorating military situation. Some excerpts of a report made by the Director of the Air Division, USAF Col James T. Nelson, of the Defence Attaché Office (DAO) in December 1973 highlighted the progress that had been realised:

'In dealing with the VNAF on a daily basis it readily became apparent that US opinion concerning the technical capacity of the South Vietnamese airman was

Most VNAF helicopter pilot training continued to be carried out in the US. Primary training took place at Fort Wolters, Texas, with an advanced course on the UH-1B/D at Hunter Field, Georgia. This VNAF cadet poses with his American instructor in front of a Hughes TH-55 Osage at Fort Wolters. (USAF)

All VNAF fighter pilots completed advanced training on the T-38 in the US. Although it was planned to establish a Talon squadron in South Vietnam, the scheme was never implemented. Instead, the cadets continued to be sent to Sheppard AFB. (USAF)

The Nha Trang Training Centre was expanded after 1972 and was home to six specialised schools, including mechanic, communication and electronics schools. This instructor is being given a course on the hydraulic system of the Skyraider. (USAF)

based on a false assumption. That assumption was that an agricultural people would require a great deal of time and training to be able to handle relatively rudimentary technical assignments. Our experience over the past year, which was a period of accelerated growth, revealed that the VNAF airman is capable of almost any technical assignment we are willing to train him for despite his primarily agricultural background …'

In particular, Nelson pointed out that although the ARVN now had fewer helicopters at its disposal since the withdrawal of US Army Aviation machines, the force made every possible effort to meet its requirements:

'The ARVN wanted dedicated helicopters, just like the US Army had when they were there. That is one area in which all the VNAF generals break their back to prove to the ARVN that they can respond in tactical requirements, airlift requirements, and so forth. The desire to prove this capability, I think, is about equal to that of US Army Aviation to prove that the VNAF can be responsive. I'm proud of them in this respect, and they're doing fine with the helicopters.'

Drawing upon his long experience with Asian air forces, Nelson made the following comparison:

'I saw the transition of the Chinese, after World War II, in becoming a nation and growing, and setting up a logistical base and becoming a self-sufficient organisation. I am also familiar with the efforts after the Korean War in getting South Korea to do the same thing. It has taken 15 to 20 years for each of these nations to achieve a capability of standing on their own two feet to a high degree. If anything, I would have said the Vietnamese's back should have been broken long ago, but they have been able to absorb it, and at a 300 per cent faster rate than either the Taiwanese or the Koreans. It is amazing what these people can do. They learn well when they learn something. I have learned, through my years of association in this country, that they have a tremendous capacity and capability of accomplishing a task. Once they're forced to do it, they can do it, but as long as somebody else will do it for them, they are going to let the other people do it. But, when you tell them to stand on their own two feet, sink or swim, they are always there and can stand up and be counted…'[17]

In order to help the South Vietnamese, for the time being the US DAO financed US civilian contract personnel. Most of them worked at Bien Hoa where Northrop established a maintenance team to assist the VNAF in preparing stored F-5s for flight. Among the other companies involved were Lear Seigler and Dynalectron. Meanwhile, General Electric was contracted to work on J85 engines.

Among the contractors was an engineer from Northrop, J. Tambini, who had also worked for the Republic of Korea and the Royal Saudi Air Forces and who described his association with the South Vietnamese as follows:

'When I arrived in Vietnam, in May 1972, the US military was almost all gone. There were a few USAF security personnel at Bien Hoa, but they were completely

The VNAF never used the Douglas B-26 Invader operationally, even if some examples were operated in South Vietnamese markings by the USAF Air Commando under the Farm Gate detachment in the early 1960s. However, when the 609th Air Commando Squadron was disbanded in November 1969, its remaining B-26Ks were stored and five of them handed over to the VNAF in 1971. The light bombers thereafter served only as ground instructional airframes for the mechanic school at Nha Trang. (Can Thep Collection)

gone within a month of my arrival. The Northrop technicians provided phase dock maintenance for their F-5s. The South Vietnamese could do the job but they didn't have enough personnel to fulfil all the requirements. The VNAF performed the launch and recovery efforts. The Vietnamese were very good aircraft maintenance technicians. All of their senior enlisted men had many years on the aircraft and were very familiar with them. The younger technicians required training, but they were very receptive to it. The VNAF were on a par with the Koreans, and they were far ahead of the Saudis.[18]

1   The Vietnamese Air Force, 1951–1975, An analysis of its role in combat and fourteen hours at Koh Tang. USAF Sout East Asia Monograph Series, Volume III, Monographs 4 and 5, p51.

2   Nguyen Van Thi, narrative about the creation of the 532nd Fighter Squadron at the Can Thep website (in Vietnamese).

3   Some 17 aircraft each of the AU-23 and AU-24 were built for the test and evaluation programme. When Project Credible Chase was finally cancelled, 15 AU-23s were handed over to the Cambodian Air Force while 15 AU-24s were delivered to the Royal Thai Air Force. The Thais were pleased with their 'mini-gunships' and ordered an additional 21 for both the Royal Thai Air Force and the Thai Air Police.

4   Pham Van Can, recollection about the history of the 427th Squadron, posted at Quang Su Khong Viet Nam website (in Vietnamese).

5   The introduction of the Hercules into VNAF service was a frustrating process. The South Vietnamese, supported by the USAF Advisory Group, regularly requested larger shipments of spares – though without successes. The issue was again raised in October 1971 when the US advisory group proposed a transport force based on four squadrons of C-130Es. Once again, the scheme was turned down on the grounds that it would require a higher maintenance skill to support the South Vietnamese Hercules, necessitate a long lead time to train aircrews and maintenance personnel, and would have a negative impact on USAF C-130 resources.

6   Nguyen Huu Chinh. The 237th Helicopter Squadron in the Battle of An Loc, unpublished report, October 2006, translated from the Vietnamese. Some excerpts are published in *Hell in An Loc, the 1972 Easter Invasion and the battle that saved South Vietnam*, Lam Quang Thi, University of North Texas Press, Denton, TX, 2009.

7   VNAF Improvement and Modernization Programme, HQ PACAF, July 1971 – December 1973. 1 January 1975 Report, Project CHECO, p9–112 about the measures taken to reduce the SA-7 threat.

8   In order to compensate this transfer of equipment to the VNAF, a new contract of USD 27.4 million was placed in March 1973 for 180 additional UH-1Hs for the US Army.

9   VNAF Improvement and Modernization Programme, HQ PACAF, July 1971 – December 1973. 1 January 1975 Report, Project CHECO, pages pp11, 36, 91.

10 The Vietnamese Air Force, 1951–1975, An analysis of its role in combat and fourteen hours at Koh Tang. USAF Sout East Asia Monograph Series, Volume III, Monographs 4 and 5, p12.

11 VNAF Improvement and Modernization Programme, HQ PACAF, July 1971 – December 1973. 1 January 1975 Report, Project CHECO, p100.

12 The RC-47s were equipped with three types of cameras, providing flexibility to meet the specific needs of the missions being planned, whether it dealt with an area target, point target, or a mapping requirement. The primary limitation of the RC-47 was of course its vulnerability. Thus the RC-47s continued to provide excellent coverage of MR III and IV, but were limited in MR II and totally unusable in MR I due to the presence of heavy enemy AAA. Consequently, as stated by a DAO Report of August 1973, 'the detection by photography of infiltration and most of the enemy activity in MR I and II is beyond the capability of the VNAF'.

13 VNAF Improvement and Modernization Programme, HQ PACAF, July 1971 – December 1973. 1 January 1975 Report, Project CHECO, p84.

14 Gurney, *Vietnam; The war in the air*, p206.

15 VNAF Improvement and Modernization Programme, HQ PACAF, July 1971 – December 1973. 1 January 1975 Report, Project CHECO, p120.

16 Ibid, p118.

17 Ibid, p124.

18 J. Tambini, email interview, 2003.

Chapter 3

THE ENEMY

The portfolio of photographs on the following pages shows some of the equipment of the North Vietnamese Air Force that opposed the VNAF during the period 1973 to 1975.

The course of the war changed radically during spring 1972 when the North Vietnamese launched a conventional offensive throughout South Vietnam, employing for the first time tanks and heavy artillery. The Communist divisions were covered by anti-aircraft defences never seen before in the South, and that forced a change of strategy in the use of air power. The VNAF was ill equipped to operate in the new high-threat environment with relatively low-performance aircraft lacking any ECM equipment. These S-75 (SA-2 Guideline) surface-to-air missile transporters of the 64th Battalion crossed the DMZ in early April and became part of the 367th Air Defence Division. The unit brought down several allied aircraft from the start of the fighting, including a USAF Douglas EB-66 Destroyer on 2 April. (PAVN)

These North Vietnamese S-60 57mm (2.24in) radar-directed anti-aircraft guns, towed by AT-L tracked tractors, are crossing a makeshift bridge installed by engineer troops, just south of the DMZ during the Easter Offensive of 1972. This battery was part of the 377th Air Defence Division that covered the advance of Division 308. (PAVN)

In addition to towed systems, the North Vietnamese also deployed self-propelled anti-aircraft vehicles equipped with 23mm, 37mm and 57mm anti-aircraft cannon. This battery of ZSU-57-2s of the 19th Anti-Aircraft Company was attached to the 203rd Armoured Brigade on the Quang Tri Front during the 1972 offensive. (PAVN)

The Vietnam People's Air Force (VPAF) was exclusively a defensive organisation, part of North Vietnam's imposing Anti-Aircraft Defence Command. It deployed four fighter regiments that were heavily engaged against American aircraft during the fighting in 1972. However, in 1973 the VPAF high command decided to reorganise its forces in order to carry out more offensive operations. Two units, the 923rd and 927th Fighter Regiments, were now devoted to ground-attack missions in addition to pure air-to-air tasks. Both of them trained their respective squadrons in close air support and interdiction tactics. A flight of MiG-17Fs from the 923rd Fighter Regiment is seen flying over a group of T-54 tanks at the completion of a joint exercise between the People's Army of Vietnam and the VPAF. (PAVN)

The North Vietnamese also deployed a substantial number of heavy machine guns to protect their forces against low-level attacks. This ZPU-4 of 14.5mm (0.57in) calibre could cause considerable damages to helicopters and FAC aircraft alike. (PAVN)

Covering the low- to medium-level altitude brackets against air attack was the 37mm cannon. This sturdy, optically sighted system was widely deployed by the North Vietnamese in both single- and twin-barrel versions. It was efficient up to an altitude of 4,500m (14,764ft). (PAVN)

During the 1972 fighting the North Vietnamese deployed the new 9K32M Strela-2 (SA-7 Grail) man-portable surface-to-air missile for the first time. It had a slant range of about 4,200m (13,780ft), a ceiling of 2,300m (7,546ft) and a top speed of Mach 1.75. The system worked only in tail-chase mode, and its effectiveness depended on its ability to lock onto the heat source of low-flying fixed- and rotary-wing aircraft. However, its appearance forced the VNAF to operate at higher altitudes in most cases. (PAVN)

Pilots from the 923rd Fighter Regiment debrief a training mission. This unit eventually combined all MiG-17s remaining in service. This agile subsonic fighter remained a potent low-level dogfighter, particularly against aircraft such as the VNAF F-5A and A-37B. (VPAF)

The 927th Fighter Regiment received the ground-attack mission as a secondary task, in addition to its traditional point defence assignment. The unit employed a mix of older MiG-21F, MiG-21PF and MiG-21PFM variants, as well as the newer and more capable MiG-21MF versions. (VPAF)

Around a hundred MiG-17 and MiG-17Fs of Soviet and Chinese manufacture were on VPAF inventory. Despite their limited range and payload, they constituted the main North Vietnamese fighter-bomber force. This MiG-17F appears to have been armed with unidentified rocket pods under the wings. Note that the MiG-21s in the background were also armed with UB-16-57-UMP rocket pods, each carrying 16 S-5 57mm (2.24in) rockets. These aircraft were from the 927th Fighter Regiment that was also assigned to ground-attack operations. (VPAF)

A camouflaged MiG-21MF of the 921st Fighter Regiment prepares for a training sortie. It was not until the delivery of the F-5E that the VNAF acquired a fighter that could compete with the MiG-21MF on equal terms. (VPAF)

After the losses suffered during the fighting of 1972, China delivered additional Shenyang J-6s to replenish the strength of the 925th Fighter Regiment. VNAF Intelligence estimated that around 80 MiG-19s were in service with the VPAF in 1974. (VPAF)

The most potent combat aircraft then in service with the VPAF was the MiG-21MF that equipped part of the 927th Fighter Regiment as well as the entire 921st Fighter Regiment. Some of the jets are seen here at Noi Bai-Phuc Yen air base in 1974. Note the Antonov An-2 in the background; these sturdy light transports were also used for clandestine supply operations inside South Vietnam. (VPAF)

The VPAF also modified some of its Ilyushin Il-14 and An-2 transport aircraft for attack missions and maritime patrol. This An-2 is armed with UB-16-57 rocket pods, machine guns as well as a bomb bay compartment in the fuselage. The VNAF took the threat seriously enough to train its A-37 pilots to engage the An-2s at low level and low speed. (VPAF)

This Il-28 of the 929th Bomber Squadron was photographed at Gia Lam airfield, Hanoi. It was painted in a typical blotched camouflage scheme, with tones of green and earth. It was over flown by an Ilyushin Il-18 from the 919th Transport Brigade, a unit that was engaged in supply missions over South Vietnam. (VPAF)

The VPAF deployed a single bomber unit, the 929th Bomber Squadron with 10 Ilyushin Il-28s. The unit had a history of establishment and disbandment; created in 1966, it was transferred to China to escape US air strikes against North Vietnamese bases, before returning to North Vietnam in 1971. It was used for a single attack mission against a Laotian outpost in March 1972 before being disbanded again soon after. Finally, it was re-established in early 1973. A crewman poses here during a training exercise taking place on an advanced airfield. Due to the very limited VNAF air-to-air capabilities, the Il-28s could prove a serious threat to the air bases in the northern part of the country, with Da Nang or Phu Bai vulnerable in the face of a surprise low-level, night attack strike. (VPAF)

Chapter 4

THE PRETENCE OF PEACE

The Paris Peace Accords were signed on 27 January 1973. The US forces had 60 days to evacuate South Vietnam while exchanges of prisoners took place. The US Navy was also ordered to sweep the mines that had been sown at the entrance of North Vietnamese ports. The USAF advisory teams attached to the VNAF – down as far as squadron level – as well as the mobile instruction teams, all departed.

The US also had to disband its general military headquarters in South Vietnam, the Military Assistance Command, Vietnam (MACV). It was replaced by the DAO that was permitted only 50 military and 1,200 civilian personnel to manage military aid to South Vietnam. However, the DAO was not authorised to continue to offer advisory services to the South Vietnamese armed forces. Some 5,237 US civilian contractors were nevertheless recruited to help the South Vietnamese in the field of maintenance; the majority of these worked for the VNAF.

Only the CIA continued to maintain a sizable presence, notably by keeping in place some 41 operational aircraft operated by its 'airline', Air America. These aircraft comprised three Curtiss C-46s, three C-47s, two C-7s, seven Volpars (turboprop-powered Beech 18s), two Pilatus PC-6s, seven Bell 204Bs and 10 UH-1Hs. Nine other aircraft

The Paris Accords demanded the withdrawal of remaining US forces as well as the end of any American advisory role. This forced the VNAF to 'go it alone'. With the passing of time and with the VNAF growing in experience, these advisers would increasingly serve more as liaison officers, to coordinate operations with US forces. This advisor is seen with Maj Dang Duy Lac, commander of the 524th Fighter Squadron at Phu Cat. (USAF)

The US terminated its direct intervention in South Vietnam on 27 January 1973. Only the CIA maintained a modicum of assets, including some 41 aircraft operated by Air America. One of the three available C-46s is seen here returning from a mission to Tan Son Nhut, behind a VNAF AC-47D from the 817th Attack Squadron.
(Author's Collection)

were stored at Tan Son Nhut. As a 'subcontractor', Air America also used some aircraft belonging to the Taiwanese national carrier, China Airlines. In reality, this served only to hide the fact that the aircraft were operated jointly by both the CIA and the Taiwanese Intelligence authority. The Republic of China Air Force's 34th Squadron, a unit dedicated to special operations, furnished the crews. The RoCAF regularly rotated two C-123Ks and a number of C-46s into South Vietnam. These 'airliners' were camouflaged, with the unusual registration in the 'ST-' range. They were therefore identified as being used for paramilitary operations.[1]

While the Americans withdrew from South Vietnam, the USAF still maintained a strong residual force in Thailand, which served as a deterrent in case of renewed hostilities. Of the 43,000 men and 500 aircraft stationed in the country, Washington

To assist their work, the International Commission for Control and Supervision (ICCS) teams used specially contracted aircraft, including 26 from Air America and 30 VNAF UH-1Hs. Note the ICCS recognition markings on this South Vietnamese 'Huey'.
(Nguyen Thanh)

Another institution that benefited from a neutral status was the Four-Parties Joint Military Commission instituted by the Paris Accords. The Commission supervised the military ceasefire, the departure of US forces and the prisoner exchanges. Its negotiators from North and South Vietnam, the Provisional Revolutionary Government representing the Viet Cong, and representatives of the United States, held meetings in a neutral enclave, Camp Davis, near Tan Son Nhut AB. Its members also used the same 'neutralised' aircraft as the ICCS. Here, a North Vietnamese Army delegation prepares to board a specially marked VNAF UH-1H. The officer on the extreme left, Col Bui Tin, would later defect to the West in the 1990s. (VNAF)

announced that 3,500 men and 100 aircraft would be withdrawn. In fact, US air operations in Southeast Asia ceased definitively only on 15 August 1973, with the conclusion of the air campaigns over Cambodia and Laos. Although it would decline thereafter, by the end of 1973 this force still consisted of the 388th Tactical Fighter Wing at Korat with F-4Es, A-7Ds and Republic F-105G Thunderchiefs, the 347th Tactical Fighter Wing at Takhli with General Dynamics F-111As, the 8th Tactical Fighter Wing with F-4D/Es and the 16th Special Operations Squadron with AC-130s at Ubon, and the 56th Special Operation Wing at Nakhon Phanom with Sikorsky HH-53s and HC-130s. The primary reconnaissance assets comprised the 432nd Tactical Reconnaissance Wing at Udorn with RF-4Cs and two squadrons of F-4Ds. There were also detachments of Lockheed U-2s at U Tapao. Strategic Air Command also maintained the 364th and 365th Bombardment Squadrons with B-52 bombers as well as the 901st Air Refueling Squadron on Boeing KC-135 Stratotankers, again at U Tapao.

While the ceasefire was in place, on 28 January 1973 at 08.00, the North Vietnamese launched a major counteroffensive in MR I to retake the harbour of Cua Viet. The squadrons from the 61st Tactical Wing of Da Nang were heavily engaged to check their advance. These A-37Bs from the 516th Fighter Squadron are having their armament checked and fused by armourers at the 'last chance area' before being launched for another attack mission. (USAF)

Over 200,000 North Vietnamese troops remained in the 'liberated zones' by January 1973. Hanoi's leaders celebrated the conclusion of the Paris Peace Accords, signalling the definitive departure of US troops, as a great strategic victory. They were now preparing for the next stage of the conflict, the total 'liberation' of South Vietnam. At the ceasefire date, ARVN troops controlled roughly 75 per cent of the territory and 85 per cent of the population.

ICCS

Meanwhile, the Paris Accords implemented the International Commission for Control and Supervision (ICCS), constituted by observers from Canada, Hungary, Indonesia and Poland. The ICCS teams had to be deployed in the field to report any violation of the ceasefire as well as to control the entry of any new military equipment. The ICCS divided the country into seven regions. In each region were a variety of team sites. Essentially, these sites were of two types: Observer Team Sites and Point of Entry Team Sites. Very quickly, however, the ICCS mission proved useless, as fighting immediately resumed. Furthermore, the North Vietnamese forbade any military inspection control in their 'liberated areas'. The ICCS had at its disposal 30 UH-1Hs provided by the VNAF. Meanwhile, Air America also furnished 26 aircraft, including 22 UH-1Hs, three PC-6s, one Caribou and a Volpar. These aircraft were in addition to those already used for 'regular service' by Air America.[2]

All aircraft flown by the ICCS benefited from a 'neutral status', and special recognition markings were applied. These consisted of three large yellow stripes around the rear fuselage and around the wingtips, and the inscription 'ICCS' above and below the wings and on the fuselage side or the fin.[3]

A VNAF A-37B from the 61st Tactical Wing at Da Nang en route to its target in an area west of the city. This area, including the infamous A Shau Valley, developed into a vast North Vietnamese logistic area, as well as supporting rear bases for several of their divisions. (USAF)

VNAF operations in MR I became increasingly contested by a growing and sophisticated air defence system. Control of air strikes by FAC aircraft was even made impossible in some areas covered by heavy anti-aircraft guns and SA-2 missiles. This U-17 of the 116th Observation Squadron was consequently restricted to operations over the less heavily defended enemy sectors. (Pham Quang Khiem Collection)

Creeping advance

As subsequent incidents would soon confirm, the peace brokered in Paris was illusory. As a result of its military losses and devastated economy, Hanoi concluded in 1973 that it could not launch a new, all-out offensive against the South for the foreseeable future. Instead, the Communists made efforts to develop their logistical infrastructure, opening new, controlled corridors that would ultimately allow the rapid deployment of troops.

Beginning in late 1973, the North Vietnamese launched a series of 'strategic raids' designed to wear down the South Vietnamese forces and to expand the 'liberated territories'. These operations initially consisted only of high-tempo guerrilla actions, but

VNAF helicopter operations in MR I were restricted in many areas due to increasing enemy anti-aircraft assets. The ARVN could no longer launch large-scale helicopter assaults against North Vietnamese rear-area logistics bases that were now well defended. The nose of this UH-1H displays the insignia of the 213th Helicopter Squadron at Da Nang. (Pham Quang Khiem Collection)

By early 1973 fighters from the 92nd Wing at Phan Rang were heavily involved in helping the ARVN repel a series of North Vietnamese offensives in the Central Highlands. This Dragonfly belonged to the 524th Fighter Squadron, one of three A-37B squadrons that operated from Phan Rang. (MAP)

A Skyraider pilot from the 530th Fighter Squadron at Pleiku receives a last-minute instruction from one of his squadron mates before a sortie. The squadron's A-1s were then engaged in supporting ARVN outposts north and west of Kontum in the Central Highlands. (VNAF)

seeing no concerted US reaction, they soon escalated into full-scale battles involving divisions and corps-sized units.

If throughout 1973 the South Vietnamese maintained the upper hand, during the following year the initiative gradually slipped into the hands of the enemy. By December 1974 the ARVN forces had beat back a coordinated series of large-scale Communist attacks, although at a heavy price: South Vietnamese losses for these alleged 'two years of peace' amounted to over 27,000 killed and 90,000 wounded.

At least as important was the fact that numerous isolated outposts had been lost, and the entire western border with Laos and Cambodia eventually came under Communist control.

Inadequacies in the High Command

South Vietnam's problems were aggravated by their own inadequate command and control, and particularly by the highly politicised structure of the military.

Constitutionally, the supreme commander of the South Vietnamese armed forces was the President of the Republic. He was advised by the Defence Minister, the National Security Council, and the Central Pacification and Development Council that

A pair of UH-1H gunships takes off for another armed patrol. These examples had not yet been modified with the infra-red suppression kit. (USAF via Robert C. Mikesh)

briefed him on military and strategic issues. In theory, the Joint General Staff (JGS) was the body charged with implementing the war strategy and conducting military operations, by combining the efforts of the ARVN, the VNAF and the VN Navy. In reality, due to the nature of South Vietnamese politics, it was President Nguyen Van Thieu alone that held such prerogatives.

Being the strongman of South Vietnam for nearly a decade, Thieu had succeeded in restoring a certain stability to a highly volatile political scene. Nevertheless, he remained cautious on military and strategic issues. He rarely shared his views with his subordinates, fearing that this would expose him to his political rivals. Because every military action had domestic political implications, all decisions were taken by the President within a restrictive circle of appointees and followers. Most of the members of this inner circle were generals who had supported Thieu during the various coups that rocked the country in the early 1960s. Collectively, these figures were part of the so-called 'Delta Clan', for they all served with Thieu in the Mekong Delta area. Down to the level of provincial chief, every post was held by ARVN officers personally appointed by Thieu, who always made efforts to avert a new coup attempt against him. Thieu dealt directly with the four Military Region-Corps commanders, who in turn exercised their authority over the provincial chiefs. Each corps commander had wide-ranging prerogatives within his Military Region, and acted autonomously as the local theatre commander. In reality, little coordination existed at the national level.

The JGS, under the command of Lt Gen Cao Van Vien, was limited to an advisory role and functioned only as a budgetary and manpower management body. Vien rarely, if ever, interfered with corps commander's operational plans and decisions, except perhaps for cross-border operations, or when General Reserve units were involved.

Helicopter operations became more costly in the face of improving North Vietnamese air defences, including the widespread use of SA-7 missiles. This UH-1H was shot down in the Central Highlands area in 1973.
(PAVN)

A pair of A-1Hs, probably from the 530th Fighter Squadron, heads towards its target. They are each loaded with two 370kg (816lb) and four 125kg (276lb) bombs.
(USAF)

The ARVN High Command was in fact plagued by incompetent, politically appointed, leaders. Throughout the conflict, the US had never combined with its South Vietnamese ally within a combined multinational general headquarters, as had been the case during the Korean War. Confined to a long period of pacification operations, the ARVN leaders had few occasions to exercise their command of modern, combined-arms campaigns. The VNAF and the VN Navy had been developed into modern tools but the ARVN commanders, unfortunately, did not know how to fully exploit them. Worse, there also existed a political rivalry between the ARVN and the VNAF following the departure of Vice Air Marshal Nguyen Cao Ky from the vice-presidency in 1971. Ky had even run against Thieu in the Presidential election the same year. Consequently, the VNAF was always suspected of being a 'possible coup force'. All of these factors combined to lessen and even damage the VNAF's own command structures.

In fact, the VNAF inherited from the Americans their own Tactical Air Control System (TACS). Even in this last field, the 'Vietnamization' policy had led to a gradual transfer of responsibility to the South Vietnamese in the period 1969 to 1971. However, the large-scale return of US air power to counter the Communist Easter Offensive in 1972 meant that it was the USAF that again ran most of the centralised command and control system.[4]

The VNAF transports redeployed the whole 22nd Division from the coastal province of Binh Dinh to Pleiku to counter an offensive of the North Vietnamese 10th and 320th Divisions in the summer 1973. This C-130A of the 435th Transport Squadron was seen landing on an advanced airstrip during a supply mission. (Pham Quang Khiem Collection)

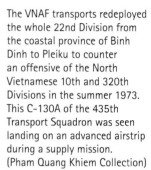

Despite the introduction of the Hercules that was intended to replace it, the C-119G was still an important asset for the VNAF after 1973. The type served with the 720th Reconnaissance Squadron, which operated them in a purely transport role since they had not been upgraded to RC-119L maritime patrol configuration. (Pham Quang Khiem Collection)

This system was based around a general headquarters, the Tactical Air Control Centre (TACC) at Tan Son Nhut that oversaw a series of regional headquarters, or Direct Air Support Centres (DASC) established at each ARVN Corps Headquarters. These latter comprised the I DASC at Da Nang, the II DASC at Pleiku, the III DASC at Bien Hoa and the IV DASC at Binh Thuy. Each DASC controlled the Air Liaison Officers (ALO) posted to the various ARVN units, as well as the local FAC squadrons. Of course, the TACC also exercised control over the air bases and the attached units deployed within their area of responsibility. However, it was one of the TACC's privileges to allocate the means necessary to meet local requirements, and to prioritise these.

Centralised control permitted greater flexibility and by virtue of the principle of economy of force, the available aircraft could be employed in the efficient way. For example, a flight of fighter-bombers that had been scheduled for a strike in the Mekong Delta could be redirected to another target in the Central Highlands.

After the American departure, there was a retrogression of the VNAF command system; now all assets were placed under the direct control of each ARVN Military Region (MR). The TACC had now lost its authority to use units from one Military Region in another, and nor did the MR Commander normally receive notification of tactical emergencies in other regions. The ARVN MR Commanders, on the authority of

The North Vietnamese increased their pressure on the Phuoc Long and Tay Ninh Provinces during the second half of 1973, threatening ARVN positions to the north and northwest of Saigon. The VNAF's 3rd Air Division at Bien Hoa was fully mobilised to counter the offensive. Here, an F-5A of the 522nd Fighter Squadron is pushed back into its revetment after a sortie.
(USAF via Robert C. Mikesh)

President Thieu, now almost exclusively employed VNAF squadrons where troops on the ground could see these aircraft providing support. Any cross-MR operations had to be approved by Thieu himself. It was now clear that the VNAF command and control system was entirely inadequate to cope with the growing North Vietnamese threat.

If versatility was ever needed it was at this time, in order to rapidly move the only flexible firepower available – air power – from area to area in order to counter the local superiority of the enemy. In fact, the centralised control of air assets, the most fundamental principle for decisive air operations, had totally vanished from the South Vietnamese strategy. The VNAF headquarters now had no identified authority for the employment of total air resources. Instead, air power was divided up into small formations, and as a consequence was improperly employed by the corps commanders, whose vision was limited to the situation in their particular corps area. Furthermore, the feeble JGS had only one senior VNAF commander on its staff and took no role in strategic decision-making.[5]

In the field, the problems were aggravated by a lack of qualified ALOs. In theory, ALOs were to be found down to battalion level. But their limited numbers forced the

The two Skyraider squadrons of the 23rd Wing at Bien Hoa were also heavily engaged in countering the North Vietnamese offensives in Military Region III during autumn 1973. This A-1H of the 518th Fighter Squadron is being directed out of its protected parking area for another sortie, loaded with 10 500lb bombs.
(Pham Quang Khiem Collection)

The C-123Ks were gradually phased out of service in the first half of 1973. Nevertheless, they continued to be of use until the end, notably in dropping supplies to beleaguered outposts such as the Ranger camp at Ton Le Chon, southwest of An Loc. The Providers were then handed over to other Asian air forces, including those of Laos, Cambodia, Thailand and the Philippines.
(Pham Quang Khiem Collection)

ARVN to use designated ARVN officers who had attended a month-long course on the employment of aircraft, strike request procedures and so forth. Since the number of such officers remained low, the ALOs were found only at regimental and divisional levels. Furthermore, most of these were inexperienced and low-ranking Army officers, or pilots who had washed-out. Others were non-rated 'observers'. Consequently, the ARVN commanders often ignored them. Efforts to post more qualified, fighter-rating officers were frustrated by assignment priorities. These reflected the prevalent attitude that the ALO's job was less esteemed and respected than that of a pilot assignment to an operational squadron. In fact, only at the Military Region level was the ALO a rated pilot.

The second-hand C-130As delivered to the VNAF came from various USAF Reserve and National Guard units, and comprised some of the oldest Hercules airframes. Among them was this example from the 435th Transport Squadron at Tan Son Nhut. It was one of the first examples built, and lacked weather and navigation radar.
(Pham Quang Khiem Collection)

New challenges

Throughout this period the VNAF was heavily engaged and progressively worn down while trying to halt the enemy advance. In fact, the VNAF aircraft had not even had time to shut down their engines when the ceasefire arrived.

Only hours before the ceasefire, which was to become effective from 08.00 on 28 January 1973, the ARVN launched an offensive to seize the Cua Viet harbour, at the mouth of the river of the same name. Situated near the DMZ, the city served as a major transhipment point for North Vietnamese supplies. At H Hour, the South Vietnamese were in control of the town and flew in international observers of the ICCS to witness this fact. However, the North Vietnamese immediately prepared a counterattack, and three days later expelled the ARVN despite intensive support from VNAF A-37s of the 61st Tactical Wing at Da Nang.

It was not only the North Vietnamese that violated the ceasefire: while attempting to consolidate their positions, the South Vietnamese regularly did the same. In February 1973 the ARVN launched an offensive to drive out the North Vietnamese 2nd Division from Sa Huyn, a small harbour at the junction of I and II Corps, and this operation was extensively supported by the 1st and 2nd Air Divisions of the VNAF.

A pair of A-37Bs of the 526th Fighter Squadron at Binh Thuy returns from an attack sortie in the Mekong Delta area. Thanks to the aggressive ARVN and VNAF stance, the South Vietnamese retained the initiative and kept control of the region practically until the end of the war.
(USAF via Robert C. Mikesh)

One of the other resident units at Binh Thuy covering the Mekong Delta area was the 526th Fighter Squadron, with its distinctive markings of white polka dots painted on blue, yellow or red tip tanks and tails. The A-37B was a good bombing platform but proved vulnerable to SA-7s and medium and heavy anti-aircraft guns.
(USAF via Robert C. Mikesh)

At Phan Rang, the 92nd Wing had mobilised its three squadrons of A-37Bs to launch a series of strikes around Bao Loc, which had come under enemy attack. A company of sappers had even entrenched inside a petrol station within the city. A flight was directed towards this target, but the aircraft were loaded with CBU-55 fuel-air explosive bombs and so the attack was cancelled; it was feared that these weapons would not only destroy the petrol station, but also the entire surrounding district. The strike was finally carried out when the aircraft had been rearmed with 500lb Mk 82 bombs. The same afternoon, a number of A-37Bs from the 534th Fighter Squadron that had been sent to Phan Thiet for a 'depot check' encountered several positions en route where the Viet Cong had raised their flags. These were methodically strafed.

South Vietnamese F-5s, A-1s and A-37s were also flying close support missions in the Central Highlands as well as in III Corps area. Throughout spring 1973 most of these sorties were in direct assistance to still small-scale ARVN operations, often 'land-grabbing' actions or repelling probing attacks carried out by the Communists against outposts manned by the Southerners. The notable exception was the heavy involvement of the VNAF's 4th Air Division from Binh Thuy in repulsing an offensive by the PAVN 1st Division against the town of Hong Nhu, near the Cambodian border in IV Corps area, in March 1974.

Crews of the 819th Attack Squadron man the night observation scope installed on the port side of the AC-119G. The aircraft had more sophisticated night sensors than the AC-47D but its weapon system was not a great improvement, with four instead as opposed to three 7.62mm (0.3in) Gatling guns. (Pham Quang Khiem Collection)

The South Vietnamese made extensive use of helicopters to haul troops and supplies despite the massive deployment of AAA and SA-7s within the combat zone. The pilots of the UH-1Hs meanwhile developed new tactics to counter the latter threat, by flying as low as 50ft (15m) in order to surprise the enemy's SAM operators. When flying at altitude, immediate evasive manoeuvres had to be taken in case of an SA-7 launch. The pilot reduced the power to idle, turned towards the missile, face-on, in the hope of breaking off the missile guidance system's infra-red lock-on. The gunners were also provided with flares that they dropped by hand to decoy the missiles. The SA-7 usually lost its tracking if the helicopter's exhaust presented an angle greater than 45° to its flight path.

In the hot afternoon hours the pilots were also advised to use concealment in clouds when possible, since the missile's crude guidance system could be distracted by the sun reflection offered by them.

ARVN soldiers board 'Hueys' of the 217th Helicopter Squadron for a troop rotation. The South Vietnamese Army still enjoyed considerable helicopter support throughout 1973 before budgetary cuts forced a reduction in availability by more than a half.
(US Army)

This 'Huey' was the personal mount of the commander of the ARVN III Corps-Military Region III, as indicated by the Roman numeral painted on the nose. However, this UH-1H was a standard transport version, not the command and control version that was better equipped in terms of communication equipment.
(Pham Quang Khiem Collection)

The big CH-47s could not fly evasive tactics, and so flare dispensers were installed, making them one of the first VNAF aircraft to benefit from this new equipment. The MJU-3B flare dispensers were also installed on some A-37s and F-5s, which entailed giving up a weapon pylon. Some 668 of the 883 flare dispensers ordered had been delivered by October 1973 and also served to equip the transport fleet. A number of A-37Bs were later modified with the internal AN/ALE-20 system that could eject up to 16 ALA-17 flares. This flare dispenser was installed at the expense of the panoramic strike camera. Some aircraft, particularly UH-1Hs, were also repainted with IR-suppressant special paint.[6]

Despite all these preventive measures, the losses to SA-7s continued to mount. Between January and June 1973, there were 22 reported Strela attacks, with eight aircraft and their crew lost: one A-37B, one F-5A, three A-1s, two UH-1Hs and one CH-47A.

A UH-1H of the 211th Helicopter Squadron at Binh Thuy inserts troops for a search and clear operation in pursuit of Viet Cong guerrillas. The disembarked soldiers would usually patrol an assigned area for three days before being picked up by another helicopter. (USAF)

'Huey' transports were usually escorted during air assaults by gunship-configured machines. The crew of this gunship has removed all the doors in order to save weight, improve visibility and facilitate their exit from the machine in case of problems. (Pham Quang Khiem Collection)

A pilot from the 718th Reconnaissance Squadron poses in front of his EC-47P. One of these valuable ELINT platforms was shot down by enemy 37mm AAA near 'Parrot's Beak' northwest of Saigon on 13 May 1974. Only the navigator, Lt Truong Tu An, managed to bail out and was taken prisoner. (Can Thep Collection)

A new ceasefire

International pressure forced the opposing parties to agree to a new ceasefire, which became effective on 15 June 1973. Although this soon broke down, the level of fighting decreased substantially during the first week of its implementation.

Thereafter, however, the Communists accelerated the pace of their attacks, profiting from Washington's failure to provide the support to Saigon that it had previously promised. In fact, such support had meanwhile become impossible: in August 1974 the US Congress adopted the Cooper Church Amendment, restricting the authority of the President to commit forces in Vietnam, Cambodia and Laos. With so much discussion with respect to the war, and the lack of support for any US military action, it was evident that Congress had no intention of permitting the White House to resume the bombing, irrespective of the scope of actions being undertaken by the North Vietnamese. The USAF squadrons maintained in Thailand as a visible display of intent should Hanoi 'significantly' violate the ceasefire thereby lost their deterrent value.

At the same time, the South Vietnamese continued to follow the strategy they had developed throughout the war. This involved a refusal to give up any piece of ground that had been gained, and an attempt to keep the enemy off balance through the extensive use of artillery and air power, with troops only being used cautiously. Over time, the leadership in Hanoi became convinced that the US would not again come to help Saigon with extensive air and naval power should South Vietnam come under a new invasion.

President Thieu therefore travelled to the US to meet President Nixon, who made efforts to reassure him. Indeed, the USAF was ordered to continue flying reconnais-

Crew of the 817th Attack Squadron run towards their aircraft during a night alert scramble. By this time, the AC-47D was now largely restricted to operating in less well-defended areas or in support of anti-guerrilla sweeps. (VNAF)

sance flights over South Vietnam until the end of 1974 in order to bolster the VNAF's meagre intelligence assets.

In the field, the international observers of the ICCS were unable to fulfil their tasks since the North Vietnamese denied them access to the areas they controlled. Two ICCS helicopters conveying observer teams were even shot down by the Communists. While the ICCS scrupulously controlled any military equipment handed over to the South Vietnamese, it was forced to recognise that none of the international observers could similarly monitor the Communist side. In fact, Hanoi now began to introduce additional forces, deploying artillery and armour inside South Vietnam.

South Vietnamese Intelligence estimated that the number of enemy tanks rose from 190 in January 1973 to 500 by mid-1974. The number of guns also rose from 220 to 715 during the same period. More worryingly, the North Vietnamese also began to refurbish 14 former French and US airstrips throughout South Vietnam, in order to accept transport aircraft. These airstrips included Dak To, Loc Ninh, Ca Lu and Dong Ha. The former airstrip of Khe Sanh was extended from 3,900 to 5,300ft (1,189 to 1,615m), rendering it capable of accommodating fighter operations. Some 24 SA-2 launchers protected the base, as well as the logistic depots of Dong Ha.

The VNAF made plans to bomb the newly refurbished air base but losses were expected to be high since no South Vietnamese aircraft was equipped with ECM equipment. In order to conserve aircraft the VNAF in I Corps area was ordered not to fly missions north of the Hue-Quang Tri area, or west of Route 1 along the Laotian border. With tacit approval, it was considered that any bombing of these Communist-controlled areas could be considered as a direct attack against North Vietnam itself, thus risking provoking heavy retaliation by Hanoi.

The faithful Skyraider was initially destined to be phased out and replaced by more modern types. Nevertheless, the VNAF continued to deploy three squadrons, appreciating the A-1's endurance and load-carrying capabilities. The 514th Fighter Squadron at Bien Hoa operated this A-1G.
(USAF)

Despite the acquisition of a limited number of O-2As, the O-1 remained the backbone of the FAC squadrons, but was now extremely vulnerable to enemy air defences. These O-1Es belonged to the 112th Observation Squadron at Bien Hoa.
(USAF)

The necessity for air defence

The threat of North Vietnamese air strikes meanwhile became reality, forcing the VNAF to establish a significant air defence organisation.

Initially the two current F-5A squadrons assumed the task, even if the mission only received a low-level priority. Pairs of 522nd Squadron F-5s armed with AIM-9E Sidewinder air-to-air missiles were standing alert at Da Nang from January 1972, and this unit usually rotated detachments of up to six aircraft at this base. The role was assumed by the newly established 538th Squadron from March 1973.

Initially, the airspace to be defended was under the responsibility of the TACC, and was controlled by its regional DASC command posts: 'Panama' at Da Nang, 'Peacock' at Pleiku, 'Pyramid' at Ban Me Thout, 'Paris' at Saigon and 'Paddy' at Binh Thuy. However, this arrangement was found unsatisfactory and with the expanding F-5 force it was decided to streamline and centralise the air defence effort. This was achieved by subdividing the country into two Air Defence Sectors (ADS): ADS North was centred at Da Nang, and ADS South was installed at Tan Son Nhut. A central Air Defence Command Post was attached to the TACC and commanded by Col Nguyen Quang Tri.

ADS North was first to be established, in early 1974, and was put under the command of Lt Col Le Xuan Lan, an officer who had just returned from Maxwell AFB, Alabama, where he was introduced to a special air defence course. The service then employed five AN/FPS-20 search radars and five AN/TPS-6 height-finding radars as part of a GCI network.

The VNAF attempted to integrate its air defence assets with those of the other services. The four ARVN air defence battalions equipped with M167 Vulcan 20mm guns, as well as some obsolete batteries of Bofors M1 40mm and Oerlikon 20mm guns were then positioned around critical strategic locations, including air bases, harbours and some important command posts. However, the planned air defence battalions attached to each ARVN division as well as the HAWK SAM battalions were never financed. In fact, until the introduction of the F-5E, the VNAF had only 40 F-5As at its disposal that

An F-5B of the 522nd Fighter Squadron departs for a target towing mission. The target dart was used for practicing 20mm air-to-air gunnery. (Anthony Tambini)

A VNAF pilot poses beside a former USAF F-5A at Bien Hoa. The jet still wears its natural metal scheme. The aircraft in the background is a former Imperial Iranian Air Force machine, painted in desert camouflage. The tempo of operations after the Peace Accord was such that the VNAF had no time to repaint its aircraft in the Southeast Asia camouflage scheme.
(VNAF)

were equipped with wingtip launch rails for Sidewinder missiles. These were distributed among three of the six F-5 squadrons that received air defence taskings: two at Da Nang, one at Bien Hoa and a detachment at Phu Cat.

The VNAF pilots flew air defence exercises and were briefed on the characteristics of the expected foes, notably with instruction films, including the Il-28, MiG-17 and MiG-19 (J-6). The MiG-21 was considered the most potent adversary, but the low-level intrusion of transport aircraft and helicopters was also taken into count, including rocket-armed An-2s. It was then decided to train some A-37 pilots for interception mission, since the Dragonfly was considered more suitable for use against enemy aircraft flying below 10,000ft (3,048m) and 200kt. A plan existed to develop a 20mm gun pod to be carried by the A-37B, but this was eventually abandoned due to budgetary constraints.

Nevertheless, the VNAF air defence system only began to be barely operational when the F-5E was introduced to service at the end of 1974. The F-5A, with no on-board radar, as well as the A-37, could only make day visual intercepts under ground-based radar control. The first F-5Es were immediately dispatched north to Da Nang to re-equip the 538th Squadron, which exchanged its F-5As. At this time the VPAF maintained four fighter regiments and a bomber squadron. VNAF Intelligence estimated that the North Vietnamese were still recovering from the heavy losses suffered during the 1972 campaign. But by 1974 the VPAF was assumed to have some 90 MiG-21s, 80 Chinese-built MiG-19s, 100 MiG-17s and 10 Il-28s. The North Vietnamese had begun a programme of ground-attack training for its MiG-17 pilots, and one of the two MiG-21

An A-37B from the 61st Wing at Da Nang returns from a combat sortie. The unit's three A-37B and one F-5A squadrons were fully committed to the defence of the northern and western approaches of Hue throughout 1973.
(VNAF)

regiments had a dual function of air defence and fighter-bomber operations. Intelligence also indicated that the most southerly VPAF base of Vinh now accommodated a detachment of Il-28 bombers, together with some armed An-2s.[7]

Going alone

The South Vietnamese were facing increasing enemy attacks now carried out at regimental and divisional strength, mainly in the II and III Corps areas. In July 1973 the VNAF's 4th Air Division was fully mobilised to support an ARVN offensive in the Seven Mountains area, between Tinh Bien and Tri Tran, against the North Vietnamese 1st Division. The A-37 wing at Binh Thuy flew numerous strikes, providing direct fire support to mobile armoured task forces. These inflicted such heavy losses upon the enemy that the 1st Division was deactivated in October. Throughout the Delta area, the South Vietnamese carried out numerous drives to wipe out enemy guerrilla pockets. The ARVN 7th Division was particularly aggressive in Dinh Tuong Province, its commander making efficient use of VNAF helicopters to deliver troops.

In order to deprive the enemy of rice, VNAF FACs and fixed-wing gunships constantly monitored the entry points and roads leading to Communist-controlled zones. However, the Communists attempted to circumvent the blockade in some areas by exporting rice to Cambodia by boat. The VN Navy made efforts to seal off this riverine traffic but could not count on VNAF cooperation since there were no maritime patrol aircraft in service.

However, the heaviest fighting took place during the summer 1973 in the Central Highlands area. In June, positions occupied by the ARVN 23rd Division at Trung Nhia, west of Kontum, were overwhelmed by a sudden North Vietnamese assault. The Communist 10th Division then entrenched in the area, supported by artillery and T-54 tanks. The South Vietnamese launched a series of counteroffensives, with heavy artillery and VNAF support, but failed to dislodge the enemy. In fact, after serious losses, the South

An O-2A from the 118th Observation Squadron at Pleiku searches for elusive North Vietnamese 130mm (5.12in) artillery during the battle of Trung Nhia, west of Kontum. The aircraft was a major improvement over the O-1 and U-17, its twin-engine configuration conferring increased reliability and survivability, although it was more costly to maintain. (Pham Quang Khiem Collection)

Vietnamese wound down the operation. They then tried once more in August but failed to advance much further. VNAF transports then redeployed the 42nd Regiment of the 22nd Division from Binh Dinh Province to Kontum for a renewed push. After heavy hand-to-hand fighting, the ARVN finally overwhelmed the enemy bunkers and trenches that had previously been pounded by VNAF A-1s and A-37s. However, the VNAF had more difficulty in destroying the elusive Communist 130mm (5.12in) artillery, even when the patrolling O-1s and O-2s spotted some of them on the move.

The North Vietnamese also tried to frustrate ARVN operations by attacking the Plei Djereng outpost. In this case, bad weather impeded VNAF support. When the weather finally improved, VNAF helicopters flew in reinforcements, but it was too late and the position was lost. Undaunted by this bad news, the ARVN II Corps tried to recapture the initiative. The plan was to lure the North Vietnamese 320th Division into flat terrain west of Pleiku and to destroy it by using the superior firepower and mobility offered by VNAF. C-130s, C-119s and C-7s began to redeploy the entire 22nd Division from the coastal province of Binh Dinh to Pleiku for the task. Unknown at this time, it was the last occasion that the VNAF would be able to mount an air bridge of this scale. However, the North Vietnamese refused to fall into the trap, and despite numerous skirmishes as well as some tanks destroyed, the 320th Division slipped back into Cambodia.

In the first week of April, the FACs discovered concerted North Vietnamese logistic preparation in the area of Duc Co and directed VNAF strikes. The A-1s and A-37s also attacked a crossing on the Se San River, near the Cambodian border, destroying 13 medium ferries and trucks.

The Communists now opened a new front when a North Vietnamese division stormed the Quang Duc outpost further south, severing the only open route to the beleaguered province of Phuoc Long in the III Corps area. The truck convoys, covered by FACs, made a long detour northwest from Saigon to the Highlands before reaching the provincial capital of Phuoc Long City. It was then vital to clear the blockade installed on Route 8B. VNAF fighter-bombers flew close support missions for the 22nd Division but its advance stalled in the face of stiff opposition. The South Vietnamese then made a series of helicopter assaults and even decided to insert a full regiment of troops on the Nhon Co airstrip. The area had been previously re-occupied by a reconnaissance platoon brought in by helicopters. The zone was still subject to sporadic enemy artillery fire but the operation continued. Six C-130As landed the 1st Battalion of the 45th Regiment on a runway targeted by artillery. In a quick turnaround, the Hercules flew out without being hit. The ARVN expanded the perimeter and secured the area, enabling the rest of the regiment to be flown in. Using a judicious coordination of artillery, close air support and helicopters, the ARVN succeeded in driving out the North Vietnamese.

In the I Corps area, the South Vietnamese were also in a precarious position, with a much-extended perimeter to defend, this stretching in a long line along the coastal plain, extending almost from the DMZ/North Vietnamese border to the boundary of the II Corps zone. This area contained important population centres including Hue and Da Nang. The enemy maintained a constant pressure on the western flank of the perimeter. It had also tremendously expanded its logistic depots at Cam Lo, Khe Sanh and A Shau Valley. The enemy build-up often now took place in full view of advanced ARVN

The C-7A equipped three VNAF squadrons, with two at Tan Son Nhut and one at Da Nang. In practice, the Caribous operated throughout the country, maintaining detachments on forward airfields to sustain the Ranger outposts. This aircraft belonged to the 429th Transport Squadron.
(Doug Lamerson)

positions. The I Corps commander bitterly complained that he could not direct heavy aerial firepower, such as B-52 bombers, against the Communist positions.

Although having little confidence in US bombing being resumed, DAO planners cooperated with I Corps in keeping target folders current, and direct liaison between I Corps and the DAO was established for this purpose. ARVN commanders had observed that since the North Vietnamese had placed thousands of tons of supplies and equipment in open, visible storage, throughout northern Quang Tri and Western Thua Thien Provinces, the B-52s could wipe them out in 10 days.

Several weeks later, the same measure was extended to the four ARVN corps areas, with a system of hotlines established to link US Support Command at Nakhon Phanom in Thailand and the ARVN Joint General Staff. The VNAF Headquarters and all four corps commanders were also given direct access to this system. Provisions of the plan included the constant updating of B-52 targets, and in the case of a major enemy offensive the ARVN was to hold its lines for seven to 15 days, allowing time for US Congress to approve the employment of US air power in South Vietnam. Later, many high-ranking officers of the DAO admitted that this arrangement was wildly optimistic and served only to bolster the morale of the South Vietnamese.

The situation also became precarious in the III Corps area. Here, the Communists expanded their logistic bases and deployed additional units that could directly attack Saigon. In fact, the Saigon-Tay Ninh corridor was regularly subjected to attacks, as was the access route to An Loc. VNAF F-5s and A-1s were regularly providing close air support to positions under attack but now faced stiff anti-aircraft opposition. Despite intensive covering air strikes, the ARVN lost the strategic position of Soui Da, which had served as a useful observation outpost. As previously indicated, Phuoc Long Province was now completely isolated. Initially, each supply convoy necessitated a combined air and ground operation. But the road link was regularly cut, forcing the VNAF to re-supply the regional capital of Phuoc Long City and the four district towns with helicopters and transport aircraft for the next 18 months. The monthly requirement was 400 to 500 tons, mostly rice, salt, ammunition and fuel.

Other isolated outposts also consumed a great deal of VNAF capacity just to keep them alive. One of these outposts was Ton Le Chon, southwest of An Loc. The 92nd Ranger Battalion held the hill and its resistance to numerous North Vietnamese assaults became legendary. The base was re-supplied using HALO parachute drops by C-130s. Many attempts were made to fly in helicopters to evacuate casualties and land replacements. With time, the enemy had dramatically increased its anti-aircraft assets in the area, including 37mm and 57mm guns, and each supply operation became more costly. Between late October 1973 and the end of January 1974, 20 helicopters attempted landings; only six managed to land and three of these were destroyed by enemy fire upon landing. The landing zone was now targeted by long-range 130mm guns as well as 160mm (6.30in) heavy mortars. In the last week of December 1973, a CH-47A from the 237th Helicopter Squadron was destroyed as it landed, the 13th helicopter to be hit by enemy fire that month. Casualties amounted to nine killed and 36 wounded. Another Chinook crashed and burned in January. As the anniversary of the ceasefire came, 12 seriously wounded soldiers remained in the beleaguered camp.

In order to ease the pressure and to disrupt the enemy's logistic preparations, the VNAF was ordered to fly a sustained interdiction campaign in October and December 1973, striking North Vietnamese supply depots in the III Corps area, situated in the Tay

Ninh, Phuoc Long and Binh Long Provinces. Exceptionally, the air assets of both the III and IV Corps were mobilised, with the F-5s of the 63rd Wing and the A-1s of the 23rd Wing at Bien Hoa committed alongside the A-37s of the 74th Wing of Binh Thuy. The operation began with an attack in late October against Xa Mat in Tay Ninh Province, a small hamlet on the border with Cambodia that served as an entry point for logistics. The raid destroyed the market, a fuel dump, and about 60 structures. Over a thousand sorties were flown, including 800 sorties directed against the huge storage complexes of Bo Duc and Loc Ninh between 7 November and 5 December. These strikes were flown against pre-planned targets and were not directed by FACs, these latter being driven out of the area by the heavy concentration of anti-aircraft fire. As expected, the South Vietnamese fighter pilots met heavy AAA and SA-7 activity, forcing them to adapt their tactics to the threat. As flak was reported up to 12,000ft (3,658m), the targets were approached at around 10,000ft (3,048m), followed by attack runs from different directions. The bombs were released between 3,000 and 7,000ft (914 and 2,134m), the aircraft spending a minimum of time under 5,000ft (1,524m) with constant jinking.

The III Corps and VNAF intelligence claimed excellent results were obtained at the Loc Ninh storage facilities, but good concealments made assessment at Bo Duc difficult. Some reports stated that the bombings yielded very poor results at this last location. An EC-47 that was monitoring enemy communications over Loc Ninh in order to collect intelligence on the strikes was brought down by 37mm AAA. Only the navigator could jump and was taken prisoner. The Communists retaliated with a rocket attack against Bien Hoa air base on 6 November, which resulted in the destruction of three F-5As.

In the long run, these kinds of sporadic interdiction campaigns did not significantly disturb the enemy's logistical build-up.[8] Moreover, the heavy tempo of operations began to exact its toll on the already used airframes that made up most of the VNAF inventory. By the end of summer 1973 cases of corrosion had been detected on many F-5A airframes. Twenty-nine F-5As were grounded as a result, while 18 other corroded airframes continued to be maintained in operational condition but required repairs as soon as possible. Treating heavy corrosion damage was beyond the VNAF's capabilities, so requests were made to send the airframes to the US for maintenance. Budget difficulties meant the scheme took over a year to implement.

The operational levels in the F-5A units began to decline markedly, reaching a low of 30 per cent for several weeks. A solution was found through the shipment of cor-

The work of the Caribous was supplemented by CH-47As. The Chinooks operated within four squadrons, and a heavy helicopter unit was allocated to each of the ARVN Military Regions.
(Long Nguyen)

A flight of Sidewinder-armed F-5As from the 538th Squadron patrols the coastline east of Da Nang. The squadron provided air defence for the northern part of the country but failed to cover the South Vietnamese Navy during naval engagements against the Chinese Navy for the control of the contested Paracel Islands.
(VNAF)

roded F-5As to a Republic of China Air Force depot at Ping Tung in Taiwan, where they were repaired under project Peace Basket. Although more affordable, the Taiwanese deal included the return of the 17 J85-13 engines that had been delivered by the RoCAF in January 1973. Maintained in store as a reserve, these engines had never been used; indeed, the original storage cans had never been opened. The first reconditioned airframes were returned to South Vietnam in April 1974.

The VNAF's limited air defence capability was clearly demonstrated on 20 January 1974 when it was unable to provide air cover to the South Vietnamese Navy during naval engagements against the Chinese Navy for the control of the contested Paracel Islands, some 230 miles (370km) east of Da Nang. The superior enemy task force sank a South Vietnamese ship and damaged three others. The 1st Air Division scrambled a flight of F-5As from the 538th Squadron followed by another flight of A-37Bs. The jets arrived too late and could only make a quick sweep of the area before being forced to retreat when they were warned that MiG-19 (J-6) and MiG-21 (J-7) fighters were being vectored towards them from Hainan Island. The enemy destroyers and missile patrol boats then covered a landing by troops that then occupied the whole groups of islands. The VNAF never dared to confront Chinese air power thereafter. Bitterly, the South Vietnamese revealed that the US Navy had provided no assistance during the fighting, not even helping in rescuing their sailors.

With the first anniversary of the ceasefire, the situation was far from encouraging. Despite blatant violations of the agreement by the North Vietnamese, Washington did not respond to Saigon's pleas. South Vietnamese Intelligence had now detected that no fewer than two anti-aircraft artillery divisions had been deployed to the South, in addition to 26 independent regiments. SA-7s could now be encountered in all four corps areas.[9]

VNAF losses continued to mount, but the scheduled replacements according to the 'one for one' basis permitted by the accords were never realised. It was a sign of harder times to come.

The newly established F-5 squadrons continued to suffer from a low operational rate during the second half of 1973 – when compared to those equipped with A-37Bs and A-1s. This was mainly due to a lack of trained maintenance personnel. The problem was partly offset by the use of contracted US civilian technicians.
(USAF)

1   Dr Joe F. Leeker. The History of Air America; E-book, University of Texas, McDermott Library. pp34–35.

2   Ibid, pp39–43.

3   Ibid, pp40–44.

4   For an in-depth analysis of the VNAF tactical control system see: 'The Vietnamese Air Force, 1951–1975, An analysis of its role in combat and fourteen hours at Koh Tang'. USAF Southeast Asia Monograph Series, Volume III, Monographs 4 and 5, pp4–12, 24–25 and 68–69.

5   A DAO Report from October 1973 described the limited role allowed to the VNAF in the control of its own forces as follows: 'VNAF Headquarters does not command or control the Air Force resources. Command and Control of strike aircraft and helicopters rests with the ARVN Corps – Military Region Commander. The monitoring of air operations by the VNAF Headquarters personnel is tempered by the quantity, quality and timeliness of data reported. Like the other components' commands and the Joint Chief of Staff itself, the VNAF Headquarters staff gets the information the Military Region Commander wants them to have, when he wants them to have it.'

6   For an analysis of the VNAF drawdown and losses for this period see 'The Vietnamese Air Force, 1951–1975, An analysis of its role in combat and fourteen hours at Koh Tang', USAF Southeast Asia Monograph Series, Volume III, Monographs 4 and 5, p51, and Robert C. Mikesh, 'Flying Dragon, the South Vietnamese Air Force', Schiffer Publishing Ltd, 2005, pp127–137. It is interesting to compare these US sources with those given by the North Vietnamese in Lich Su Quan Chung Phong Khong, Volume 3, p260. There were few discrepancies between them. For example, the Communists claimed 124 VNAF aircraft shoot down between 28 January 1973 and 31 October 1974, a figure that was slightly inferior to the US estimate, that included 38 fighters, 65 helicopters, 15 observation, and six transport aircraft. The SA-7 system was credited with 25 kills from this overall total.

7   Contrary to the very rich air combat experience of the VPAF, the VNAF air defence potential was considered, as stated in a DAO Report of July 1973, as being marginal: 'In the Air Defence role, the VNAF is handicapped by aircraft which have no capability (because of available weapons) in the front intercept environment. In addition, (again because of weapons) they are constrained to a clear air mass situation and stern attack geometry. Geographical shape and radar masking give VNAF little early warning. The command and control system, although responsive, is still not quick enough to take advantage of early warning. In the air superiority role, the VNAF faces more experienced pilots flying equipment that is similar in capability. This will result in a serious disadvantage during the learning curve until the VNAF pilots gained experience in air-to-air combat. Neither training resources nor supervisory incentive are sufficient to overcome these deficiencies in the near future.'

8   The VNAF could never provide a sustained interdiction campaign against the enemy lines of communication. By comparison, the USAF flew an average of 200 daily strike sorties, in addition to those of the AC-130s, during each dry season. Consequently, the North Vietnamese were able to develop a new logistic corridor, known as the 'Ho Chi Minh East Trail' on the eastern slopes of the Annamite Mountains chain, inside South Vietnam proper in addition to the other branch that runs along the Laotian and Cambodian borders.

9   The North Vietnamese sources indicated that 68 additional SA-7 launchers had been sent as reinforcement into South Vietnam at the end of 1974. With those already there, they had at their disposal some 794 missiles available at the beginning of 1975. See Lich Su Quan Chung Phong Khong, Volume 3, p257.

Chapter 5

FIGHTING THE POOR MAN'S WAR

Outside Vietnam, political considerations now began to weigh heavily on the support that the South Vietnamese could expect to receive. The US Congress began impeachment proceedings against President Nixon in the wake of the Watergate scandal. On 9 August 1974, Richard M. Nixon, the last steadfast supporter of South Vietnam, resigned the presidency, to be replaced by Gerald R. Ford.

The trend of diminishing aid to Saigon then accelerated. US military assistance fell from USD2.924 billion in 1973 to USD1.185 billion in 1974, a reduction of nearly two thirds. During a meeting of the Politburo in Hanoi, this news was received with the recognition that 'now Saigon was forced to fight a poor man's war'.

The soaring prices of imported oil, resulting from the Yom Kippur War, also had a negative impact on the readiness of the VNAF, which saw its fuel reserve slump to just half of its requirements. Later, the situation improved slightly when Saudi Arabia, known for its staunch anti-communist policy, agreed to sell oil to South Vietnam at a preferential rate. Budget cuts also translated into a reduction in the deliveries of ammunition and spare parts as well as some maintenance programmes. Many airframes that were scheduled for overhaul or other lesser maintenance works were instead maintained on the flight line and flown to their limits.

By early 1975 the prospect of winning the war had become bleak for South Vietnam. Despite its best efforts, Saigon was now diplomatically isolated, while Washington had decided to abandon its ally. Even after a group of Senators made an inspection tour of air bases and received a brief on the debilitated status of the VNAF, the US position remained intractable.
(Nguyen Van Khoi)

The VNAF training system was still functioning at its full capacity by early 1974 before the implementation of budget cuts. Lt Pham Quang Khiem poses here in front of a T-41D of the 918th Air Training Squadron at Binh Thuy in January 1974. The aircraft was probably making a stop at the base in the Mekong Delta area during a navigation exercise from its home base of Nha Trang. (Pham Quang Khiem Collection)

The number of US civilian contractors working for the VNAF was further cut due to budget restrictions, falling from 5,237 to 2,823. In spring 1974, the VNAF was forced to terminate the contracts of US technicians working at its 22 aerial logistics sites. Many lesser bases and airstrips were closed down or saw their activities reduced, including Hue, Chu Lai, Phu Bai, Cam Ranh Bay and Ban Me Thout East. These bases remained open but had no permanent units assigned and served only as refuelling points or auxiliary deployment airfields.

Another concern was the poor state of communications and electronic equipment due to a lack of spare parts and depot maintenance, as well as cuts made in terms of contracted US technicians. Consequently, by early 1974 the VNAF navigation aids were suffering nearly a non-operational rate of nearly 50 per cent. At the time, only six of the 11 Tactical Air navigation (TACAN) sites remained operational. Only four of the seven ground-controlled approach radars were functioning, as well as three out of five AN/FPS-20 radars and two of five AN/TPS-6 radars. The situation improved slightly when VNAF technicians were sent to the US for additional training under Operation Commando Gopher.[1]

With no aircraft replacements in the pipeline, the VNAF was forced to adopt a cautious policy to conserve its strength in case of an all-out North Vietnamese offensive.

The VNAF operated 10 AN/FPS-20 and AN/TPS-6 radars for air defence, but only two thirds of these were operational. This was due to a lack of spare parts, limited depot maintenance and a reduction in the number of contracted US technicians. This radar station was positioned atop a hill near Da Nang and covered the border with North Vietnam. (USAF)

In order to limit its losses, particularly to SA-7s, the VNAF fighter squadrons received an order to operate at higher altitudes. However, when ARVN troops were in contact with the enemy, the tactic was to press on to support the friendly troops as best as possible. This Skyraider is pulling out from a low-level napalm pass.
(Pham Quang Khiem Collection)

Pilots were ordered to operate from ever higher altitudes, under radar guidance when practical, in order to avoid losses when targeting enemy positions or depots behind the front lines.

The tactic was based around the use of the AN/TPB-1A Beacon Only Bombing System (BOBS) ground-based radars. The VNAF received four of the five planned AN/TPB-1A systems in addition to the two AN/MSQ-77 radars left over by the Americans. These served as the basis for three fixed BOBS sites: Bien Hoa, Pleiku and Da Nang. At this last location, a VNAF CH-47 moved the radar from its initial emplacement at Phu Bai to Hill 625 of Son Cha Island in Da Nang Bay.

The A-37B was the most favoured platform for these high-altitude, level-flight, bombings under guidance. Using BOBS, it was able to bomb in adverse weather or at night. The A-1, also beacon-equipped, could also fly BOBS but was limited to daylight

These F-5As were in the process of being serviced by Northrop-contracted American technicians at Bien Hoa. The US cuts of two thirds of the planned military aid budget for 1974 led to the departure of more than half of them.
(Anthony J. Tambini)

missions and could not get above the heavy flak (larger than 37mm calibre). The F-5A, not beacon-equipped, was the least well suited for these kinds of operations, due to its basic weapons aiming system. As a result, the accuracy of the F-5A was consistently poor. Sometimes F-5As teamed up with an A-37B, flying as a pathfinder, and dropped their bombs on the command of the beacon-equipped Dragonfly.

However, when friendly units were in contact with the enemy, the VNAF showed no reluctance in taking risks, flying at low level to give close support. But here also efficiency and accuracy decreased, since heavy AAA often forced the accompanying airborne FACs out of the area. Many ARVN commanders began to complain that they were not receiving the same level of air support as given by the Americans.

The last offensive

The balance of the war meanwhile began to tilt favourably towards the enemy. Hanoi expanded the scope of its attacks, now carried out at the corps level, in order to inflict a maximum of casualties on the ARVN. AT the same time, the Communists began to threaten important population centres including Da Nang and Hue. Even Saigon's northern approaches were threatened.

Before the reduction in US military aid began to take effect, the South Vietnamese decided to launch an offensive for the last time, in April 1974. This would attack the 'Angel's Wing', a salient that served as an important Communist base on the Cambodian border and which threatened Tay Ninh. The operation involved 20 battalions, organised in four armoured task forces. Air support was provided by assets of both the III and IV Corps, including the fighters from Bien Hoa, and those at Binh Thuy. The offensive also aimed to destroy the North Vietnamese 5th Division. But pre-empting the ARVN move, the North Vietnamese attacked the Duc Hue outpost first on 27 March. The local defenders resisted fiercely, thanks to effective VNAF support, but an A-1 and an O-1 were brought down by SA-7s.

The ARVN armoured task forces received excellent VNAF support and nearly wiped out the North Vietnamese 5th Division during the attack on the 'Angel's Wing'. These M113 APCs are being supplied by VNAF 'Hueys' in a clearing in Cambodia. (VNAF)

ARVN troops wait to be picked up by the 'Hueys' of the 43rd Wing in order to embark on a search operation.
(US Army)

Next, the South Vietnamese pushed on towards Cambodia, encountering fierce resistance at Long Khot and Svay Rieng. The main thrust was spearheaded by a heliborne assault including 54 UH-1Hs. VNAF fighter-bombers inflicted serious casualties on enemy troops and destroyed many equipment depots. On 29 April, some 200 F-5 and A-37 attack sorties were flown against a single depot and AAA positions alone. The operation was concluded by 10 May, by when the South Vietnamese withdrew from Cambodia after inflicting such serious losses to the 5th Division that it would be withdrawn from fighting until the end of the war. The operation was characterised by audacity, speed and excellent ground-air coordination, all of which provided Saigon's troops with clear advantages.

A UH-1H of the 215th Helicopter Squadron at Nha Trang loaded with crates of rations at an ARVN outpost. The squadron insignia, representing an elephant, was painted on the nose. The aircraft also wore an unusual two-tone camouflage scheme.
(Pham Quang Khiem Collection)

Battle for the Iron Triangle

A pair of A-37Bs heads towards its target. In order to reduce losses that could no longer be replaced, they often attacked at high altitude, in level flight, under the guidance of the BOBS ground-based radars.
(VNAF)

Despite the best efforts of the South Vietnamese, it was the turn of the North to take the initiative, and launch a series of multi-division offensives in the three northernmost corps. The first thrust began at the end of April, when the Communists launched an all-out offensive against the Ton Le Chon outpost. The base had survived only thanks to VNAF support, but now the situation became untenable for the besieged rangers. No helicopters could land and the defenders had to be re-supplied by HALO drops from C-130s. On the night of 11 April, the last survivors fought their way out of the outpost and succeeded in reaching An Loc.

This Communist success was followed by an effort by two divisions along the Song Be and Saigon Rivers, north of Saigon, with the aim of pushing south as far as possible to position artillery that could threaten the capital itself, as well as the adjacent air bases of Tan Son Nhut and Bien Hoa. The North Vietnamese reoccupied the northern part of the former 'Iron Triangle' area, and the South Vietnamese required a three-phases offensive, and six months, to expel them. The urgency of the situation required that IV Corps divert part of its assets to support the fighting. In addition, some close air support sorties by A-37s of the 74th Wing at Binh Thuy were flown from altitudes above 10,000ft (3,048m), but were mostly ineffective. This brought considerable criticism upon the VNAF, but the commander of the 4th Air Division, Brig Gen Nguyen Huu Tan, explained that the radar-controlled bombings were justified since he felt he could otherwise not sustain the expected loss rate. It took many efforts by the JGS and the VNAF commander before the different corps commanders accepted the fact that they must share their air assets in the case of 'surging' crises.

Correspondingly, by the end of 1974, reports indicated that VNAF units were ready to accept losses if necessary to support troops in contact. The ARVN commanders expressed satisfaction with the support they received, including that from the 4th Air Division.

By the end of June and early July 1974, VNAF F-5s and A-1s from Bien Hoa were heavily engaged in the support of the ARVN offensive in the 'Iron Triangle'. Between 27 June and 1 July, 250 strike sorties were flown in support of an armoured task force that had suffered heavy casualties. In August, North Vietnamese sappers infiltrated the approaches of Bien Hoa AB and intermittently pounded it with 122mm (4.80in) rockets that damaged several F-5s and destroyed 500 napalm canisters.

Skyraiders from the 23rd Wing at Bien Hoa were engaged extensively during the fighting for the 'Iron Triangle'. The 518th Fighter Squadron operated this A-1E.
(Pham Quang Khiem Collection)

The 1st Air Division at Da Nang was also fully mobilised during spring and summer 1974 to help the ARVN repel several North Vietnamese divisional assaults in the provinces of Quang Tien and Quang Ngai. In April 1974 the commander of the 427th Transport Squadron, Lt Col Pham Van Can, recalled one mission to support an advanced outpost:

'At around noon, we had a surprise inspection by the commander of the I Corps, Lt Gen Ngo Quang Truong, accompanied by the boss of the 1st Air Division. After touring the hangars and attending my briefing, Gen Truong suddenly asked me, 'Can you give me 15 Caribous for tomorrow? I need to deploy reinforcement troops to the Duc Pho outpost'. I replied that I needed to check the status of the aircraft with my Mechanic Officer, Lt Col Nguyen Binh Tra. He assured us that 15 C-7s would be available for tomorrow even if his men had to work all the night.

'As promised, the reinforcement battalion boarded the 15 Caribous on schedule. The first aircraft landed on the airstrip without problems. The next began his approach, piloted by the squadron's deputy, Maj Nguyen Ba Dam. Suddenly, the enemy AA opened fire. A shell nearly severed half of the aircraft tail, while another set on fire the starboard engine. Miraculously, Dam succeeded in making a crash-landing 5km [3.1 miles] away in a clearing. His co-pilot had a broken leg. They were quickly picked up by a 'Huey'.[2]

The next communist advance targeted the area of Duc Duc. Here, VNAF F-5s and A-37s helped to stabilise the situation. On 19 July a column of enemy tanks was discovered and attacked with bombs and rockets. The Communists were now entrenched in a line of crests on Ky Vi Mountain and held the ARVN forces at bay. The A-37s flew 18 attack sorties but to little effect.

On 25 July the North Vietnamese resumed their attacks, and the 1st Air Division flew 67 attack sorties on the 25th and 57 on the 26th, trying its best to blunt the offensive and destroying or damaging several pieces of armour. Another attack was also gearing up against Thuong Duc. The base was completely encircled and its commander requested the evacuation of the wounded. However, the VNAF 'Hueys' could not land due to heavy 23mm and 37mm anti-aircraft fire. On 4 August the A-37s attacked the flak emplacements but could not silence them sufficiently for the helicopters to fly in. The next day an airdrop of supplies was made, but all eight bundles fell outside the perimeter. The VNAF tried to destroy them but an A-37B was brought down in the

A VNAF pilot, probably from the 544th Fighter Squadron at Bien Hoa, poses with his F-5A in early 1974. The jet is a former USAF aircraft delivered at the end of 1972 during Project Enhance and is still to receive camouflage.
(VNAF)

This F-5A from the 542nd Fighter Squadron at Bien Hoa was also received during Project Enhance. Unlike many other airframes taken on charge at the same time, it received the yellow and black chequered identification band of the 63rd Wing. Strangely, the nose of the aircraft was painted black, although it did not contain radar.
(Anthony Tambini)

By early 1974, the F-5 squadrons finally reached an acceptable operational level when they received their complement of planned maintenance personnel. This bombed-up F-5A was waiting at Bien Hoa for the next mission. (USAF)

The 2nd and 6th Air Divisions in II Corps made great efforts to support ARVN forces battling to preserve a string of outposts northwest of Pleiku in the final months of 1974. One of the most heavily engaged units was the 524th Fighter Squadron at Phan Rang. (USAF)

attempt. The small garrison fell on 7 August. The situation in I Corps was now so serious that Saigon released its last strategic reserve, the 1st Airborne Brigade, which was flown into Da Nang by C-130s and C-119s by 8 August. The reinforcements enabled the enemy advance to be checked along the Que Son Valley, but the fighting lasted into autumn 1974, the ARVN losing some 4,700 men.

The 2nd and 6th Air Divisions in II Corps were also supporting the ARVN forces battling to preserve a string of outposts northwest of Pleiku. Most of these had succumbed to the enemy by the end of summer, as at Dak Pek where 70 A-1 and A-37 sorties could not prevent its fall. The South Vietnamese pilots pressed home their attacks despite heavy 37mm AAA fire, and knocked out several tanks. Some posts survived, as at Plei Me, where the local Rangers counted on fighter-bombers and fixed-wing gunships to resist 29 consecutive days of siege.

A declining force

By mid-1974 the effects of the budget cuts had become clear. The lack of spare parts and the fact that many of the airframes received already had high utilisation hours resulted in many aircraft beginning to show signs of technical unreliability. A report by Brig Gen Dung Dinh Linh, deputy chief of staff for materiel, indicated that the trans-

The reduction in helicopter operations began to have adverse effects on the ARVN, including a shortfall in medical evacuations. In order to solve the problem, the VNAF decided to centralise the medevac operations by establishing the 259th Helicopter Squadron. This group-sized unit maintained detachments of eight to 12 'Hueys' at most of the major air bases. This UH-1H from Detachment H operated in the Mekong Delta area. (US Army)

port assets were the hardest hit. First of all, the UH-1H fleet saw operational levels slump to an average of only 50 per cent. The maintenance units were forced to cannibalise airframes to maintain the others in operational status. Furthermore, some aircraft experienced problems with their transmission gearboxes that required long periods of immobilisation.

The state of the CH-47As was even more debilitating. Many had reached the end of their useful lives and required a complete overhaul that was beyond the scope of the VNAF maintainers. The 241st Helicopter Squadron at Pleiku suffered the lowest operational rate; on some days the unit could make available only a single Chinook for the entire II Corps. Additionally, a number of Chinooks remained grounded as they were modified with flare dispensers.

The fixed-wing transport fleet also began to experience technical problems. The three C-7 squadrons saw their availability decline steadily. The Caribous suffered engine problems, a lack of spare parts, corrosion, and some structural cracks. By the end of 1974, only a third of the fleet was operational at any given time.

The three Caribou squadrons were disbanded for budgetary reasons. Their role of STOL transport was handed over to the Chinook units. The crews of the 427th Transport Squadron pose here for a group photo at Da Nang some time just before the disbandment of the unit. (Pham Van Can)

The mainstay of the VNAF transport fleet was its two Hercules squadrons, and these began to experience fuel leakage problems. The maintenance crews were forced to work ceaselessly to cure the leaks. Some airframes also revealed structural cracks on the wing spars and undercarriage. Most of the VNAF's requests to send its C-130As back to the US for overhaul were now turned down. The last time that such an arrangement was made was in August 1973 when three airframes were ferried to the US and replaced by another three refurbished examples, provided by a USAFRES squadron. From a fleet of 32 airframes, only eight to 14 could be made available on any given day. The situation improved slightly at the end of 1974 when some aircraft were sent to Singapore for heavy maintenance work on their cracked wing spars. Out of 19 aircraft that experienced wing spar problems, 12 had initially been scheduled to be sent to the US for rebuilding, within the 1975 Fiscal Year appropriation.

During the same period of time in early 1975, the number of C-130s available on any given day increased to between 16 and 18. Without much hope, the Air Division of the DAO suggested that all C-130As should be replaced by the more modern C-130E. Washington politely turned down the request. Instead, the VNAF was now forced to assign many tactical transport missions to the ageing C-119s and C-47s that were now taken out of storage. In fact, the older C-47s and C-119s enjoyed an improved operational rate, in no small part due to the fact that they were serviced by very experienced mechanics well accustomed to their machines.[3]

The constant fighting, the scarcity of spare parts and the lack replacement aircraft, all contributed to wear down the VNAF by summer 1974. During the first three months of that year, some 39 aircraft had been shot down. By the end of June, the total number of aircraft brought down since January 1973 had risen to 84 –17 of which due to SA-7s. Consequently, throughout the first nine months of 1974, the number of flying hours was down by more than 100,000 hours, but the accident rate went down too. This key indicator of professionalism in war was a great testimony to the efforts of the VNAF airmen: the accident rate was slashed from 9.9 accidents per 100,000 flying hours to 6.8.

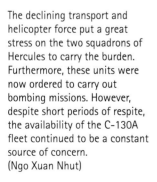

The declining transport and helicopter force put a great stress on the two squadrons of Hercules to carry the burden. Furthermore, these units were now ordered to carry out bombing missions. However, despite short periods of respite, the availability of the C-130A fleet continued to be a constant source of concern.
(Ngo Xuan Nhut)

Another US blow

It was in this context that a drastic new reduction in US military aid was announced. In September 1974 the Congress appropriated only USD700 million for South Vietnam during Fiscal Year 1975. This figure only met half of the already austere VNAF requirements, and some USD46 million had to be assigned to US DAO operations, leaving just USD654 million for direct support.

The South Vietnamese were now required to take drastic measures to conserve their equipment and ammunition, and to cut operating costs. The VNAF acted swiftly. In late November 1974 a decision was taken to deactivate 10 squadrons and put into storage all the aircraft that were considered the most difficult to service. Originally, it was envisaged that 224 aircraft would be retired, including the 52 remaining C-7s, 61

In order to reduce demands upon maintenance, among the VNAF aircraft put into storage in autumn 1974 were the 31 surviving O-2As from a total of 35 initially received. This O-2A was from the 110th Observation Squadron of the 41st Wing at Da Nang.
(Pham Quang Khiem Collection)

With the O-2As put into storage, the O-1s continued to soldier on until the end of the war. However, they proved so vulnerable that on many occasions VNAF fighter-bombers had to attack without FAC control.
(Pham Quang Khiem Collection)

During the summer of 1974 the last 61 A-1s were put into storage and no additional pilots converted on the type. The VNAF subsequently terminated training on the Skyraider, previously undertaken at Hulburt Field, Florida. This picture shows the last group of South Vietnamese pilots qualified on A-1s, 72-4A, from 1974.
(Byron Hukee)

A-1s, 31 O-2As, 34 AC-47D and AC-119G gunships, 31 UH-1Hs, as well as all the U-6s, T-41Ds and T-37Cs. However, it remains unclear if this plan was fully implemented.

The decision to disband the last three Skyraider squadrons was taken due to the poor condition of the remaining airframes. The aircraft were old and had been flying combat missions with a 3g restriction for some time. Their instruments had deteriorated to the point where they could only fly clear-weather day sorties. Furthermore, they had become increasingly vulnerable to enemy air defences, with 10 examples shot down since January 1973, including five by SA-7s.

It seems that the decision to ground the 819th Attack Squadron and its AC-119Gs was rescinded. The 817th Attack Squadron was indeed disbanded, but most of its AC-47s were simply disarmed and returned to cargo configuration.

The tasks previously performed by the C-7s were reassigned to the four CH-47 squadrons. The stored aircraft had their engines dismounted and their status was regularly checked such that they could be quickly returned to operational condition if required. Some 500 technicians were especially devoted to this monitoring task.

The Skyraiders of the 23rd Wing of Bien Hoa are seen here being mothballed for storage. Before putting the aircraft inside hangars, the mechanics had to remove the engines, which were stored separately. The F-5A in foreground was from the 536th Fighter Squadron that operated from the same base.
(Anthony Tambini)

The 530th Fighter Squadron was one of the three Skyraider squadrons that were disbanded. It had been the last unit established on the A-1, at Pleiku in December 1970. The squadron's 'Jupiter' radio call sign quickly became famous throughout the Central Highlands area in which its pilots operated efficiently, notably helping to blunt the massive North Vietnamese offensive of spring 1972. These A-1Es and A-1Hs from the unit are seen departing for another sortie from Pleiku. Contrary to the Skyraiders of the 23rd Wing at Bien Hoa, which wore a chequered yellow and black band around the fuselage, those at Pleiku had no distinctive unit markings. Pilots of the squadron are also seen posed in front of their Operations Room at Pleiku. (Robert D. Young)

Most of the personnel from the disbanded units were reassigned to the remaining squadrons with a resultant net increase in the readiness levels of operational aircraft. For the first time, the VNAF had a surplus of pilots. However, squadrons without pilots retained their number plates as an administrative measure. A cadre of personnel was maintained, assigned to base duties and awaiting reassignment. Morale hit rock bottom in the grounded units. When the process of disbandment ended, a material assessment at the end of December 1974 indicated that the VNAF now fielded a force of 1,484 aircraft. A total of 299 aircraft had been lost due to combat, operational causes or transfers since the Peace Accord. A DAO report of September 1974 listed 154 aircraft destroyed by the enemy, including 74 helicopters (five CH-47s and 69 UH-1s), 21 observation aircraft (16 O-1s, one U-17, one U-6 and three O-2s), five transports (two C-7As and three C-47s), four fixed-wing gunships (two AC-119s and two AC-47s), one EC-47 electronic warfare aircraft, as well as 49 fighter-bombers (10 A-1s, 19 A-37s and 20 F-5s, including two RF-5As).

Sixty-six other aircraft were listed as having been transferred back to the USAF, including four C-47s, 19 C-123Ks, eight C-119s, and 35 O-1s. Most of these transfers comprised aircraft sent back to the US for maintenance but then impounded there when the required work was not budget-funded. Other aircraft were likely never returned to the US due to their obsolescence, such as the O-1s and C-123s that were handed over to allied Asian air forces or scrapped. Sixty-two other airframes were lost in accidents or to other operational causes.[4]

In order to compensate for the drop in VNAF airlift capacity, the CIA was forced to increase its Air America assets to continue to support its own operations. The number of transport aircraft increased to 36, of which 24 aircraft, including 16 UH-1Hs, were stored at Saigon. Other aircraft on strength included one C-46, three C-47s, one C-7, eight Volpars, eight PC-6s, nine Bell 204Bs and six UH-1Hs. Meanwhile, the Air America commitment in support of the ICCS had now been reduced to one C-46, one Volpar and 12 UH-1Hs.[5]

The VNAF was forced to cut back its helicopter operations in the second half of 1974. The lack of spare parts and fuel meant the ARVN could now only count upon around half the helicopter support that it was used to. This UH-1H of the 51st Wing is returning to its base at Da Nang.
(Author's Collection)

Budgetary reductions also had a profound impact on the operational rate of the Chinook squadrons. Like the 'Huey' units, these suffered from a lack of spare parts and the cancellation of scheduled maintenance. Many Chinooks had reached the end of their useful lives and required a complete overhaul. Some squadrons had to contend with six to eight operational machines instead of the planned 18.
(USAF)

One of the most detrimental effects of these cost-saving measures was the total disruption of the VNAF training programme. In view of the gravity of the situation, it was considered necessary to focus all available resources on combat operations for the foreseeable future. Training was cut down to a minimum level. First, 400 jet and helicopter pilot students undergoing training in the US were recalled. Over 1,000 trainee airmen earmarked for flight and non-flight jobs undergoing English-language training were turned into infantrymen. At the ATC, the training syllabus was also slashed. Undergraduate pilot training, suspended with the withdrawal of the T-41D, was resumed on U-17s at Nha Trang. The grounding of the T-37C also interrupted the final basic training class at Phan Rang. The students completed their course on a number of detached A-37Bs. With the graduation of the last class of students at the end of 1974, training was suspended altogether.

The first Tigers

The only positive among this raft of bad news was the delivery of the first brand-new F-5Es. Right from the start, tentative plans were prepared for the new aircraft to form the backbone of the VNAF, with some 300 airframes envisaged for delivery.

Originally, Fiscal Year 1973 planning had proposed a fighter structure of eight squadrons of F-5Es and 12 squadrons of A-37Bs, together with the replacement of all A-1s and F-5As. Meanwhile, at the time of the ceasefire, some 57 F-5Es had already been budgeted for the VNAF, a figure later extended to 126 machines by 1974, including 28 two-seat F-5Fs and 18 RF-5Es. Negotiations also took place with Northrop concerning another batch of 71 aircraft for Fiscal Year 1976.

However, budget constraints only saw funding for 90 aircraft, amounting to USD220 million, to be delivered between July 1973 and December 1974. The programme was further mired by delays both in the budget appropriation process and by production problems. A first group of South Vietnamese pilots was sent to Williams AFB to train on the F-5E in summer 1973. In addition to the mechanics and other specialists, 126 personnel were trained as instructors on the F-5E.

The first F–5Es were delivered in March 1974. A total of 126 personnel were trained as instructors on the F–5E. These experienced F–5A pilots transitioned without many problems and would form the backbone of the units to be converted.

The VNAF finally received its first four F-5Es in the course of Operation Pacer Line. These arrived at Bien Hoa on 13 March 1974. Fourteen other airframes quickly followed, these being diverted from a batch ordered by the Imperial Iranian Air Force.

The first unit to exchange its F-5As for the Tiger II was the 538th Squadron at Da Nang. The re-equipment of this unit was assigned top priority in order that it could fulfil the air defence mission covering the border with North Vietnam. The unit became fully operational on the F-5E in July. However, delivery of the F-5Es, taking place in the midst of budget restriction measures, led to much criticism among the armed forces. The ARVN, accustomed to receiving the bulk of US military aid, was now bitterly opposed to a plan that absorbed roughly a third of the meagre defence expenditures. Ultimately, the VNAF was forced to cancel part of its F-5E acquisition programme.

Eventually, South Vietnam received only 54 F-5Es, the remaining 36 aircraft being cancelled and the funds then recovered and channelled to more vital operational needs.

The VNAF finally received its first four F-5Es under Operation Pacer Line on 13 March 1974, quickly followed by 14 other aircraft diverted from a batch ordered by the Imperial Iranian Air Force.
(USAF)

The first F-5Es re-equipped the 538th Squadron based at Da Nang. The others were delivered to the 542nd and 544th Fighter Squadron at Bien Hoa. This F-5E was presented during an inspection for officials at the VNAF Headquarters. The aircraft was shown with the vast array of weapons that it could carry, including bombs, rocket pods, and AIM-9E Sidewinders, as well as cluster bomb dispensers. (Anthony Tambini)

Although the VNAF was allocated USD183 million for Fiscal Year 1975 – representing only 44 per cent of its requirements – almost this entire budget was allocated to the re-equipment of three squadrons with the F-5E. The remaining aircraft were delivered in two additional batches of 27 and nine airframes, respectively. The 71 other F-5Es intended for the VNAF for Fiscal Year 1976 were later acquired by the USAF to equip its Aggressor squadrons.

A priority plan for installing radar homing and warning sets and built-in flare dispensers on F-5As, RF-5As and F-5Es, in order to improve survivability in high-threat areas, was also cancelled due to a lack of funding.

The remaining F-5Es re-equipped the 542nd and 544th Fighter Squadron at Bien Hoa. During the transitional period, both units continued to operate their F-5As. The last F-5Es were pressed into service in February 1975. Northrop Contractor Anthony J. Tambini recalled that *the introduction of the F-5E into Vietnam went very smoothly.*[6]

Despite the introduction of the F-5E, the VNAF continued to train F-5A pilots in air-to-air combat tactics. Seen beside the Tiger II during the same inspection, 63 Wing at Bien Hoa also displayed a Sidewinder-armed F-5A. (Anthony Tambini)

The twin-engine configuration of the F-5 series was a safety measure greatly appreciated by its pilots. This F-5A was hit by a SA-7 but the pilot managed to return to Bien Hoa. The aircraft is a former Iranian machine and still wears desert camouflage. (Anthony Tambini)

'*There was a short period of transition and then the aircraft went into service*'. However, it was found that the aircraft was not particularly cost-effective considering the level of improvement that it brought in. '*Although a great aircraft, it was too little too late. The F-5A was a better aircraft, in my opinion, for ground support of ARVN forces. It cost less, was easier to maintain and carried a similar ordnance load as the F-5E.*'

The new fighter supplemented the older F-5A rather than replacing it outright. None of the governments that had 'lent' their F-5As to South Vietnam had requested their returns. Meanwhile, the Tiger II represented a significant improvement in both air-to-air and ground-attack capabilities. The fighter was beacon-equipped, allowing BOBS attacks, while its lead-computing gun sight provided greater precision in delivering ordnance.[7]

Fuel shortages

Other conservative measures concerned the fuel allowance. This was centrally controlled for the three branches of the armed forces and was funded at USD60 million. Here also the VNAF had to fight with the ARVN and the Navy to maintain its own fuel requirements at just below 50 per cent of the required level. As a result of fuel shortages, ARVN truck transportation was cut in half while VNAF helicopter operations were reduced by 70 per cent compared to 1973. Except for emergencies, combat movement of troops by helicopter was limited to the infrequent insertion and extraction of Long-Range Patrols into enemy territory. The fighter-bomber force also saw its allocated flight hours cut by 51 per cent.

The transport force was meanwhile restricted to the most urgent requirements, such as air drops in support of several isolated outposts or special operations. Maj Hung of the 435th Transport Squadron remembered one of these missions:

'*It was 28 December 1974, the 16th birthday of my son. I was requested by the Squadron Commander, Lt Col Lam Van Phieu, who received me with a grave face. I wondered what I had done wrong. Maybe the model kit of a Hercules that I had assembled for him had been broken? No, it was still there on his desk. In fact, he told me that I had been requested for a special mission on behalf of the Special Forces of the ARVN Technical Directorate. Usually these kinds of missions were rather risky and tricky. I then remembered another flight completed for them where I had dropped blocks of ice on parachutes over enemy territory. The purpose of the mission was to lure the North Vietnamese into believing that a commando team had been parachuted into the area when they discovered the empty harnesses. That prompted a vast manhunt. An RF-5A was subsequently sent to take pictures of the disclosed Communist positions.*

'*This time, it was to make two drops of non-specified items near Loc Ninh, then the seat of the 'Provisional Revolutionary Government' of the Viet Cong, near the Cambodian border. Suffice to say that the area would be strongly defended by anti-aircraft artillery. With the help of my navigator, Maj Tu Thanh, I carefully checked all the latest Intelligence data to plot the route by trying to bypass the most well defended areas, notably the plotted positions of 37mm and 57mm AA guns. Never-*

theless, the intended drop zones were all ringed by guns and I had even to overfly an enemy armoured unit. And they would probably have the feared SA-7s. I hoped to surprise the enemy by flying very low and fast.

'*When I came to check the loads, there were two square wooden crates of one metre long and one metre wide. No one knew what they contained, even if some speculated that there were electronic sensors inside. But I didn't believe it because they would not survive a high-speed, low-level drop. On the tarmac were assembled some senior officers who had come to wish us goodbye, including the 53rd Wing Deputy Commander, Col Bui Huu, as well as Maj Ha Hau Sinh of the 5th Air Division. I finally boarded the aircraft with my co-pilot, Maj Phan Vu Dien. Both of us had put a flak jacket over our survival vests and brought along an M16 rifle with 10 clips of cartridges. The navigator for his part had put two additional flak jackets under his feet!*

'*After taking off in complete radio silence, I turned northeast towards the small airstrip of Song Be, west of Phuoc Long City. That part of the flight was conducted at 10,000ft [3,048m] and the loadmasters in the cargo compartment were instructed to scrutinise outside to warn of any SA-7 launches. If anyone saw the brilliant white plume of a departing missile, he must immediately reach one of the command panels and pull the release button to drop flares. In fact, each VNAF C-130A had been modified to carry two 'boxes' containing a total of 32 flares. The procedure was simple and none of the loadmasters had received any particular training to do this, although each of them had received an un-translated, English technical manual for the system. Reaching Son Be, I simulated a landing approach by reducing speed, and lowering flaps and wheels, while dispersed petrol lamps illuminated the strip. But at the last moment, I turned sharply and took the direction of Loc Ninh at treetop level.*

'*The weather was perfect, with the noon illuminating the landscape. The overflown area was flat, with jungle crisscrossed by rice fields and small, scattered hamlets. I pushed forward the throttle with the flight mechanic surveying the temperature of the turbine inlets. Normally, a C-130A was limited to 280kt at sea level but here the indicated airspeed was in the red while we were flying slightly over 300kt! Despite the speed, I had the curious impression that everything was moving in slow motion. I was so concentrated on the flying that I grasped only fleeting details of what happened around the first drop zone. Suddenly someone had dropped two flares that bounced over the ground, illuminating the whole area as if was day. I then turned towards the next DZ around 2km [1.2 miles] away and which I reached by cutting across the southern part of the city. Here also, the drop was done quickly.*

'*It was only now that my co-pilot asked me if I had seen all the tracers converging on us since the beginning of the run, as well as the SA-7s – a real firework display! That stunned me, for I had not had the impression that we were under enemy fire. I had also not seen the enemy tanks. I just remembered seeing some dark silhouettes. And maybe a North Vietnamese atop what could be a tank turret who intently followed us while smoking his cigarette. The adrenalin that overflowed my body began now to recede as I pressed on at low level for 15 more minutes and crossed the Cambodian border. I then dropped the two external fuel tanks before turning back towards South Vietnam. Slowly I began to relax, climbed back to altitude and contacted Paris Control for a direct approach into Tan Son Nhut. Jokingly, my co-pilot told me that I must concentrate on the landing in order to improve my night flying*

The North Vietnamese increased their pressure during the second half of 1974 by attacking Saigon's northern perimeter with two divisions that attempted to reoccupy the 'Iron Triangle' area. The VNAF flew an all-out effort with squadrons from both the III and IV Corps. This A-37B was probably from the 546th Fighter Squadron at Binh Thuy.
(Pham Quang Khiem Collection)

skill. Both of us laughed for we had previously served together with the 817th Attack Squadron on the AC-47D and were very comfortable with night operations. When I stopped, I was greeted by a worried Squadron Commander who was overjoyed to see us alive.[8]

All the restrictions imposed on operations caused a most adverse psychological effect among the VNAF. Soldiers went to fight knowing that they would no longer benefit from the support of the VNAF or artillery as in the past. Medical resources were also fast declining. The worsening economic situation of the country, with rampant inflation, also shook the morale of the South Vietnamese. An August 1973 DAO fact sheet pointed out that since 1964, the real purchasing power of the soldier and the civil servant had declined by 78 per cent! The average airman's salary was USD17.28; the

By late November 1974 it had been decided to launch F-5 operations using their full load of ammunition, contravening the reduced bomb-carrying policy previously followed. This F-5A is loaded with four 500lb (227kg) Mk 82 bombs equipped with extended fuses. These allowed the bombs to explode above the surface of the ground, maximising the blast effect.
(Anthony Tambini)

monthly cost of feeding one individual on the South Vietnamese economy was USD15. This left a balance of a mere USD2.28 for supporting the rest of his family. The situation was such that without exception, the South Vietnamese commanders would have preferred payment in food for their troops instead of currency.

Even if VNAF personnel benefited from better living conditions, cases of malnutrition were commonplace – even among flying personnel. In order to sustain their families, many took second jobs after normal military duty hours, or sought help from relatives. Others pilfered what was at hand for resale.

Seen in this light, it was not a question of how corrupt a person became, but how honest he remained. Some hideous practices even began to surface, and several reports indicated that in the Mekong Delta area, certain helicopter pilots evacuated wounded soldiers only if they were paid. Such practices remained marginal, but the fact that they existed at all illustrated the fast declining morale of the troops.

In order to alleviate the problem, it was decided to set up a dedicated medevac helicopter unit, the 259th Squadron with 109 UH-1Hs. In fact, based on its size, it was closer to a group than a squadron. The unit was divided into eight detachments, each with eight to 14 'Hueys', which were assigned at major air bases throughout South Vietnam.

Nevertheless, compared to the ARVN, the South Vietnamese airmen continued to feel that they belonged to an elite within their country's military. The VNAF had the lowest desertion rate of the armed forces. Recruitment, when compared to the other services, was extremely selective. The DAO cited as an example of VNAF morale an incident that occurred during February 1973 at Phu Cat AB. The base, while considered a 'hardship assignment' in the eyes of the VNAF, was one of the best disciplined. At the time of the ceasefire, a Viet Cong force was in the city of Phu Cat. The ARVN had been unable to expel them. The VNAF base commander gathered his airmen together, equipped them with flak vests and weapons, attacked the city, and drove out the enemy. This outstanding example of discipline and spirit was a source of pride to the VNAF. In fact, despite being constantly subjected to Communist propaganda pointing out the corruption and ineptitude of their political leaders, few VNAF airmen had ever envisaged switching sides. Only a single case of defection occurred in 1974 when a 'Huey' pilot flew his helicopter into North Vietnam.[9]

One of the helicopter pilots, from Detachment H of the 259th Squadron at Can Tho, recalled the deteriorating conditions of late 1974 under which he was forced to operate:

The VNAF had reinforced its helicopter assets devoted to the support of the Vietnamese Navy's riverine operations in the Mekong Delta. The number of gunship 'Hueys' was increased in order to provide an on-call strike capability. This UH-1H was escorting a convoy of barges sailing up the Mekong River towards Cambodia. (VNAF)

'It was late when I landed and went towards the parking area of the 249th Squadron flying CH-47s. I was tired and hoping to find something to eat at their mess. But, looking at my watch, it appeared that this would surely now be closed. I had no choice but to walk back to my squadron mess, which was little further away. Suddenly, coming from the opposite direction, I saw a group of civilians with a young woman trotting at their head. I did not want to cross their path for my flight suit was soaked by perspiration that added to the strong odour of the dead bodies that I had loaded today in my Dust-Off 'Huey'. Nevertheless, she came directly towards me, tears in her eyes, and asked me if I knew that a Chinook had gone down. I replied that I had heard something about it. 'Please, do you have any news about my husband?' He was the co-pilot of the new squadron's commander who had been on an orientation flight. His name was Tran Van Hoa. I froze on the spot, not knowing what to tell her. I demurred and said that I knew nothing.

'A flow of images came back into my memory while the other members of her family dragged her away. Hoa was one of my closest friends. We graduated in the same class in the United States. We were then posted together to the 217th Helicopter Squadron at Pleiku, in the Central Highlands. However, he dreamed of returning to his native lands in the Mekong Delta area. He tried to persuade me to apply with him for a transfer to a new squadron there, explaining, 'You see, Can Tho is a good place to live and the girls are the most beautiful...' He was finally selected for a conversion course on the CH-47 and saw his dream fulfilled. For the next three years, I continued to operate from Pleiku and saw Hoa only occasionally. By mid-1974, I was selected to follow a course on the Chinook but budgetary cuts stopped my training. I found myself without an assignment. My old squadron at Pleiku had no place left and finally I was posted to the 259th Squadron, flying medevac missions. I was based at the smaller airfield, adjacent to the city of Can Tho, while Hoa operated from the more important base of Binh Thuy, outside the town. However, since my arrival, I had more occasions to come over to Hoa between two sorties. He told me to be careful because the enemy had deployed plenty of AAA in the area, and many

The C-7A continued to provide logistic support to the advanced outposts. This Caribou was seen on an airstrip in the Central Highlands in 1974, sharing the ramp with several O-1s, during the fighting around Quang Duc. (Author's Collection)

Despite growing maintenance problems with the C-7 fleet, the VNAF continued to be able to maintain a good operational rate within the three squadrons of Caribou by early 1974. They proved to be invaluable for the medium-capacity transport role and even supplemented the Hercules, which had a lower operational rate. These aircraft from the 431st Transport Squadron were photographed at Tan Son Nhut. (Robert D. Young)

SA-7s. We promised to see each other again at his home, where he intended to present his family.

'I was then sent to Tan Son Nhut to pick up a new 'Huey' out of maintenance. I flew back home with a group of officers who came along for a ride. Suddenly, I was ordered to land at the Moc Hoa outpost and to drop my dejected passengers there. I met an ALO who told me that a Chinook had just been brought down in the area. He was following the Ap Bac River when it was hit by a SA-7. The missile literally cut the CH-47 in two. The helicopter had on board a platoon of troops and there were probably no survivors. A search party tried to collect the remains but the bodies had been spread over a vast area. Only the tail of the Chinook had been located on a rice field. They had not yet located the cockpit or the bodies of the pilots. I spent the rest of the day ferrying back to Can Tho the gruesome remains. It is now only that I realised that among the victims was my dear friend.'[10]

1   VNAF Improvement and Modernization Programme, HQ PACAF, July 1971 – December 1973. 1 January 1975 Report, Project CHECO, pp158–163.

2   Phan Van Can, narrative on the history of the 427th Squadron, on the Quan Su Khong Viet Nam website (in Vietnamese).

3   VNAF Improvement and Modernization Programme, HQ PACAF, July 1971 – December 1973. 1 January 1975 Report, Project CHECO, see pp81–91 about the DAO discussions concerning the C-130A maintenance difficulties.

4   Phan Van Can, narrative on the history of the 427th Squadron VNAF, on the Quan Su Khong Viet Nam website (in Vietnamese)

5   Leeker, 'The History of Air America', University of Texas, McDermott Library, pp40–44.

6   J. Tambini, email interview, 2003.

7   A DAO Report of 9 August 1973 summarised as such the advantages of the introduction into service of the F-5E: 'The F-5E is faster and vastly more manoeuvrable than the F5A. It has a greater range, a lead computing sight, search and track radar and a missile in-range computer. Furthermore, the F-5A is restricted to clear air mass for its engines has tendency to ice up and the pilot uses only eyeball to determine when in range to launch the AIM-9 missile. Because of thrust to weight ratio, wing loading and extreme flight stability, the F-5E will, pilots being equal, more than match the MiG-21 in the standard manoeuvring combat arena. Its area of potential superiority is much greater than the MiG-21 and gives the F-5E the upper hand whereas the F-5A is a match for the MiG-21 in a very restricted environment.'

8   Nguyen Hung, narrative on the history of the 435th Squadron VNAF, Can Thep website (in Vietnamese).

9   VNAF Improvement and Modernization Programme, HQ PACAF, July 1971 – December 1973. 1 January 1975 Report, Project CHECO, p179.

10 Narrative about operations of the 259th Helicopter Squadron by a former VNAF helicopter pilot at the 'Can Tho. Can Thep' website (in Vietnamese).

Chapter 6

BEGINNING OF THE END

Immediately exploiting the new geopolitical situation, Hanoi further accelerated the pace of its attacks during late 1974, focusing particularly on the Central Highlands as well as the strategic I Corps area. The purpose was to expand a new logistic corridor, running parallel to the famous Ho Chi Minh Trail, but on the eastern slopes of the Annamite Mountains range. From this new route, the North Vietnamese consolidated their positions and now tried to isolate Kontum, Da Nang and Hue. If they succeeded in achieving this aim, the ARVN would be isolated in fragmented pockets and would have to devote many scarce resources to try to reverse the situation. This would also force the VNAF to sustain these enclaves with air bridges.

While it was clearly wiser for the ARVN to reduce its front lines by abandoning the most exposed positions and towns, President Thieu flatly rejected such a proposition out of fear that a radical redeployment would cause a collapse in the morale of the country, undermining his own power.

The Communists acted methodically but also cautiously since they were still unable to guess the exact intentions in Washington. Each successive offensive was viewed with trepidation by Saigon, which still hung on to the hope that the latest attacks could

These A-37Bs from the 92nd Wing at Phan Rang flew an interdiction sortie in the difficult monsoon weather, searching for enemy trucks in the Central Highlands Area in 1974. They tried to slow down the North Vietnamese efforts to open a new logistic corridor on the eastern slopes of the Annamite Mountain chain. (VNAF)

be considered enough of a 'blatant violation of the ceasefire', thus forcing the US to resume its military aid.

The greatly diminished VNAF was now trying to support the harassed ground units as best as it could. One of the most critical problems was the restriction put on the use of ammunition in order to preserve stocks. Only USD9 million was available for the air force's ammunition in the entire budget for Fiscal Year 1975. This allowed for a war reserve of just 60 days of accelerated-pace operations.

Correspondingly, the fighter squadrons were ordered to reduce their bomb loads from four to two bombs for the F-5, and from eight to six, and then finally to four for the A-37. Upon re-evaluation of this policy in late November 1974, it was decided to return to normal loads while reducing the number of sorties per aircraft.

The effect of this decision was to force the ARVN to evaluate more thoroughly the requests for air strikes, and approve only those that were worthy of a full expenditure of ordnance. It was in the opinion of the USAF officers at the DAO that the reduction in sorties improved the overall effectiveness of the strikes, as well as preserving the potential of the airframes. The scarcity of resources also forced the corps commanders to release at least some of their own assets, around 25 per cent, to be centrally utilised by the TACC. This allowed the VNAF to regain more tactical flexibility. VNAF Intelligence also pointed out that fighters taking off were now regularly reported by a network of North Vietnamese observers. By operating outside their corps area, they could mislead the enemy and strike with surprise.[1]

The 2nd and 6th Air Divisions spent the last months of 1974 supporting the ARVN outposts west and northeast of Kontum, as well as on the Gi Plateau. The A-37s from the 92nd Wing at Phan Rang and those of the 532nd Squadron at Phu Cat took many risks in bad monsoonal weather and mountainous terrain to deliver bombs and rockets over the beleaguered Army positions. In early October, the VNAF tried without success to support the important Trung Nhia outpost. A battalion of reinforcements was preparing to be brought in by the helicopters of the 72nd Wing at Pleiku but enemy artillery bombardment of the intended landing zone was such that the scheme was dropped at the last moment. The position fell soon after.

Interdicting enemy logistics

From September a great effort was also directed against the steady development of a new enemy logistic corridor, Route 715, leading due east towards the Binh Dinh Province's coasts. The VNAF helicopters infiltrated long-range reconnaissance patrols to lay mines and sabotage trucks and road-building equipment. The O-1s directed long-range 175mm (6.89in) artillery as well as air strikes.

One of the most frequently attacked targets was the Duyen Binh Bridge on Route 14. It was brought down several times but on each occasion was quickly rebuilt. Meanwhile, the assaults became increasingly costly due to increasing AA fire. Intelligence then indicated that the enemy had directed a unit of T-54 tanks coming from Cambodia towards the bridge, and a strike by 16 A-37Bs was directed to attack the flak positions on the surrounding ridges. They were then followed by 16 more A-37Bs that made a BOBS-directed formation bombardment. The carpet of bombs destroyed the bridge before the tanks could cross.[2]

A still from a video showing a VNAF UH-1H gunship in early 1975. The poor view nonetheless illustrates well how the infra-red suppression kit worked. The helicopter carried two 2.75in (70mm) rocket pods as well as two Miniguns in the doors. (Author's Collection)

One of the controversial measures taken in order to adapt to budget cuts was the reduction of allocated aircraft ammunition. Consequently, the number of bombs carried was often cut in half. This F-5A of the 63rd Wing at Bien Hoa illustrates this practice, with only two instead of the usual four bombs loaded. The measure was later rescinded since it was found more profitable to launch fully loaded aircraft on fewer sorties. This also preserved flight hours and improved airframe readiness.
(Pham Quang Khiem Collection)

Night interdiction sorties were also flown by AC-119s and BOBS-directed A-37s against the enemy depots north of Kontum, these raids including aircraft of the 63rd Wing at Bien Hoa as well as F-5 detachments deployed at Pleiku and Ban Me Thuout East, where the newly resurfaced runway had been lengthened to accommodate jet operations. The 540th Fighter Squadron and its F-5Es was also deployed to Phu Cat for two weeks.

Persistent VNAF interdiction efforts inflicted heavy casualties among enemy work parties and temporarily stopped further extension of the road.

In January and February 1975 the VNAF also flew daily attack sorties against enemy communication lines in the Darlac Plateau. In one instance, at the end of February, a convoy of several hundred trucks was sighted and attacked with spectacularly destructive effect. However, the North Vietnamese subsequently began operating corps-sized formations of ground units inside the I ARVN Corps area. The bloodiest battle of this period saw the Airborne Division of the ARVN pitted against the entire 3rd Corps of the North Vietnamese Army in a bloody attrition battle in the hills just west of Da Nang, and notably around Hill 1062. VNAF A-37Bs and F-5Es from Da Nang flew numerous strikes, with a quick turnaround between missions since the targets were getting ever closer to their base.

The 63rd Wing at Bien Hoa also participated in this campaign. Detachments of F-5s were deployed at Pleiku and Ban Me Thuout East. Here, a flight of F-5As from the 522nd Fighter Squadron heads towards its target in bad monsoonal weather.
(VNAF)

By December 1974 the ARVN and the VNAF had managed to force the enemy away and thus put Da Nang outside the range of Communist artillery. The North Vietnamese subsequently deployed their 324B Division to launch an attack in the Hue area and on the Hai Van Pass. Despite the gallant defence of the ARVN 1st Division, the enemy succeeded in bringing several 85mm (3.35in) artillery pieces within range of Phu Bai AB and put the latter under attack. The local installations were severely damaged in the process. Although the 1st Division eventually forced the North Vietnamese out of the area, this was the bloodiest campaign of the 'ceasefire' period, costing South Vietnam as many as 2,500 casualties among the paratroopers alone.

The A-37Bs of the 92nd Wing at Phan Rang played an important role in the fighting in the Central Highlands at the end of 1974. This aircraft from the 524th Fighter Squadron is being prepared for the next sortie in the standard configuration of four external fuel tanks and six 500lb bombs.
(USAF)

Despite the gallant defence of the ARVN 1st Division, the North Vietnamese 324B Division succeeded in digging in 85mm (3.35in) D-44 guns on the hills of I Corps sector, within range of Phu Bai AB. The base installations were severely damaged by the shelling.
(PAVN)

By late 1974 the area between the DMZ and the west of Hue was firmly in North Vietnamese hands. The Communists installed many logistic depots around Dong Ha and in the A Shau Valley. They also rebuilt the old US airstrip at Khe Sanh, scene of fierce battles in 1968. VPAF transports and helicopters now used the extended runway.
(USAF)

Similar hard-fought battles also took place in Quang Ngai Province where the 2nd Division suffered heavy losses while losing control of the towns of Minh Long and Gia Vuc. Some strikes in support of local ground units were flown by A-37s from the II Corps area.

The VNAF was forced to drastically curtail its helicopter operations by early 1975. Gone were the days of large-scale, regimental-size, air assaults. Most of the missions now consisted of logistics support tasks as well as the insertion of small reconnaissance teams. (VNAF)

Sustaining ARVN outposts within enemy-controlled areas became increasingly costly. Many outposts could only be supplied with parachute drops and occasional helicopter landings. They were now targeted by heavy artillery and were often ringed by anti-aircraft guns and SA-7s. Each supply operations now required flak suppression, while the helicopters had to be escorted by gunships. (ARVN)

The North Vietnamese methodically expanded their logistical routes and depots in preparation for a new, large-scale offensive. They tried by any means possible to eliminate the South Vietnamese advanced positions that could impede their move. Passing the wreckage of a VNAF UH-1H gunship, these Communist troops had just overwhelmed a Ranger position in the Central Highlands at the end of 1974. (PAVN)

Fall of the Flying Dragon

Attacks on the A Shau Valley

During late 1974 the North Vietnamese dramatically expanded their logistic efforts in all of northern South Vietnam. Aerial reconnaissance, by both the VNAF and USAF, revealed new storage zones at Ruong Ruong, south of the A Shau Valley, where two truck parks and one tank parks were found, together with a 150,000-gallon fuel tank farm, connected to pipelines. More worrying was that in the process of reconnoitring the area in November 1974, a USAF RF-4C as well as two Firebee RPVs (one at Quang Tri and one at Dong Ha) were shot down by the Communists. As a result of these losses, Washington suspended even this low-profile reconnaissance programme – leaving the South Vietnamese to deal with the situation with the few reconnaissance assets at hand. Furthermore, a precious RF-5A was brought down in I Corps Area, killing one of the few reconnaissance-qualified pilots, 1st Lt Nguyen Anh Tuan. Another RF-5A was lost soon after on take-off from Da Nang due to fuel contamination in January 1975. Meanwhile, Hanoi went as far as to protest against overflights by USAF Lockheed SR-71s, in December 1974.

Since the VNAF sorties faced ever-stronger enemy air defences, its aircraft began attacking parts of the enemy logistical build-up with the help of night-time BOBS guidance. The main targeted zones were the A Shau and Ben Vanh Valleys. The attacks were usually carried out from altitudes of between 10,000 and 15,000ft (3,048 to 4,572m), by formations of between 20 and 24 A-37Bs, which dropped their bombs simultaneously, on the command of the radar controller.

An RF-5A was brought down in I Corps Area, killing 1st Lt Nguyen Anh Tuan, at the end of 1974. The few remaining RF-5As could not hope to compensate for the withdrawal of USAF reconnaissance aircraft.
(USAF via Robert C. Mikesh)

Washington had allowed a low-profile reconnaissance programme to continue, using RF-4Cs, U-2s, SR-71s and RPVs, but now suspended it altogether in December 1974. This left the South Vietnamese to rely on the few reconnaissance assets they had, including this EC-47D from the 716th Reconnaissance Squadron at Tan Son Nhut. It was mainly used to intercept radio communications.
(USAF)

The logistical complexes of Dong Ha and Khe Sanh were heavily defended by several regiments of AAA as well as SA-2s, and the VNAF lacked the ECM equipment to attack these positions. This crew of a SA-2 battery from the 367th Anti-Aircraft Missile Regiment was ready to repel 'any VNAF air strikes'. Other SA-2 sites were also positioned across the DMZ in North Vietnam.
(PAVN)

VNAF A-37Bs and F-5Es from Da Nang flew numerous strikes, with a quick turnaround between missions, in order to support the ARVN in blunting an offensive launched by the North Vietnamese 3rd Army Corps west of the city. This Dragonfly from the 61st Wing is being directing towards the runway, fully loaded with six 500lb bombs.
(USAF)

Sometime in late December 1974 a particularly successful operation was carried out against a North Vietnamese position that had been plotted some 50km (31 miles) west of Da Nang, on the Fai Foo Peninsula. The area was hit by a formation of 24 A-37Bs from the 61st Wing armed with CBU-24A/B cluster bombs. Numerous secondary explosions were observed and an EC-47 that was monitoring enemy communications indicated that a command post had been hit, killing several high-ranking North Vietnamese officers.

Large formations of F-5s and A-37s were also deployed for CAS operations. Targets that would previously have been hit by only a pair of fighters now regularly received

Only the A-37B and the new F-5E were capable of BOBS bombing. In order to fully exploit this tactic, which reduced the risk of AAA and SA-7s, the VNAF devised plans to use the Dragonfly as 'pathfinder' for F-5As. The A-37B would guide a group of F-5As under the instructions of the ground-based radar controller. It then dropped its bombs on his command, and the F-5A pilots followed suit. (Pham Quang Khiem Collection)

The 1st Air Division also carried out night BOBS strikes against enemy concentrations. This A-37B was photographed while returning from a night attack sortie. (VNAF)

up to three flights – one of which was usually deployed for flak suppression – in an attempt to divert the attention of the enemy gunners. Furthermore, in an attempt to reinforce the air assets of I Corps, the 536th Squadron at Bien Hoa was transferred its F-5As to Da Nang in March 1975. During the early months of 1975, the two F-5E squadrons at Bien Hoa also rotated detachments to Da Nang to reinforce the local 538th Fighter Squadron, maintaining air patrol alerts to counter any North Vietnamese air attacks.

Facing simultaneous North Vietnamese offensives on several fronts by early 1975, the VNAF took radical measures that fully mobilised its forces. All available technical personnel as well as instructor pilots were posted to reinforce the operational units. All training activity was suspended and the Air Training Centre closed. These cadets of Class 75 were the last to receive their wings. They celebrated with the traditional bath after concluding their primary training. (Can Thep Collection)

The Skyraiders at Bien Hoa were soon back in service for the final battle for South Vietnam. However, the A-1s of the 530th Fighter Squadron at Pleiku had not been taken out of storage.
(Pham Quang Khiem Collection)

Awaiting a major North Vietnamese offensive, the VNAF decided to resurrect part of its Skyraider fleet in January 1975, and the 514th and 518th Fighter Squadrons at Bien Hoa were brought back to life. Some members of the latter unit are seen at that time. Kneeling, third from left, is the Squadron Commander, Lt Col Nguyen Quang Vinh.
(Nghia Tran Ta)

Nevertheless, by January 1975 the situation was considered critical enough for the VNAF to come to the decision to reactivate the 514th and 518th Fighter Squadrons, equipped with Skyraiders, at Bien Hoa. Due to the poor state of their aircraft, these two units elected to share all the available airframes, which were regrouped into a common pool.

C-130 bombers

Searching for a solution for its lack of firepower, the VNAF eventually decided to use C-130 transports for bombing missions. Since C-130 crews regularly performed radar-guided HALO supply drops with a good recovery rate on the ground, why not deliver bombs or napalm in the same manner?

The idea developed by the South Vietnamese was to carry out attacks from high altitude and saturate potential targets with a large number of bombs, while aiming with the help of BOBS system. The first test took place in late 1974. Initially, most of the attacks were carried out using the established supply-dropping techniques, with airborne extraction of parachute-retarded pallets of 55-gallon oil drums, filled with napalm or even waste oil and gasoline. The drops were usually conducted from 10,000ft (3,048m) and soon it was found that the same accuracy could be achieved with the drogue parachutes deleted.

Nearly all C-130 attack missions – which were codenamed 'Hoa Cong' (Fire Support) – saw the deployment of fire-bombs, each aircraft carrying 12 pallets with four drums that would burst on impact and usually ignite an area some 1,300ft (396m) long and 700ft (213m) wide.

During the last weeks of the war, the C-130As went on to use the same technique for dropping bombs in direct support of ARVN units, and with great success. These 'Hoa Loi' operations usually saw the deployment of 32 500lb (227kg) Mk 82 bombs, installed

The VNAF compensated for its lack of firepower by using C-130 transports for bombing missions. The aircraft conducted area-coverage bombing under BOBS radar guidance. The C-130s could carry a sizeable load ranging from 24 M117 bombs to 48 napalm tanks. (Pham Quang Khiem Collection)

on eight pallets. Other configurations included 48 250lb (113kg) Mk 81 bombs, or 24 750lb (340kg) M117 bombs. These attacks were usually carried out from altitudes between 4,572 and 7,315m (15,000 and 24,000ft), always with BOBS support. The C-130s became so popular they were soon nicknamed 'BC-130' or 'mini B-52'.[3]

Test of resolve

While South Vietnam began to shudder under the repeated assaults of the Communist forces, and without much reaction from Washington, during a special meeting of the Politburo in Hanoi in November, the North Vietnamese decided to launch their final campaign for the 'liberation' of the South.

Based on the experience of the 1972 Easter Offensive, as well as different campaigns carried out since the 'ceasefire', the plan envisaged a cautious, phased offensive that would extend for two years. The North Vietnamese were fully aware of the crippling conditions faced by the South Vietnamese armed forces, and particularly the VNAF, but they still highly regarded their residual combat capabilities. Consequently, they envisaged a first phase offensive for 1975 that would in particular target the Cen-

An O-1E, probably from the 114th Observation Squadron at Nha Trang, searches for enemy activity in the Central Highlands area. The O-1s also directed long-range artillery against North Vietnamese positions and engineering efforts to build new logistic corridors. (Pham Quang Khiem Collection)

The three A-37B squadrons of the 71st Wing at Binh Thuy were dispatched in support of ongoing fighting in the III Corps area. These missions were in addition to those flown at lower level, within their own IV Corps Area. These armourers were photographed loading Mk 82s on a Dragonfly.
(Pham Quang Khiem Collection)

tral Highlands in order to cut the country in half. The isolated I Corps area would be attacked thereafter. The last phase of the offensive would be postponed until 1976 and would aim at Saigon and the Mekong Delta area. The Communist leaders were ready to deploy the entire North Vietnamese Army for this operation.

Due to disputes concerning possible reactions from the US, Hanoi eventually decided to launch an 'ultimate test', the purpose of which was to take a major town in South Vietnam, if possible a provincial capital. If the Americans did not react, then the definitive invasion of the South could be launched. The choice fell upon the city of Phuoc Long, north of Saigon, which had been isolated from the rest of the country for some time.

While preparing this operation, the North Vietnamese decided to launch a diversion that would disperse the ARVN III Corps assets. Correspondingly, Communist units first attacked a number of outposts in Tay Ninh and Long Khanh Provinces. One of these positions was Nui Ba Den, atop a mountain and serving as a very useful observation position. Due to the massive deployment of flak, re-supply by helicopter soon became impossible. Before too long, the local garrison began suffering water shortages, even though it still had enough food and ammunition. On several occasions, VNAF 'Hueys' attempted to reach the strongpoint but were driven off. Additionally, an F-5A participating in CAS efforts was shot down. Eventually, out of water, the Nui Ba Den position was overwhelmed. Another, division-sized attack took place against the city of Hoai Duc, northeast of Saigon. The ARVN counter-attacked, inserting two battalions of the 18th Division by helicopter.

The Battle of Phuoc Long

The assault on Phuoc Long began on 13 December 1974, and was carried out by the North Vietnamese 301st Army Corps. The outlying district towns fell in succession, despite the VNAF flying dozens of CAS sorties. The adjacent Phuoc Binh administrative sector was soon isolated and had to be re-supplied by air drops. Helicopters also landed inside the town, together with liaison aircraft such as U-17s and U-6s that used

On 22 December 1974, after
losing two C-130As, the VNAF
put an end to the air bridge
to sustain the garrison of
Phuoc Long. Only helicopters
continued to land inside the
town, together with liaison
aircraft. This U-17A from the
124th Observation Squadron at
Bien Hoa was perhaps involved
in these missions.
(USAF)

the main street near the market place as an improvised runway. The ARVN still held
the town's airfield at Duc Phong where, despite artillery shelling, C-130As and CH-47As
landed to bring in six additional 105mm (4.13in) howitzers and fly out refugees and
injured soldiers. However, on 21 December a C-130A was heavily damaged by artillery
and another example that landed supplies and a team of medics was shot down the
next day – despite direct support from several FAC aircraft and helicopter gunships.
This brought the air bridge operation to an end. The ARVN forces continued to resist
desperately, now concentrating within several isolated pockets. After fighting back
several assaults, however, they were overrun on 26 December 1974.

Lacking the will to deploy the sole ARVN's Airborne Division for a major counterattack, President Thieu refused to authorise a corresponding plan. He considered it a
misuse of resources to deploy this crack outfit, which was vital for the survival of the
entire I Corps. Furthermore, due to the geographic isolation of Phuoc Long, any counteroffensive in that area would depend heavily upon airlift to deploy and supply the
troops, as well as combat aircraft to support them. To mount the operation as planned,
two UH-1H and one CH-47A squadrons would be required to augment assets of the III
Corps – in addition to other tactical aircreft. The Huey-squadrons could be taken from
II and IV Corps assets, but the Chinooks were not available. The CH-47 units of the II
and IV Corps – 241st and 249th Squadrons, respectively – were newly activated and
bellow their authorized personnel strength, each being able of providing only six to
eight sorties a day, which was exactly what their own Corps required. Phuoc Long had
to fight with what was on hand.

The combat assets of the VNAF were deployed in the area from 1 January 1975, and
flew an average of 100 attack sorties per day. However, the North Vietnamese retaliated by infiltrating a sapper team into Bien Hoa, which shelled the local installations,
damaged one runway, set several buildings ablaze and interrupted the operations.

Too little, too late

When Saigon finally realised the seriousness of the situation, on 3 January 1975, a
desperate decision was taken to insert a part of the elite 81st Airborne Ranger Group,
usually engaged in commando operations. By this time, Song Be airfield was already
partially occupied by the enemy, which controlled one end of the runway and deployed
several T-54s nearby. A series of vicious attacks by VNAF F-5s stopped the North Viet-

This flight of F-5As from
the 522 Fighter Squadron is
preparing to take off for a
close air support mission with
Mk 82 and napalm bombs
during the Phuoc Long Battle
in January 1975. The armourers
are 'cocking up' the 20mm
nose guns.
(USAF)

namese advance, but these then began concentrating flak in the area. The RF-5As were active as well, flying more operational sorties by 6 January than had been allocated to them for the entire month. The RF-5As were tasked with searching for enemy positions – particularly for seven recently deployed 37mm AA guns. An additional problem was the fact that the auxiliary helicopter landing zone near Lai Khe, south of Phuoc Long, was already under artillery fire.

Despite the difficulties, the proud Rangers were willing to conduct what was certain to be a sacrificial operation. Two companies were assembled at Bien Hoa AB on 4 January but poor weather frustrated their first two landing attempts. At 0800 on 5 January, 60 tactical sorties cleared a helicopter landing zone east of the city. At 0900 the first wave of 'Hueys', escorted by helicopter gunship, landed the first company. At 1100 another wave of helicopters landed the remaining troops. Several helicopters were hit but miraculously none were brought down.

Once on the ground, the commandos immediately found themselves in the middle of an armoured assault, which developed into furious street battles between the greatly depleted defenders and a number of T-54s. Several North Vietnamese tanks were destroyed on 6 January, but by dawn the next day, the invaders were effectively in control of Phuoc Long. The last surviving Rangers fought their way out of the encirclement: after four days spent searching for them, the 'Hueys' retrieved 121 troops, most of them wounded. The VNAF had lost 10 aircraft during the battle. The first regional capital in South Vietnam had fallen – without the slightest sign of protest from Washington.

The ARVN was unable to mount a counteroffensive to save Phuoc Long. In a desperate move, it was decided to insert members of the elite 81st Airborne Ranger Group as reinforcements. The Rangers are seen here assembling at Bien Hoa before boarding the 'Hueys'. (US Army)

An F-5A is prepared for another sortie. During the battle of Phuoc Long, the 63rd Wing at Bien Hoa tried to support the besieged defenders, its F-5s flying dozens of strike missions, as well as flak suppression operations against the enemy batteries that ringed the city. (Pham Quang Khiem Collection)

In addition to the efforts of the 3rd Air Division at Bien Hoa and the 5th Air Division at Tan Son Nhut, the 4th Air Division at Binh Thuy also supported ongoing operations in the III Corps area. Here, an A-37B of the 546th Fighter Squadron heads towards its target. (USAF)

An armourer reloads the guns of an F-5A with 20mm ammunition. The proximity of the new front allowed a quick turnaround between sorties. However, the North Vietnamese attempted to disrupt VNAF operations by intermittingly attacking Bien Hoa AB with rockets.
(VNAF)

Ten VNAF aircraft were lost during the Phuoc Long Battle. This F-5A of the 63rd Wing at Bien Hoa carries a rare Multiple Ejector Rack (MER) that allowed it to carry up to six Mk 82 bombs. A small number of these MERs were delivered together with the new F-5Es.
(Pham Quang Khiem Collection)

An F-5A from the 63rd Wing at Bien Hoa takes off for a CAS mission. It is loaded with four LAU-61/A rocket pods, each with 19 2.75in (70mm) rockets. Rockets fitted M247 HEAT warheads were the usual configuration for anti-tank missions.
(Pham Quang Khiem Collection)

1   'The Vietnamese Air Force, 1951–1975, An analysis of its role in combat and fourteen hours at Koh Tang'. USAF Southeast Asia Monograph Series, Volume III, Monographs 4 and 5, see pp68–69 for the VNAF inadequate tactical control system.

2   Tranh Dinh Giao, narrative on the VNAF BOBS operations, on the Quan Su Khong Viet Nam website (in Vietnamese).

3   Interview Chau Huu Loc, former VNAF officer with the Air Logistic Command.

Chapter 7

ABANDONING THE NORTH

With the Phuoc Long campaign successfully completed, the North Vietnamese feverishly began the planning for their next step – an offensive in the strategically important Central Highlands area, code-named 'Campaign 275'.

In Saigon, it was now all too clear that 1975 would see the beginning of the Communists' final, all-out offensive. However, nobody knew when and where would this take place.

In January 1975, the VNAF received a visit from the USAF C-in-C, Gen David C. Jones, who came to assess the situation. This was already very bad, the month proving a very costly one for the VNAF, and particularly its 74th Wing, based at Binh Thuy. Between 22 and 26 January, the Dragonflies of the unit had extensively supported the ARVN 7th Division's attempts to stop a division-sized attack in the northern Kien Tuong Province near Cambodia. Five A-37Bs were shot down by Sa-7s, and North Vietnamese teams armed with this weapon further increased their tally at the end of January to ten aircraft throughout South Vietnam. Among their victims was a C-123K of China Airlines, brought down on 3 January near Nha Trang while operating on behalf of the CIA.[1]

Lt Gen Tran Van Minh therefore made a correspondingly pessimistic report to Gen Jones. Even if the VNAF was still able to 'hold the line', the budget restrictions imposed by the US had considerably diminished its capabilities. A December 1974 DAO report already indicated that from an authorised strength of 64,905 officers and airmen, the

A USAF inspection team in January 1975, at the eve of the North Vietnamese general offensive concluded that VNAF maintenance was in good condition, particularly for the fighter force. Its operational ready rate was better than 70 per cent. These mechanics were servicing the J85-GE-17A engines of an A-37B. (USAF)

The North Vietnamese had introduced additional SA-7s by early 1975. In January the launcher teams raised their tally to 10 VNAF aircraft shot down, including five A-37Bs. The SAM teams were helped by the fact that the South Vietnamese pilots now flew at low altitude to provide close air support to their ground troops. (PAVN)

air force could call upon 62,585 personnel, which meant that its personal strength had dropped to 96.4 per cent. Although this followed the then prevalent pattern within the USAF, there were also several shortages in particular skill levels, notably in seven- and nine-level airmen. A number of evaluations showed that maintenance had improved, though the overall operational readiness rate of 70 per cent was still unsatisfactory. Particularly poor was the readiness rate of 30 per cent for the remaining C-130As, and around 50 per cent for the entire transport force.

The operational rates for the other aircraft were higher than the fighters, with the exception of the AC-119. Due to this aircraft's inadequate radar, the AC-119 offered only limited utility during adverse weather operations.[2]

However, these figures were somewhat misleading, due to the fuel restrictions that hampered the number of sorties that could be generated. The most striking aspect was the fact that the VNAF had to reduce its tactical helicopter operations by 70 per cent. An evaluation of the TACC, made in December 1974, indicated that it was functioning in a satisfactory manner although complete use of the system was not being made due to restrictions imposed by the corps commanders. The in-commission rate was reported as 90 per cent, based on a USAF team visit in January 1975. It was assumed, therefore, that the TACC was fully capable of handling the sorties that the VNAF could generate in the offensive.

It was reported that the VNAF had approximately 390 fighters on strength, comprising A-37s and F-5s. With an in-commission rate of 70 per cent, there should have been a force of 273 aircraft available for operations. Based upon USAF experience with A-37s in Vietnam, the VNAF ought to have been able to generate a sortie rate of at least two per operationally ready aircraft per day. However, reports indicated that there were some difficulties in meeting such a rate due to poor logistical support from the US.

In fact, the A-37 squadrons generated on average less than 0.5 sorties per operational aircraft per day. The programmed 4.246 tactical sorties at that point failed to reflect the severity of the North Vietnamese threat. Nevertheless, the VNAF commanders assured that in case of emergency, they had sufficient capability to put up a major

Capt Hoang Gia Vien from 536th Fighter Squadron could count himself very lucky. His F-5A was hit by an SA-7 as he pulled out from a low-level bombing pass. Fortunately, the missile only disabled one of its two J85 engines, allowing him to land safely at Bien Hoa. (Northrop)

The 1st Air Division at Da Nang had been reinforced since the end of 1974 and now had two F-5 units. These were the 536th and 538th Fighter Squadrons, equipped respectively with F-5As and F-5Es. The new F-5Es were just reaching operational capability in January 1975 and were immediately thrown into combat in order to counter a North Vietnamese offensive along the Song Bo River corridor, which aimed to cut Route 1 between Hue and Da Nang. These two rare views show an F-5E from the 538th Fighter Squadron practicing a scramble during an air defence alert exercise. The nose gear unit had been raised by 13in (33cm) to allow a shorter take-off roll. (Anthony J. Tambini)

effort. This, they argued, could reach the level achieved in 1972, with surges of up to 504 tactical sorties per day. This did not take into account the enemy defences and the losses that would have been incurred. If the VNAF had flown at these higher rates, attrition would probably have been approximately three aircraft per hundred sorties. This rate was fairly consistent with USAF and Israeli experience when operating in very high threat areas. But without replacement aircraft, it was clear that the VNAF would have only a limited ability to sustain operations over longer periods of time. Gen Minh argued that in case of an all-out offensive to conquer South Vietnam, it would have been correct to sacrifice its fighters in a last-ditch stand, hoping the US would replenish the force or perhaps introduce USAF fighter units.[3]

The USAF inspection team also indicated that they were some problems with the supply chain. In December 1974, the supply fulfilment rate from the depot was running at 34 per cent. Chronic problems with the depot were still prevalent, notably in regard to the accounting procedures to determine where the parts were. VNAF logisticians were still coping with the problem with the help of US civilian contractors. There was also a backlog of engines for overhaul.

This latter could have become a factor with time, but it did not limit the operational readiness of the force at the time being. Units were not replenishing bench stocks, and in time this too would have a limiting effect. Ammunition and fuel stocks were declining, but these were estimated as sufficient for approximately 55 to 60 days during an accelerated rate of operations. It was concluded that even though stocks were dwindling, this factor should not limit the capability of the VNAF to fly an all-out effort of several weeks' duration.

Ceding to Minh's pleas, Gen Jones decided to intercede with Washington in order to help improve VNAF readiness. First of all, within the 1975 Fiscal Year limits, he succeeded in securing new and additional munitions (the budget allocated to the VNAF for that month was barely USD6 million). Furthermore, the cost of these munitions had increased due to high inflation, with an average of 27.7 per cent increase in price between time of request and time of appropriation.

The base of Da Nang received intermittent rocket harassment firing from the North Vietnamese by January 1975 on. They destroyed this A-37B from the 61st Wing. The mechanics were removing the wreckage of the aircraft that had caught fire just in front of its protective hangar.
(Pham Quang Khiem Collection)

It was due to this last measure that the VNAF was able to appropriate some CBU-55 fuel-air explosive (FAE) bombs, in addition to the usual rockets and general-purpose bombs. FAE had already been in use with the VNAF on a limited basis since 1972, with a devastating effect on enemy infantry. The USAF also transferred from its stocks 15 15,000lb (6,804kg) BLU-82 'Daisy Cutter' bombs stored in Thailand. These were to be dropped by the C-130As. Using the same techniques employed for high-level napalm attacks, the huge 'blockbuster' ammunition was reserved for high-value targets. The blast effect was sufficient to level anything within a diameter of 150m (492ft). A selected group of highly experienced pilots was gathered and trained in dropping the huge bomb. The training was delayed by various factors, notably waiting for VNAF explosive ordnance specialists to receive correct training on the new ammunition. The lack of required fuses, which arrived only erratically, also plagued the programme, combined with the fact that the local USAF 7th Air Force did not assign a high priority to the programme. It was only in early April 1975 that the first two pilots were qualified: Maj Nguyen Tan Ming from the 435th Squadron and Capt Ngo Xuan Nhat from the 437th Squadron.

Gen Jones also ordered the urgent deliveries of spare parts for the C-130s from Pacific Command stocks. Their arrival by early February greatly improved the availability of the two Hercules squadrons, allowing 16 aircraft to undergo the process of Programmed Depot Maintenance.

One of the most combat-capable units at Da Nang was the 516th Fighter Squadron. It had a distinguished record of uninterrupted combat operations since its creation as the 2nd Fighter Squadron on the T-28D at Nha Trang in December 1961. It was then renumbered and moved into Da Nang in February 1964. The unit exchanged its Skyraiders for the A-37B in 1969. Some of the squadron's pilots pose here for a group photo in front of the Operations Room in January 1975.
(Vo Ngoc Cac)

An A-37B from the 528th Fighter Squadron is serviced at Da Nang. The unit was one of the three Dragonfly squadrons operating this base, and was the second to be raised on the type in December 1970.
(USAF)

Surprise blow in the Central Highlands

While VNAF commanders were planning how best to cope with the major enemy offensive that was now expected, the North Vietnamese moved first by unleashing a sudden stroke in the Central Highlands. The South Vietnamese had expected an attack here, but most of their plans focused around the Kontum and Pleiku areas. In fact, the Communists had secretly moved an entire army corps down south to attack Ban Me Thuot, the rear logistical base of the ARVN II Corps. In order to keep this massive deployment and logistic preparation a secret, the Communists mounted a sophisticated deception campaign that was directly targeted against the strongest element of the enemy's intelligence apparatus: the electronic and aerial reconnaissance assets of the VNAF. Strict radio silence was imposed on all units involved in the offensive. North Vietnamese deception personnel sent hundreds of fake radio messages, conducted unconcealed truck movements, and conducted bogus road-building operations. All these efforts were recorded by VNAF EC-47s, RF-5s and O-1s. The resulting intelligence misled the II Corps Commander into believing that the true attack would occur in the northern part of the corps' area of responsibility.[4]

On 4 March the North Vietnamese isolated Ban Me Thuot by cutting Routes 19 and 21. As the roadblocks could not be cleared, it was decided on 9 March to insert a battalion of Rangers at Phung Duc, an outpost northeast of the town, to block any enemy

The North Vietnamese began their offensive in the Central Highlands in late March 1975. This type of North Vietnamese regimental command post participated in the sophisticated deception campaign that masked the build-up of forces in the area.
(PAVN)

The North Vietnamese radio deception campaign in the Central Highlands was monitored by the VNAF RC-47Ds, EC-47Ds and EC-47Ps from the 716th and 718th Reconnaissance Squadrons of the 33rd Wing. This EC-47P from the 718th Reconnaissance Squadron was photographed at its home base of Tan Son Nhut.
(David Mesnard via Jean Pierre Hoehn)

The North Vietnamese assault against Ban Me Thout took place on 4 March 1975. Despite stubborn resistance, the outnumbered defenders were soon overwhelmed. The Communist soldiers assaulted the town's air base, moving towards the radar station with its associated Control and Reporting Post (call sign 'Pyramid'). The antennae of the AN/FPS-20 and AN/TPS-6 radars can be seen in the background.
(PAVN)

The town's air base was heavily hit by enemy artillery that destroyed 13 UH-1Hs of the 2nd and 6th Air Divisions. This group of North Vietnamese soldiers is passing a destroyed 'Huey'; an artillery shell has severed the helicopter's tail boom. (PAVN)

advance there. However, it was now late and the local airstrip, which was used only occasionally by Air Vietnam DC-3s, had no lightning system for night operations. The six C-130As that were already airborne were instead ordered to land at Phu Cat and wait for the dawn.

The main North Vietnamese assault took place soon afterwards. It included three divisions supported by tanks and three anti-aircraft artillery regiments. The town's air base was heavily hit by artillery that destroyed a CH-47A, an O-1 and six UH-1Hs of the 6th Air Division. Four of the seven UH-1Hs of the 2nd Air Division were also destroyed on the ground, although three damaged 'Hueys' managed to escape to Pleiku. By afternoon, the outnumbered defenders – a single regiment and some regional troops – had already lost half of the city.

In order to support the defenders, the VNAF flew 196 sorties in the course of the first two days of the battle, including 158 by A-37s, 30 by F-5s and eight by AC-119s. These sorties helped knock out 13 tanks, but the bad weather hampered the provision of close air support.[5] Meanwhile, intense AA fire shot down three helicopter gunships and three A-37Bs, and considerably reduced the ability of the FACs to direct bombardment. The 92nd Wing at Phan Rang paid particularly a heavy price with two A-37Bs shot down and two others badly damaged by 37mm flak.

At the town's air base, the local commander of the Control and Reporting Post (call sign 'Pyramid'), Lt Col Tran Dinh Giao, received bad burns to his face but continued to direct air support. In spite of all these efforts, the North Vietnamese tanks eventually pushed inside the base and Giao was forced to call air strikes directly onto his bunker. By mistake, one of the attacking VNAF aircraft hit the communications centre of the ARVN sector headquarters, compounding the difficulties of guiding the fighter-bombers.

The battalion of Rangers that was waiting at Phu Cat AB was finally loaded in helicopters and sent in the direction of Ban Me Thuot. However, when the 'Hueys' approached the city, the anti-aircraft fire was such that after waiting in a holding pattern to find a suitable landing zone not under enemy artillery fire, the battalion's commander eventually opted to land at Buon Ho, 30km (19 miles) northeast of the intended target.[6]

The loss of Ban Me Thout

The last pockets of resistance in Ban Me Thout were overpowered after 32 hours of high-intensity combat. Outside the town, some Ranger troops still held the base of Phung Duc as well as the airfield at Ban Me Thuout East. They were ordered to resist until reinforcements could be flown in. However, the concentration of flak was meanwhile so great that no helicopters could land there: two UH-1Hs and a CH-47A were destroyed attempting to bring in supplies. Instead, it was decided to insert the 45th Regiment of the 23rd Division into a new landing zone at Phuoc An, 30km (19 miles) east of Ban Me Thuot.

In order to bolster the helicopter assets of II Corps, detachments of four other 'Huey' squadrons, provided by III and IV Corps, were dispatched to Pleiku, as well as four CH-47As from IV Corps. On its side, I Corps sent a detachment of five 'Hueys' from the 239th Squadron at Da Nang. At Pleiku AB, they were met by intermittent North Vietnamese 122mm (4.80in) rocket shelling that had already destroyed three A-37Bs on 11 March. The regiment was lifted from Pleiku on 12 March by 90 helicopters, including just six CH-47As. With available Chinook numbers so limited, only a battery of 105mm (4.13in) howitzers could be brought in to support the regiment. The rest of the 23rd Division was then to be flown in to Phuoc An and attack in a westerly direction to link up with the defenders of Phung Duc. They would reoccupy Ban Me Thuout East Airfield and this would serve as a strongpoint to retake the city.

The link-up manoeuvre was launched on 15 March but, without armour or artillery support, it stalled in the face of the North Vietnamese 10th Division. The ARVN was

A group of proud North Vietnamese soldiers poses with the wreckage of one of 13 destroyed UH-1Hs, caught by surprise on the ground at the Ban Me Thout. However, three damaged 'Hueys' managed to escape to Pleiku. It is interesting to note that the Communists hold a Viet Cong flag rather than that of North Vietnam, maintaining the fiction that they were local 'native insurgents' and not part of a regular foreign invasion army. (Vietnam News Agency)

The first South Vietnamese initiative to retake Ban Me Thout was an airborne assault carried out by the 45th Regiment, 23rd Division, into a landing zone at Phuoc An. The VNAF was by now overextended in several theatres and had great difficulty in assembling enough helicopters for the operation. Finally, by calling on the assets of II, III and IV Corps some 90 machines could be assembled. Troops are seen here boarding the 'Hueys' for the initial assault. (US Army)

only supported by VNAF fighters and helicopter gunships, which faced a strong flak opposition. The command and control helicopter that flew over the area to direct the operation was damaged, wounding the 23rd Division's commander. The VNAF flew an average of 60 to 70 strike sorties per day during the offensive, but the task force was pushed back three days later to Khanh Duong, at the entrance of the M'Drak Pass.

Four aircraft were lost during this failed counteroffensive. One of them was an A-37B from the 534th Squadron that was hit by an SA-7 after a bombing pass over Phung Duc. Both pilots ejected successfully: one landed atop the Rangers' command post, while the other drifted away and landed in the jungle. He managed to reach the

The troops inserted at Phuoc An received an order to link up with ARVN forces that still maintained a foothold at Ban Me Thuout East Airfield. But, facing strong opposition and without armour support, the counteroffensive failed. The VNAF lost over 20 aircraft during the battle, including this UH-1H captured by the Communists at Ban Me Thuout East Airfield. (PAVN)

ground and then escaped the enemy, racing towards a clearing where he was picked up by a group of M113 APCs.

The state of affairs was temporarily stabilised at Khanh Duong when the entire 40th Regiment of the 22nd Division was inserted here by helicopter. The situation for the Rangers at Phung Duc now became desperate. The defenders were re-supplied only by HALO drops from C-130As and C-119Gs. But now most of the bundles were falling outside their shrinking perimeter. On 18 March, after a week of fighting, the survivors broke out and escaped in small groups. Despite the gallant efforts of the South Vietnamese airmen, Ban Me Thuot was definitively lost, the VNAF suffering a loss of no fewer than 20 aircraft and helicopters in the course of the battle. Attrition included four precious CH-47As and a TACAN station.[7]

The VNAF could mobilise only six CH-47As during the attempt to retake Ban Me Thout. These helped to bring in a battery of 105mm (4.13in) howitzers at the Phuoc An landing zone. Two other Chinooks had already been destroyed during the initial fighting inside the city.
(US Army)

Thieu's gamble

On 14 March 1975, while the offensive to retake Ban Me Thout was taking place, President Thieu flew to Cam Ranh Bay AB to meet the commanders of the I and II Corps. Already convinced of the probable failure of the Ban Me Thuot operation, he then ordered a complete redeployment of ARVN forces in the northern half of the country, including the evacuation of Pleiku and Kontum.

The stunned ARVN commanders protested vehemently. Even today it is difficult to understand the rationale behind such an extreme decision, in which nearly half of South Vietnam was abandoned to the enemy. President Thieu later argued that his decision permitted the ARVN to concentrate its remaining forces and shorten the logistic lines. Other ARVN officers suggested that such a radical decision had been taken to force the US to react and to implement the promised equipment and air power support. Consequently, holding the Hue and Da Nang enclaves would provide bridgeheads for a new US ground intervention. Indeed, several days later Thieu dispatched Nguyen Tien Hung, his special envoy, to Washington with several letters from former US President containing promises of support in the case of a new Communist invasion.[8] However, there was no positive reply from Washington and whatever Thieu's real motives might have been, nothing of the kind had been previously planned by the ARVN JGS: instead, the evacuation of each unit was left to the responsibility of local commanders.

On 14 March 1975 it was decided to abandon to the enemy nearly the whole northern part of the country. The VNAF Headquarters was not even informed of the fateful decision despite the fact that its transport aircraft would be destined to play a crucial role in the evacuation process. This C-130A from the 435th Transport Squadron was photographed at the Ban Me Thout East Air Base some weeks before it was taken by the North Vietnamese.
(Pham Quang Khiem Collection)

The VNAF commander, Lt Gen Tran Van Minh, was a recognised leader who had led his forces into one of the most challenging reorganisation and expansion process. Due to his illustrating the South Vietnamese high command inadequacies, he was not even represented in the National Security Council while his units were placed directly under the command of each ARVN Corps Commanders.
(USAF)

Thieu's gamble was about to set off a chain of events that would lead to the total collapse of South Vietnam.

Evacuation of Pleiku

Speed and secrecy were the order of the day for the evacuation of the Central Highlands but the cumbersome and fragmented South Vietnamese chain of command meant the operation was flawed from the start. The lack of cooperation between the ARVN and the VNAF only exacerbated the problem. The withdrawal would take place along Route 7B, a long disused track with many destroyed bridges. However, it was reasoned that since Route 19 linking Pleiku to the coast was already cut, it was the only alternative left.

Immediately after the meeting with Thieu, the headquarters of I and II Corps were ordered to operate accordingly. I Corps was in the worst position, since it received the order to concentrate its remaining forces around enclaves in the areas of Hue and Da Nang, and to abandon the rest of the country to the Communists. This meant that significant contingents of ARVN and VNAF were left cut off, hundreds of miles behind enemy lines.

The task of II Corps was not much easier and its commander was therefore in a rush: he ordered Brig Gen Pham Ngoc Sang, GOC 6th Air Division VNAF, to evacuate his aircraft and personnel from Pleiku AB. Technically, this was a manageable task. But practically, Sang was left with only 48 hours to implement this order! The bewildered officer dispatched his deputy to Saigon to meet the C-in-C VNAF, Gen Tran Van Minh, to seek the help of some C-130As: this meeting was the first time that Minh became aware of Thieu's decision, as well as the decision to evacuate Pleiku – even though an entire division of his force was directly involved.

Minh required several hours to receive the approval of the Army Transportation Division, which had operational control of the airlift resources as a theatre asset, in order to release the C-130As for such a priority task. He then put in charge of the

When the 6th Air Division was ordered to evacuate from Pleiku AB, the unit was left with barely 48 hours to do so. This UH-1H from the 72nd Wing was unloading the belongings of VNAF personnel at Nha Trang AB.
(David Butler)

In addition to the C-130As, the VNAF also fully mobilised its other transport aircraft in the vast redeployment of forces that took place at the end of March 1975. The C-119Gs of the 720th Reconnaissance Squadron were involved alongside the Hercules and C-47s.
(USAF)

operation his deputy, Maj Gen Vo Xuan Lanh, who flew to Pleiku to supervise the task. Throughout the night eight C-130As, together with some C-119Gs and C-47s, shuttled in and out of Pleiku, moving equipment and personnel to Phu Cat and Phan Rang. At dawn, the aircraft of Air America joined the effort, as did those of the national carrier Air Vietnam. At that point, there was no contact between the ARVN and the enemy troops, even if the base was intermittently shelled by artillery. Most of the personnel of the 6th Air Division were occupied in getting their families out. The weather on 15 March was bad and no Hercules could be flown into Pleiku.

As could have been expected, the departure of the troops caused panic in the town and thousands of civilians joined the long column. Others poured into the airfield hop-

The evacuation of II Corps along the disused Route 7B turned into a rout. The North Vietnamese moved into Pleiku City without much resistance. This aerial reconnaissance photo, probably taken by an RF-5A of the 522nd Fighter Squadron on 19 March 1975, shows the abandoned aircraft at the local air base.
(USAF)

Triumphant North Vietnamese troops cheer their victory at Pleiku. These soldiers are posed beside the huge tropospheric scatter, trans-horizon antennae near the air base. These were part of the South Vietnamese long-range national communication network, linked to US installations in the Pacific Area.
(Vietnam News Agency)

ing to catch a flight out. An Air America C-46 with 51 seats took off with no fewer than 142 armed soldiers on board; one C-47 carried 80 refugees instead of the usual 30, and a Bird Air DC-6, from another CIA 'contracted airline', flew out with no fewer than 340 passengers on a single flight!

As the weather lifted, Gen Sang elected to try and get the rest of his people out in broad daylight along the road towards the coast, even though he knew this would be extremely hazardous. However, he had no other choice since the North Vietnamese had meanwhile moved in anti-aircraft guns around Pleiku AB and an Air Vietnam DC-3 had been brought down while taking off.

On 17 March the air bridge was suspended altogether due to increasing enemy artillery fire on the base. By this time, nearly all operationally ready aircraft and almost all of the personnel of the 6th Air Division had been flown out. The GOC 6th Division had performed tremendous work and exhibited great courage in the handling of a chaotic situation. However, he had to leave 32 aircraft in flyable storage behind, including 21 A-1s of the disbanded 530th Fighter Squadron, 11 O-2s of 118th Observation Squadron, four O-1s, as well as a single examples of the C-47, C-7 and C-119. A lack of time meant that no attempt was made to put these aircraft in commission. Therefore, hardly any of these aircraft were destroyed, the most noticeable exception being 10 operational UH-1Hs that had been sent to Camp Holloway Airfield, in order to hide them from the enemy's harassing artillery fire. As no pilots came to pick them up, the local armoured troops tossed hand grenades into their cabins before withdrawing.

Only very contradictive evidence is available in regards the destruction of fuel and ammunition dumps in Pleiku. However, the Control and Reporting Post (call sign 'Peacock') and the local BOBS station were destroyed, partly by a team of CIA agents that had been inserted by an Air America PC-6. The loss of this installation significantly hampered all future VNAF operations over the Central Highlands.

Rout in Cheo Reo

After hearing reports of the long column of ARVN troops and civilian refugees retreating along Route 7B from Phu Cat and Nha Trang, the North Vietnamese deployed their 320 Division – supported by tanks and two AAA regiments – in pursuit. Initially, the ARVN withdrawal went well, until the column reached the Cheo Reo fording, where it came across another column of several thousand refugees. The Communists caught up and deployed their artillery to shell the area, irrespective of the presence of civilians. The survivors could not say how many were killed, but the North Vietnamese fire was reported as being to intense that the entire town of Cheo Reo was set on fire.

There is no indication that an emergency plan was put into operation to use air power from other corps areas to help stabilise the retreat. Disorganised by the evacuation of Pleiku and nearly paralysed by the chaos that reigned on the ground, as well as the lack of FACs, the VNAF attempted to provide support. VNAF transport units became engaged in some supply drops, but there is no evidence indicating any kind of a major effort against enemy artillery or ambush sites. The A-37s flew only 20 CAS sorties between 16 and 18 March, but mostly attacked North Vietnamese units around Cheo Reo. Two A-37Bs of the Phu Cat-based 532nd Squadron are known to have been shot down in the process: 1st Lt Chan Van Yen was KIA during a mission over the Chu Pao Pass, while 1st Lt Pham Vang was shot down over An Khe and his whereabouts remain unknown. On 20 March, a flight of Dragonflies mistakenly attacked a battalion of Rangers, causing heavy casualties. After this tragedy, the fighters were only engaged in interdiction operations, attempting to slow the North Vietnamese pursuing forces; instead, CAS missions were flown by helicopter gunships.

From 20 to 23 March, some eight to 12 fighter sorties were permitted each day to attack the bridges built by the enemy. For example, on 21 March four A-37Bs destroyed a semi-submerged bridge at Ai Nu. The important Dak To Bridge that resisted several strikes was finally brought down by a flight of A-37Bs of the 548th Fighter Squadron led by Maj Nguyen Tien Xuong, a day later. Some missions were also directed towards Pleiku to destroy the equipment abandoned there, but during a strike against this air base another A-37B was shot down, on 20 March.

The VNAF attempted to support the withdrawing column along Route 7B from Phu Cat and Nha Trang air bases. However, air support became almost impossible due to the chaos reigning on the ground and the lack of FACs. Two A-37Bs from the 524th Fighter Squadron are making a rocket pass against an enemy column.
(VNAF)

After a mistake that saw the retreating South Vietnamese on Route 7B attacked by A-37Bs, it was decided to restrict CAS to the helicopter gunships. The crew of this gunship are attempting to save a group of refugees. (US Army)

The North Vietnamese captured several operational – or otherwise 'quickly repairable' – aircraft at Pleiku AB. This group of their soldiers is seen inspecting an abandoned 'Huey'. (PAVN)

On the same day the head of the column withdrawing from Pleiku was again stopped at the Song Ba River. The tanks and trucks had torn up the ford so badly that pierced steel planking had to be placed on the riverbed. This was delivered by VNAF CH-47 helicopters that also flew in a bridge section to the site, 1.5km (0.9 miles) downstream from the ford. The 'Huey' squadrons also flew dozens of sorties to bring in supplies, and pick up stranded troops or refugees. In many instances, the pilots had to make a 'touch and go', for their helicopters were literally swarmed by panicking people, many of whom would hang on the landing skids.

During the last week of March, the retreat from Pleiku turned into a rout, as the entire road towards the coast was filled with withdrawing military and fleeing civilians. The endless column, named the 'convoy of tears' by the press, was increasingly fragmented and fought desperately to escape.

The Central Highlands retreat turned into a rout all the way from Pleiku to the coast. Many VNAF pilots took great risks to pick up terrified civilians fleeing the enemy artillery shelling. This mother and child were fortunate enough to be flown out by a 'Huey' gunship. (US Army)

Many VNAF pilots took great risks to fulfil their duty, even if they did not always adhere to their orders. Typical for this period was the story of Capt Huynh My Phuong of the 229th Helicopter Squadron, who flew a UH-1H gunship. Although ordered to fly attacks on North Vietnamese troops only, on several occasions he landed to pick up refugees. On one such sortie, Phuong embarked panicking civilians atop a hill but later found that a group of children had been left on the ground without their parents. Tears in his eyes, he tried to swing his helicopter around to rescue them. He could not, however, as he already had so many aboard. After refuelling, Phuong returned to the same location but the children were no longer there. Next, he saw a Communist mortar team opening fire on the convoy of refugees. Together with his wingman he destroyed the enemy position using unguided rockets and then landed again to pick up refugees. As Phuong's gunners ran out to help children and old people, several bewildered soldiers also scrambled aboard. Phuong stated that on several occasions the people he had rescued were forced by local ARVN troops to pay for their journey. But he also reported that many of his squadron's pilots had paid from their own pockets for the rice that they dropped to the refugees.[9]

Collapse of II Corps

By late March 1975, a mechanised task force consisting of Rangers with some armour support was the last organised ARVN unit that continued fighting and pushing on towards the coast. This column, followed by an estimated 60,000 refugees, was resupplied with ammunition by two CH-47s on several occasions, but continued suffering losses in the course of several ambushes set up by the Communists.

If the situation for II Corps was critical by late March 1975, it became almost catastrophic on 2 April, when North Vietnamese tanks entered Tuy Hoa harbour, thus severing the strategic coastal Route 1 that ran from Saigon to Hue. In this way, the remnants of II Corps were cut in two, and more than 140,000 refugees were unable to escape from Binh Dinh Province.

The fighter-bombers of the 2nd and 6th Air Divisions did their best to slow down the enemy advance from the Central Highlands towards the coast. This A-37B of the 92nd Wing is ready to be launched for another attack sortie, loaded with six 500lb bombs. (USAF)

Panicking refugees rush towards a VNAF CH-47A as the air base at Tuy Hoa is evacuated. The town fell on 2 April 1975, when North Vietnamese tanks entered the harbour. The town was the last hope for many of the 200,000 refugees fleeing in that direction; only some 60,000 are estimated to have survived. (US Army)

With their tanks now in Tuy Hoa and Ban Me Thout, the North Vietnamese threatened the VNAF bases in the Nha Trang area from two directions. In order to protect the area, the ARVN swiftly deployed the 3rd Airborne Brigade, freshly released by I Corps, and rushed this unit towards the M'Drac Pass to block the advance of the Communist 10th and 316th Divisions. This crack paratrooper outfit fought tenaciously and with great skill, but there was only a finite amount of time in which even the best unit could hold out under such conditions.

Despite some 200 combat sorties flown by A-37Bs within only five days, around a dozen night interdiction sorties flown by AC-119s, and even more efforts by helicopter gunships, the outnumbered paratroopers were eventually forced to withdraw. As usual, the North Vietnamese flak was heavily represented, and it shot down one O-1 and one A-37B, while another Dragonfly was knocked out by a SA-7. Unsurprisingly, on 2 April 1975 the pursuing North Vietnamese reached the outskirts of Nha Trang, now protected by only a few minor regional units, most of which fled at the first sight of the enemy.

On the verge of moral collapse, the GOC II Corps, Maj Gen Pham Van Phu, abandoned his command, embarked in his personal helicopter and flew directly to Saigon. He was put under house arrest and later committed suicide when the North Vietnamese entered the capital.

The ARVN tried to block the enemy advance towards Nha Trang AB at the M'Drac Pass with the 3rd Airborne Brigade. However, the Paratroopers failed for they lacked artillery and armours and could count only on VNAF support like this A-37B from the 92nd Wing. (USAF)

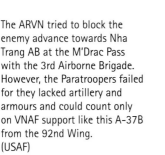

The loss of Phu Cat, Nha Trang and Cam Ranh Bay

Left without any choice, the VNAF immediately ordered the evacuation of the air bases at Phu Cat and Nha Trang, both of which were about to be overrun. Angry and full of mistrust for their superiors, the VNAF officers literally kidnapped high-ranking ARVN officers at Nha Trang, requesting the return of Gen Phu in order to defend their air bases.[10]

As in the case of Ban Me Thout, only very few efforts were made to destroy a number of crucially important ground installations and heavy equipment left behind at Phu Cat and Nha Trang. Most of the aircraft stored or parked there, including dozens of T-41Ds and T-37Cs, were simply abandoned, as the VNAF mechanics assigned to the local units fought their last battles as simple infantry troopers. Their pilots had only a little more luck. The A-37 pilots of the 532nd Squadron flew repeated missions to cover the evacuation by sea of the 22nd Division from Qui Nhon harbour. They continued attacking the approaching enemy until the last ship and boat had left the area. Their commander then gathered the remaining 30 pilots, as well as 10 from the disbanded 530th Squadron of Pleiku, who were in the process of converting from A-1s to A-37s, to tell them that it was time to abandon the base and fly to Nha Trang. Once there, the entire formation was ordered to refuel and immediately take off for Phan Rang. The pilots remained only one day at this base, until ordered to redeploy to Tan Son Nhut. After spending some days in Saigon, they were finally moved for the last time to Binh Thuy, where they were incorporated within the local 74th Wing.

The evacuation of Nha Trang was thus undertaken in haste and in a state of almost complete chaos, with the air base practically overrun by thousands of refugees that broke through the perimeter fence. The VNAF flew out as many aircraft as physically possible, usually all loaded with personnel and families, but also many civilians, amid another series of dramas. In one instance, hundreds of armed soldiers and their families, most of them mounted on motorcycles, met a C-130A that had just landed with a load of three pallets of mines and hand grenades. Weighing up his chances, the pilot

The outnumbered 3rd Airborne Brigade was forced to withdraw from the M'Drac Pass, several paratrooper battalions being picked up by helicopter and sent to Phan Rang. Sometimes, the enemy attacked the pick-up zones, forcing a hasty evacuation, with some troops hanging on the landing skids as the 'Hueys' departed under North Vietnamese artillery shelling.
(US Army)

On 3 April 1975, the North Vietnamese entered Nha Trang AB practically unopposed. They occupied the installations of the 62nd Wing and those of the Air Training Centre. Among the captured aircraft were these B-26Ks that were used as ground instructional airframes. The North Vietnamese immediately deployed 57mm (2.24in) S-60 AA guns to protect the base.
(PAVN)

The base of Phu Cat, home of the 82nd Wing of the 6th Air Division, was evacuated when there were no more ground forces to protect it. The North Vietnamese captured these CH-47As of the 241st Helicopter Squadron. The machines appeared damaged and could not fly away. (PAVN)

prudently decided to turn around and take off without making a stop, and divert to Phu Cat instead. His request to return to Saigon was denied, however, and the C-130 was ordered back to Nha Trang. Obeying, the pilot took off from Phu Cat among gaggles of helicopters that had begun the evacuation. Once airborne, he tentatively suggested dropping his cargo over the sea, since the enemy would otherwise capture all the ammunition. But orders were orders and he landed back at Nha Trang. The pilot stopped on a taxiway where the aircraft was unloaded. As he moved onto the apron, the Hercules was literally flooded by refugees. With great difficulty, the crew fought to close the doors and flew out with over 300 people on board!

Cam Ranh was evacuated under similarly chaotic circumstances during the first week of April, leaving a huge air base complex and the vast harbour practically untouched in the hands of the enemy. Within only 15 days, the VNAF had thus lost three major air bases in the II Corps area. Yet more distressing events were about to take place in the northern part of the country.

The fall of Hue

Since January 1975, I Corps was facing increasing enemy pressure west of Hue and in its southern sector around Tam Ky. The VNAF provided valuable support but by early March the 1st Air Division was ordered to stand down in order to conserve its assets for an expected major enemy offensive. As of that date, the division still had no fewer

An F-5A from the 536th Fighter Squadron is towed towards its alert pad at Da Nang. The unit assumed the air defence mission with the locally based F-5Es of the 538th Fighter Squadron. (Pham Quang Khiem Collection)

The 61st Wing still included 72 A-37Bs that represented a potent attack force, reinforced by some 20 F-5As and 16 F-5Es. A Dragonfly from the 516th Fighter Squadron is seen here ready for another mission. (USAF)

than 344 aircraft on strength, including the 61st Wing with 72 A-37Bs, 20 F-5As and 16 F-5Es available; the 51st Wing with five UH-1H and one CH-47A squadrons (totalling 192 helicopters), plus an entire squadron of stored C-7s.

In early March, the North Vietnamese increased their pressure along the Song Bo River corridor, aiming to cut Route 1 between Hue and Da Nang. The strategic fire-support base 'Bastogne' was lost to a Communist assault, but was then retaken by the ARVN. The VNAF reacted vigorously, destroying several T-54 tanks, but two A-37Bs and two UH-1Hs were shot down between 9 and 13 March.

Another major North Vietnamese concentration of troops was meanwhile detected at Thu Bon, west of Da Nang, and subjected to the most fierce attack flown by the VNAF up to that date: a formation of nine C-130As under BOBS guidance bombed the area, each simultaneously disgorging a total of 32 Mk 82 bombs, saturating the target zone with no fewer than 288 weapons. The results of this mission remain unknown, however.

Despite such operations, the district capital of Tam Ky was soon under enemy artillery fire and between 10 and 13 March the VNAF lost two further A-37Bs and a UH-1H in the defence of the town.

President Nguyen Van Thieu took the fateful decision of a complete redeployment of the ARVN forces in the northern half of the country for the second half of March 1975. He is seen here inspecting ARVN outposts by early 1975 aboard some VNAF 'Hueys'. (VNAF)

During the battle of Da Nang, the VNAF lacked comprehensive reconnaissance assets to asses the fluid and quickly changing military situation in the ground. Its FAC aircraft were furthermore held down by intense enemy flak. Some sorties were flown by a detachment of RF-5As of Bien Hoa. (USAF)

It was under these dire circumstances that the JGS ordered, on 12 March, the reassignment of the crack Airborne Division to the central reserve at Saigon. The redeployment would take more time than expected due to the lack of air transport assets, which had been mobilised for the ongoing battle for Ban Me Thout. Therefore, the decision was taken to evacuate most of the unit by sea.

On 14 March, the GOC I Corps returned from the Cam Ranh Bay conference and held a meeting with his staff. He detailed his new strategy for the defence of the area centred on Da Nang, with the evacuation of Quang Tri and Hue, and his intention to establish a major defensive perimeter, anchored at the Hai Van Pass, just north of Da Nang. This defensive perimeter was to include positions of the 1st and 3rd Army Divisions, as well as the Marine Division, with the 2nd Army Division in reserve. Maximum conservation of resources would be in effect until the main battle for Da Nang was joined. In particular, the VNAF units deployed in Da Nang had to be used cautiously, since their presence was offsetting the balance against the much superior North Vietnamese forces that were about to launch their onslaught.

However, chaos had begun to spread to Da Nang by this time, and it appears that the CO 1st Air Division VNAF, Brig Gen Nguyen Duc Khanh, was not even invited to this meeting.[11]

The resulting lack of coordination and cooperation between the ARVN and VNAF, as well as contradictory orders issued by President Thieu were soon to lead straight to another disaster.

On 16 March 1975 the units ordered to withdraw into the Da Nang perimeter began pulling out from their positions. However, discipline and unit cohesion soon collapsed and panic spread among the military and civilians alike. In the southern sector, two North Vietnamese divisions overran the ARVN units, forcing a hasty evacuation of Quang Ngai City. Many of the troops left in their outlying positions had to be extracted with the help of VNAF helicopters. Even though this operation was undertaken in good order, most were flown directly to the piers in Da Nang harbour and then evacuated by sea.

Next, the North Vietnamese launched their major attack from the north, involving three divisions that pressed in the direction of the high ground west of the city. As the regional troops began to abandon their positions around Quang Tri and join the mass of refugees that clogged the roads leading towards the south, the major Army units soon began to disintegrate in that sector as well.

Although there had been some rocket attacks against Da Nang AB, destroying an F-5E, the 1st Air Division had suffered no major blow to its operational capabilities by this time. On the contrary, in accordance with the I Corps Commander's directive, the VNAF flew very few sorties. In fact, only an average of 40 strike sorties per day was authorised, and no consideration was given to an accelerated rate to facilitate the withdrawal. One of the main concerns was the conservation of ammunition, as the main ammunition dump in Da Nang had been destroyed by enemy sappers in early January 1975, and had since been only partially replenished.[12]

Since Thieu's instructions concerning the defence of the ancient Vietnamese capital of Hue remained vague, there was plenty of uncertainty among the local commanders. Eventually, the evacuation of the city was only launched on 17 March, since Thieu rescinded the order three days later than everywhere else. Instead, he directly ordered the Marines and the armour to move to the north of the Hai Van Pass – away from the area. As ever more refugees kept flowing into Da Nang, the local roads were soon nearly impassable, causing massive delays in troop movements. It proved practically impossible to regulate this human deluge. Important passes in Route 1 were frequently jammed, delaying troop movements.

It was under such circumstances that the North Vietnamese resumed their major offensive, aiming at first isolating Hue from Da Nang. The 324th and 325th Divisions attacked west and southwest of Hue, converging on Phu Loc, to cut Route 1. The VNAF directed 33 sorties by A-37s and F-5s against the 324th Division on 21 March, helping to stop its advance at La Son. The 325th Division took over Hill 500 but thanks to very efficient VNAF support it was expelled from this position and Route 1 remained open – at least for the time being.

Adding to the general confusion, for a third time, on 25 March, another order was delivered to I Corps regarding the fate of Hue City. President Thieu changed his mind one more time, and ordered the withdrawal of all forces south of the Hai Van Pass. The order was delivered in the course of a speech aired on National Radio and Television almost simultaneously, the President announcing that the old imperial city would be defended at 'all costs'.

Contradiction and confusion in the orders accelerated the breakdown of ARVN and civilian morale. The Marines fought their way out from Dan Cau Hai Bay on an improvised pontoon bridge consisting of semi-sunk civilian ships, and reached Da Nang after an enforced march in good order, even though without their heavy equipment. On 26 March, the North Vietnamese flag was raised over the old Imperial Palace of Hue.

Disaster at Da Nang

While the evacuation of Hue took place, another presidential order fell upon a stunned I Corps Staff. The Marine Division, extracted from Hue under great difficulty, was to be evacuated to Saigon. The departure of the Marines meant that the last hope of maintaining a bridgehead at Da Nang had vanished. Inside the city, the refugees' problems overwhelmed the local authorities. Over one million people wandered the streets without food or sanitation. Added to these were thousands of deserters that sometimes exchanged gunfire with the police and looted the shops. Eventually, the crumbling ARVN perimeter left Da Nang AB within enemy artillery range.

People tried to escape the Da Nang enclave by every means possible as the North Vietnamese approached. Scenes of chaos soon spread to the air base, where VNAF security troops had difficulty in restoring order and were soon overwhelmed. These desperate refugees are attempting to embark on one of the chartered US aircraft.
(Vietnam News Agency)

The North Vietnamese divisions that converged towards Da Nang were protected against VNAF air strikes by an imposing air defence system. This battery of 57mm AA guns had just been positioned on the northern perimeter of the enclave. (PAVN)

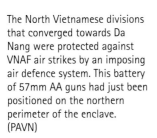

Not knowing the real intention of the ARVN, the VNAF Commander, Lt Gen Tran Van Minh, decided to take things into his own hands. On the night of 26 March he dispatched his deputy, Maj Gen Vo Xuan Lanh, to Da Nang to asses the situation. He was directed to save as many assets as possible but still maintain a residual force to sustain the Da Nang enclave. Above all, Minh wanted to save his most modern equipment, notably the F-5Es. They were some arguments against maintaining them at Da Nang, since a North Vietnamese air strike now would have devastating effects on the base. Only a few days earlier, a pair of MiG-21s on a reconnaissance mission approached undetected at low level and thundered over the airfield, taking everybody by surprise. The two MiGs popped up and went down the length of the runway at full speed before veering northwards. It was the first time that an enemy aircraft had overflown a VNAF base. Concluding that the situation was very bleak, Minh agreed to evacuate both the 536th and 538th Squadrons, equipped with F-5As and F-5Es, respectively. As of 26 March, there were three F-5As and two F-5Es awaiting repairs. After frantic efforts, including the help of some US civilian contractors, two F-5As were made operational by cannibalising the third example. Both F-5Es were repaired and made flyable, but one aircraft had a defective directional gyro. Although not a safety issue in the given situation, for some reason this Tiger II was not flown out.[13]

The F-5As took off first, on the afternoon of 27 March. The F-5Es were checked for the return trip to Bien Hoa – though not without a 'last bang'. Under the command of Lt Col Le Xuan Lan, the Air Defence System North's Commander, the jets were fully bombed up and flew a BOBS attack against North Vietnamese positions west of Da Nang. After releasing their bombs through the overcast, they flew south.

With the F-5Es out of the way, the North Vietnamese pushed on Chu Lai. After causing the collapse of another unit of I Corps ARVN, they captured the local air base in an intact condition as well.

On 27 March, the first US commercial jets chartered for the evacuation of US citizens and other foreigners landed in Da Nang, including World Airways Boeing 727s and Continental Air Service Douglas DC-8s. Initially, the Americans planned to airlift about 14,000 people in daily runs between Da Nang and Cam Ranh. However, Cam Ranh fell a few days later and meanwhile the news of the evacuation spread within the Da Nang perimeter: the airport was besieged by a frantic crowd that swamped the runways and mobbed the aircraft. The VNAF security troops had difficulty in restoring order. An Air America C-46 barely managed to evacuate the team of US civilian contractors working on the maintenance of VNAF aircraft. Among them was J. Tambini, still working for Northrop:

'The night prior to our departure the base was hit by 40 122mm [4.80in] rocket rounds. We were informed that evening that we would be evacuated out the next day. We went to the base, at what was left of base operations installations, and it was packed with Vietnamese attempting to depart. World Airways 727s were coming in and being mobbed by the Vietnamese. I then saw a C-47 with no markings on it that taxied to the base operations and shut down. Two men came out and were dressed in combat fatigues without any markings on them. I talked to one of them, an American, and asked what they were doing at Da Nang. He told me that they were on their way to Hue to blow up the LORAN station there. I was surprised and asked him if he knew that Hue had already fallen to the Communists. He shrugged and said yes. They departed shortly thereafter. We were then contacted by Air America personnel and driven to another location where an Air America C-46 was waiting to take us. The aircraft was already full with what appeared to be Vietnamese dependents. We sat on the floor in the aisle.'

That night, eight C-130As landed to pick up VNAF personnel but were soon overwhelmed by civilians and Army troops. Capt Nguyen Van Chuan, the pilot of one of the Hercules remembered that he had considerable difficulty in restoring order in the fully loaded cargo compartment:

'While directing my aircraft towards the runway an UH-1H helicopter hovered just in front of us, seemingly attempting to make me stop. I did not, for it became obvious that the pilot wanted me to take his family, who were in the helicopter. Sorry, there was no room anymore. No sooner had the helicopter moved away than a truck pulled in front of us. The driver jumped out and pointed an M16 rifle at the cockpit, giving the appearance that he would fire without hesitation. He then motioned that he too wanted to have a ride on the plane. I gave a thumbs-up ok signal to the man, and motioned for him to meet the plane at the end of the runway. He seemed satisfied and sped away to the take-off end of Runway 18. But when I reached the runway entrance, there was no hesitation nor did we ask to get clearance from the tower for take-off… After landing in Son Nhut, I counted more than 200 passengers coming out of my C-130!'

The next day, enemy artillery began to hit Da Nang AB, suspending the civilian air bridge altogether, as four North Vietnamese divisions and a tank brigade pressed upon the western and southern flanks of the defensive perimeter. Leaning upon the fire-support base 'Baldy', the 3rd Division ARVN held off another attack on the western side of Da Nang, while the VNAF knocked out a number of tanks despite intense anti-aircraft fire. The air force also made great efforts to destroy the enemy's camouflaged artillery positions – although with minimal results. The O-1s operated as FACs, guiding A-37Bs and the counter-battery of the 175mm (6.90in) guns.

The pull-out operation from Da Nang began on 28 March, with VNAF transports reinforced by those of Air Vietnam, Air America, as well as US chartered commercial jets. This C-47 of Air America was photographed after landing a team of CIA agents who came to Hue to destroy the local LORAN station. (Anthony J. Tambini)

However, the ever increasing shelling of Da Nang AB gravely disrupted subsequent air operations. Under fire, civilians took cover inside the aircraft shelters, making the servicing of parked aircraft impossible. In the light of corresponding reports, Gen Minh ordered the evacuation of as many operational aircraft as possible from Da Nang. Mechanics tried now to make the Caribou of the 427th Transport Squadron flyable again. Before too long, thousands of people gathered at the air base, attempting to climb on anything offering the hope of escape. Some departing pilots told of seeing a UH-1H on the maintenance ramp fully packed with people waiting for the flight crew, not realising that the helicopter did not have rotor blades.

The end of Da Nang began when the 3rd Division was ordered to pull back towards the city in order to shorten the defensive lines. Once on the move, the unit began to disintegrate, as its officers and soldiers defected en masse in order to search for their families. Hastening the final collapse of I Corps ARVN were also rumours – possibly spread by Communist agents – that a secret agreement had been reached for a new partition of the country.

By the night of 28 March, left with only vague directives from Saigon, the GOC I Corps, Lt Gen Ngo Quang Truong, decided to evacuate what was left of the Da Nang garrison. He ordered the displacement of all units during the night towards three embarkation points where Navy ships would pick them up. That same night three other C-130As landed but only one could pick up refugees before the situation spiralled completely out of control. The two other aircraft made a quick turnaround for a hasty departure. At daybreak, the artillery fire increased, making evacuation of the remaining aircraft more hazardous. About half of the A-37Bs had been evacuated, most of these making final bombing sorties before recovering at Phang Rang for refuelling and continuing towards Bien Hoa or Tan Son Nhut.

The fate of the remaining aircraft was bleaker. It was impossible to service them, left alone to move them around on a base flooded by refugees and leaderless soldiers. Suddenly, during a lull in the artillery barrage, a lone World Airways Boeing 727 appeared and landed. Two M113 APCs escorted the airliner to the parking area. A huge crowd surged forward when it stopped. In a shameful scramble, hundreds of desperate soldiers fought their way through the refugees and began to climb aboard. The aircraft's captain moved forward while dozens were still clinging to the rear door. While accelerating on the runway, the airliner was pursued by countless cars and motorcycles. Worse yet, several soldiers who were clinging to the landing gear were crushed to death when this was retracted. Landing back at Saigon, the crew counted 330 passengers on board.

A C-7 of the 427th Transport Squadron that had just been returned to operational status took off, fully loaded with refugees. It was followed an hour later by another Caribou that launched despite a crippled engine. The pilot eventually shut it down and managed to limp to Tan Son Nhut on the remaining engine. One of the last departing aircraft was an AC-119K of the 821st Attack Squadron on temporary duty at Da Nang and piloted by Capt Vinh Pho. He later reported that he had to taxi over 100 dead bodies on the ramp before he could make it to the runway.[14]

The helicopters and observation aircraft lacked the range to escape south since many of the air bases on their route were already in Communist hands. Consequently, many helicopter pilots flew their machines to the pick-up points at the end of the Hai Van Pass or at the foot of the Marble Mountain, hoping to embark on a ship. Others

On 29 March 1975, the ARVN tried to evacuate its remaining forces in Da Nang by sea, using three embarkation points on the beaches east of the city. Many helicopters lacked the range to escape south, so their pilots flew to the end of the Hai Van Pass or the foot of Marble Mountain where they hoped to embark on a ship.
(Tran Khiem)

flew to Cu Le Re Island, some 40km (25 miles) west of Chu Lai. The island served as an Air America base and as a regrouping point for the ARVN before their transhipment towards the south. Dozens of other helicopters tried their chance anyway, pressing south as far as possible before landing in enemy-controlled areas. Others chose to ditch at sea, hoping to be rescued by passing ships. The crews of the 213th and 239th Helicopter Squadrons apparently attempted a concerted evacuation plan on the night of 28 March. About half of their 'Hueys' took off and pressed on south in very bad weather. Less than a quarter of them succeeded in reaching Phu Cat AB a few hours before this was also overrun. After refuelling, they continued to Nha Trang then Saigon. Capt Nguyen Gioang of the 239th Squadron later recalled:

'Time and again, many of my wingmen would announce that they were out of fuel and forced to land in the areas controlled by the enemy. One crew was even heard saying a goodbye to everybody before choosing to crash at sea, killing themselves, rather being captured by the Communists.'[15]

The evacuation by sea encountered problems of its own. All the naval vessels reached their designated rendezvous points as planned, but the tide was low and the troops thus had to wade and swim towards them while being shelled by enemy artillery. It is unlikely to ever become known how many were killed by artillery shells or otherwise drowned.

The lack of clear directives and collapse in control led to many VNAF personnel, including a great number of pilots, being trapped in Da Nang. In a last desperate attempt, a group of 12 C-130As was again dispatched to rescue them. When they arrived over the besieged air base around midday on 29 March, their crews found North Vietnamese tanks at both ends of the runway.

Another plan envisaged picking up a group of pilots who had moved to the alternate airfield of Marble Mountain, by using A-1E/Gs. The plan called for each Skyraider to pick up five to six stranded pilots after a quick turnaround on the ground. A formation of armed A-1Hs would provide close support to cover the whole operation. However, before this rescue attempt could be launched, even that base had fallen.

North Vietnamese sappers move into a revetment that contained a damaged VNAF UH-1H at Marble Mountain airfield. This former USMC base was used by the VNAF as an auxiliary establishment to train helicopter pilots. (PAVN)

Another aircraft captured at Marble Mountain airfield was this O-1E. It probably belonged to the VNAF 120th Observation Squadron. Shrapnel from exploding artillery shells damaged the aircraft. (PAVN)

On 30 March the Communist tanks rolled into the second largest city in South Vietnam. They captured 169 aircraft, including 29 A-37Bs and one F-5E. Only a few communications and radar facilities at Monkey Mountain – the alternative command post of I Corps – had been sabotaged, though it remains unknown if the same was the case with the local Control and Reporting Post and the BOBS station. The total VNAF losses during the final campaign in the Da Nang area amounted to some 268 aircraft – valued at USD106 million – written off as of 4 April due to all causes. Furthermore, the air force lost USD48 million worth of ammunition and USD68.6 million worth of spare parts and support equipment. These losses did not include the irreplaceable facilities such as air bases, depots, and radar and communications installations.

THIRTEEN ABANDONED/DERELICT C-7s

This aerial view shows part of Da Nang AB now in the hands of the North Vietnamese. It was probably taken by an RF-5A from the 522nd Fighter Squadron. It is clearly apparent that the installations remained mostly intact, together with the parking areas and runways. (USAF)

North Vietnamese soldiers pose in front of the entrance of the 1st Air Division Headquarters. The fall of Da Nang AB was the worst setback suffered by the VNAF so far, far outweighing in terms of materiel loss what had happened in the II Corps area. (PAVN)

The North Vietnamese captured 169 aircraft, including 29 A-37Bs and one F-5E, on Da Nang's main and auxiliary airfields and landing pads. This poor but interesting view shows some of the Dragonflies still parked in their protected revetments, with a 'Huey' in the background. (PAVN)

On 30 March 1975, the North Vietnamese stormed Da Nang AB, HQ of the VNAF's 1st Air Division, and one of the largest in South Vietnam. These Communist soldiers are moving through the parking area of the 427th Transport Squadron with its mothballed C-7As. (PAVN)

North Vietnamese soldiers pose on a captured A-37B for a propaganda photo. The aircraft was found at the entrance of the main runway, still loaded with two 750lb and six 250lb bombs. (PAVN)

The North Vietnamese captured dozens of helicopters inside the Da Nang enclave. These 'Hueys' were found inside a hangar in various states of maintenance. There was no time to make them operational in order to evacuate them. The helicopter with the Red Cross painted on the nose was probably from the detachment of the 259th Helicopter Squadron, a unit devoted to medevac operations. (Vietnam News Agency)

The North Vietnamese found these two UH-1Hs on the embankment of the Do Toa River in the southern part of Da Nang City. The 'Hueys' from 51st Wing seemed to be abandoned intact in a small landing pad within an ARVN base. (PAVN)

These three UH-1Hs were captured at Da Nang's Navy Headquarters. The machines seem to be intact and attracted the curiosity of the soldiers of the PAVN's 126th Naval Infantry Brigade that helped to take the city. (PAVN)

1   Dr Joe F. Leeker. The History of Air America; From Vietnamization to the end 1969–1975 E-book, University of Texas, McDermott Library. p34.

2   'The Vietnamese Air Force, 1951–1975, An analysis of its role in combat and fourteen hours at Koh Tang'. USAF Southeast Asia Monograph Series, Volume III, Monographs 4 and 5, p62.

3   Ibid. pp63–65.

4   Victory in Vietnam; The official history of the Pople's Army of Vietnam, 1954–1975. The Military History Institute of Vietnam/translated from the Vietnamese by Merle L. Pribbenow. Kansas University Press, 2002, see pp361–367 about the deception operations carried out by the North Vietnamese prior to the offensive against Ban Me Thout.

5   The breakdown for each type of aircraft and number of sorties could be slightly inferior to the missions actually flown. The figures were in fact given by the North Vietnamese that reported only the number of sorties that their troops could observe over the battlefield. See Lich Su Quan Chung Phong Khong, Volume 3, p272.

6   Ibid.

7   Tran Dinh Giao, narrative about the final moments of the Ban Me Thout Control and Reporting Post (call sign 'Pyramid'), at the Quan Su Khong Viet Nam website (in Vietnamese).

8   Nguyen Tien Hung was South Vietnam Minister of Economic Development and Planning. After the war, he published in exile a series of books that provided additional insight on America's relationship with South Vietnam during this crucial period.

9   The story of Capt Huynh My Phuong was published in Newsweek magazine on 2 April 1975.

10 Stephen T. Hosmer, Konrad Kellen, Brian M. Jenkins. The Fall of South Vietnam; Statements by Vietnamese Military and Civilian leaders. Crane, Russack & Company, Inc, New York 1980, p203.

11 'The Vietnamese Air Force, 1951–1975, An analysis of its role in combat and fourteen hours at Koh Tang' USAF Southeast Asia Monograph Series, Volume III, Monographs 4 and 5, p75.

12 Since February 1975, the O-1s in reconnaissance missions had detected a dramatic increase in the communist logistic preparations around Hue. On 17 February a FAC discovered a big enemy convoy of trucks moving toward a ridge line some 28 miles southwest of the city. Several new field artillery positions were also identified in the area, along with bulldozers building new roads toward friendly positions. However, I Corps headquarters failed to act on this intelligence and no air strikes were ordered.

13 J. Tambini, email interview, 2003.

14 Robert C. Mikesh. Flying Dragons; the South Vietnamese Air Force. Schiffer Publishing Ltd. Atglen, USA, 2005. See pp143–144 for a description of the evacuation of Da Nang.

15 Nguyen Gioang, narrative about the evacuation of his unit from Da Nang at the Quan Su Khong Viet Nam website (in Vietnamese).

Chapter 8

TARGET SAIGON

The ARVN withdrawal from Hue took the North Vietnamese by surprise. Still, it did not take long for the Politburo in Hanoi to decide to adapt its plan for phased offensives against the South. Even if it lacked specific details about the intention of its enemy, it was clear that Saigon was about to implement a vast redeployment of its forces. Taking profit of the chaos created by the deliberate abandonment of the northern provinces, it was therefore decided to launch an all-out offensive – that would soon take the name 'Ho Chi Minh' – directly against the remaining forces concentrated around Saigon. The 1st Mechanised Army Corps, held in reserve, was sent down the Ho Chi Minh Trail, together with all of its armoured and mechanised units, as well as several additional anti-aircraft units.

Other North Vietnamese units pushed south along the coastal road, taking one town after the other, and from the Cambodian border towards Saigon. The ARVN stiffened its resistance, supported by what remained of the VNAF. But now it was too late, and nothing could stop the Communist tidal wave. In Washington, President Thieu's special envoy found most of the doors closed. No one wanted to hear from him about President's Nixon letters and the promises of US air support. President Thieu's poker game had turned against himself and his country.[1]

This aerial reconnaissance photo of Da Nang, taken a week after the North Vietnamese had overrun it, showed that it was already in use by the Communists. The VPAF moved in very quickly and employed the base for bringing in supplies with its own transport aircraft. The photo reveals the presence of one Antonov An-24, one Il-14 and one Mil Mi-6 helicopter. (USAF)

The VPAF stepped up its transport missions towards the South, bringing in urgent supplies and deploying technical teams to take over newly conquered air bases. The crew of this Mil Mi-8 of the 919th Transport Brigade was planning a next supply sortie from the recently occupied Da Nang AB. By this stage, the VPAF had put into service only a small number of Mi-8s, with eight machines delivered by the Soviets in 1974. (VPAF)

The VNAF met immensurable problems while attempting to cope with the task of withdrawing units from long-established bases, or at least withdrawing its crucially important aircraft and personnel. Most of the aircraft arrived on their new bases in the south without ground support equipment, lacking spares and even the most basic tools. Nearly all the educational facilities had been lost and no replacements could be expected soon from the schools. At least as important was the lack of personnel – notably mechanics and other specialists – many of whom had been killed, captured, or abandoned in enemy territory. The evacuated airmen were therefore integrated into current units or were regrouped under the units that were the most intact and that had been able to escape.

But the most serious problem was taking on charge the evacuated personnel and their families. Few facilities existed and many airmen had to cope alone when it came

Despite the catastrophic losses falling upon the South Vietnamese armed forces, the VNAF 'esprit de corps' prevailed. These pilots of the 540th Fighter Squadron at Bien Hoa continued to carry out their missions with determination despite the gloomy situation. The F-5A in the background is a former Imperial Iranian Air Force example. (Can Thep Collection)

to finding accommodation, or even the simplest place for their dependants to live. A number of pilots simply vanished from their units for a time in order to take care of their loves ones. Morale was low among the evacuated and their pessimism and anger towards the catastrophic military decisions could not be contained for long. However, the traditional VNAF 'esprit de corps' prevailed and the slump in morale was far less severe than among the ARVN ranks. In fact, the massive influx of refugees from the north acted as a plague in the areas held by the Army. They carried with them demoralisation and fear, and many positions were lost soon after being hit by 'the refugee wave'. But surprisingly, in many places, the ARVN stood its ground and fought heroically: the furious battles that ensued in the last weeks of the war included some of the heaviest fighting of the entire conflict.

All-out battle

Between 10 March 1975, when the Battle of Ban Me Thuout began, until 10 April 1975, by which time all the air bases in the northern half of South Vietnam had been evacuated, the VNAF had flown 3,468 close air support sorties, 1,349 interdiction sorties, and 123 reconnaissance sorties. Despite the gravity of the situation, it appeared that only around 500 additional sorties had been generated, compared to the scheduled working plan. It was true that the rapid collapse of the ARVN and the loss of air bases gravely disrupted any concerted effort to increase the rate of sorties. During that same period, the transport squadrons also flew 1,669 sorties, carrying 54,000 passengers and 4,500 tons of cargo. The Hercules fleet also transferred North Vietnamese prisoners to Phu Quoc Island, while some 5,200 tons of supplies had been dropped to besieged garrisons.[2]

In this period of time, the VNAF lost 39 fixed-wing aircraft shot down and had to abandon no fewer than 387 others. A census of 4 April indicated that the VNAF had now shrunk to a total of 976 operational aircraft. In the face of such dire circumstances, it was decided to reactivate as many of the aircraft that had been placed in storage as possible.

At Tan Son Nhut the 429th and 431st Squadrons were resurrected on C-7As. By the end of March, Washington dispatched Gen Frederick C. Weyand, US Army Chief

Many units evacuated were assigned to new bases, but these were often without technical support and tool kits, while many of their mechanics could not be evacuated. This A-37B from an unidentified unit was departing for another mission from Tan Son Nhut. (William Liddell)

F-5As from the 63rd Wing at Bien Hoa head for a CAS mission, armed with napalm tanks. By early April 1975, the ARVN was hastily reorganising its forces in the hope of halting the North Vietnamese offensive. It continued to hold a last foothold in the II Corps area, centred upon Phan Rang City and its air base. The VNAF's 3rd Air Division at Bien Hoa and 5th Air Division at Tan Son Nhut were redirecting a great part of their resources to sustain the battle.
(USAF)

of Staff, to Saigon to assess the situation. There he met the ARVN and VNAF commanders who renewed their pleas for a strong commitment by the US towards their country. The VNAF commander again raised the question of direct USAF intervention, stating that this alone could turn the tide. He also requested an urgent reinforcement programme for the VNAF to offset its losses. Weyand further requested an exceptional aid of USD44.9 million for aircraft spares and support equipment, as well as USD21 million to reconstitute the airborne munitions stocks. Finally, he also expressly asked for funding as quickly as possible in order to repair two of the five C-130As stranded in Singapore for overhaul.

The US Congress turned down every one of these demands.

These circumstances forced the ARVN to allow more latitude to the TACC in its use of the remaining assets. The VNAF then began to conduct a more coordinated battle along the following guidelines:
- Around 100 daily strike sorties for III Corps,
- 60 for IV Corps, and
- 20 to be reserved exclusively for use against targets of its own determination.[3]

However, few interduction missions were flown against the advancing North Vietnamese motorised columns. In fact, the TACC that could control the strikes had been

Unable to monitor enemy movements, VNAF gunships consequently made only occasional interdiction missions, flying most of their missions at night in support of ground forces in direct contact with the enemy. This is an AC-119G of the 819th Attack Squadron at Tan Son Nhut.
(Pham Quang Khiem Collection)

greatly diminished with the loss of half its DASCs and the few remaining FAC aircraft. Once more, the lack of reconnaissance assets precluded the exact assessment of enemy deployments. Instead, most of the strikes were directed to support troops in contact.

When it came to transportation activities, the C-130 fleet was meanwhile primarily devoted to bombing missions, with some eight to 12 aircraft available daily for this task. From 1 to 19 April, some 153 C-130 bombing sorties were flown. Among the targets attacked by the Hercules were an enemy corps headquarters, suspected concentrations of troops, convoys and a SA-2 site that was being set up. There were also some strikes against the lost air bases of Phuoc Long, Nha Trang and Pleiku. The purpose here was to crater the runways in order to deny their use by enemy aircraft. In the course of these missions, VNAF C-130s deployed nine 'Daisy Cutter' bombs. The first was dropped on enemy positions north of Khanh Hoa, quickly followed by a second, west of Nha Trang. Two more pilots had been qualified to drop them: Capt Mac Huu Loc and Nguyen Que Son.

North Vietnamese transport aircraft were deployed in support of the Army advance towards the South as well, primarily to bring in urgent supplies and deploy technical teams to take over newly conquered air bases. From 29 March to 30 April, the 919th Transport Brigade flew 163 fixed-wing aircraft sorties, carrying 6,250 passengers and

The North Vietnamese offensive against the remaining ARVN forces concentrated around Saigon was to involve the strategic reserve as well as all available armour. The defenders of the capital would soon face four Army corps and could count only upon the VNAF to offset the balance. Here, a VNAF A-37B, probably from the 546th Fighter Squadron at Binh Thuy, heads towards its target. (Pham Quang Khiem Collection)

The VNAF conducted a more coordinated and efficient battle during the last weeks of the war. With ARVN Headquarters relinquishing some of its authority over air assets, the VNAF now had the right to allocate a number of sorties against targets of its own determination. These armourers are reloading bombs on A-37s of the 74th Wing at Binh Thuy. (Pham Quang Khiem Collection)

120 tons of equipment, including 48 tons of 100mm (3.94in) tank shells. These figures did not take into account additional missions carried out by helicopters. A former VNAF C-119G and some U-17s were also pressed into service. The Flying Boxcar was used to transport a commando of Viet Cong conscripts who originated from Saigon. With their knowledge of the city they were to be used as guides for the North Vietnamese columns progressing towards the town.[4]

The road to Saigon

The ARVN defensive perimeter was meanwhile re-established along two front lines, protecting the northern and western approaches to Saigon. What was left of II Corps was reduced to holding the last few coastal towns.

On 6 April the 2nd Airborne Brigade was flown into Phan Rang and moved north to block the PAVN advance along the coast. Nearly all supplies for the paratroopers, as well as for air operations at the base, including aviation gasoline and jet fuel, were transported by VNAF aircraft as well.

The three A-37B squadrons of the Phan Rang-based 92nd Wing under Col Le Van Thao flew an all-out effort. They were reinforced by a detachment of four A-1s under Maj Le Thuan Loi, while helicopters flew teams of the elite Strategic Technical Directorate to infiltrate northeast and northwest of the city. However, the respite was short, as the airborne brigade was quickly ordered back towards Saigon, to be replaced by a Ranger group and an ARVN regiment.

The troop rotation was nearing completion when heavy fighting broke out on 12 April, after the North Vietnamese attacked the northern perimeter of Phan Rang with two divisions, as well as cutting the retreat Route 1 towards the south. About half of the regional battalion in charge of the defence of the air base had deserted, forcing the VNAF mechanics to fight as soldiers to defend it. Targets struck were so close to the airfield that pilots hardly had time to get their gear up before dropping their bombs. In a rush, most of the pilots helped load their aircraft with bombs and flew mission after mission as the enemy approached the gates of their air base, destroying half a dozen of tanks in the process.

Despite all its efforts, the situation eventually became untenable. The stubborn GOC 6th Air Division commander, Brig Gen Pham Ngoc Sang, had already overseen the hasty departure from Pleiku AB. He was now determined to save as many aircraft at Phan Rang as possible. He stayed until the end to supervise the operation and refused to be evacuated. By noon on 15 April, the enemy tanks broke through the city's

The paratroopers fought tenaciously to block the Communist advance along the coast, supported by VNAF air strikes. This F-5A from the 63rd Wing at Bien Hoa, loaded with four 750lb bombs, departs for another mission. (USAF)

In addition to committing its entire battle corps into the South for the final offensive against Saigon, the North Vietnamese also dispatched more than half of their Air Defence Command assets. By early April 1975 these comprised more than 48 anti-aircraft regiments with more than 2,600 guns as well as two regiments with 48 launchers for SA-2 missiles. A column of these missiles is seen here on Route 1.
(PAVN)

With direct US intervention in this stage of the conflict now more than remote, the North Vietnamese were preparing to transfer additional anti-aircraft defence assets to participate in the final assault against Saigon. In addition to the 367th and 377th Anti-Aircraft Divisions already committed, the Communists were now deploying the 375th Anti-Aircraft Division. This battery of SA-3s from the 375th Division was preparing to move south.
(PAVN)

A Mi-6 embarks troop reinforcements heading South. The VPAF operated 12 of these heavy transport helicopters at the time. They were much appreciated for their load capacity, range and speed.
(VPAF)

Mainstay of the VPAF helicopter fleet in 1975 remained the Mil Mi-4. The piston-engine machine, which entered service in 1958, constituted two thirds of the medium helicopter fleet. The Mi-4 was used extensively thereafter for clandestine supply missions over Laos and South Vietnam.
(VPAF)

centre and overwhelmed the last ARVN positions. Gen Sang was taken prisoner by the Communists, who also captured two A-37Bs, two C-119Gs and two AC-119Ks. Two days later, the town of Phan Thiet, the last foothold in MR II, was evacuated.

On 19 April an Air America Volpar was hit by flak in the area of Phan Rang while it was searching for a lost CIA agent. The aircraft came down on a beach and the crew was quickly retrieved by an Air America 'Huey'.[5]

Meanwhile the city of Da Lat had been evacuated, including the ARVN National Military Academy. The local university also possessed a small nuclear research reactor and the US authorities were willing to evacuate the fuel rods. Two C-130Es from the USAF's 374th Airlift Wing landed at the local airfield on 31 March. One aircraft evacuated the South Vietnamese scientists and their families towards Saigon, while the other embarked the nuclear fuel rods in lead-lined caskets. These were handed over to a C-141 at Clark AB in the Philippines to be transferred to the US.

All the North Vietnamese regular battle corps, some 19 divisions, were now converging upon Saigon.

Bombing the Palace

On the morning of 8 April 1975, there was plenty of activity at Bien Hoa. Dozens of aircraft – F-5s, A-1s and A-37s – were in the process of being prepared for the numerous strike sorties scheduled for the day. The enemy pressure was such that even the standing alert patrol of F-5Es had been stripped of their AIM-9E Sidewinder missiles to be assigned to ground-attack tasks.

In the 544th Fighter Squadron's Operations Room, the pilots were poring over their maps in order to plan the assigned missions. They had just attended a meeting held by the squadron's commander, Maj Vo Van Si, who informed them of the latest developments on the different fronts, as well as the sorties assigned to the unit. He also enquired as to the availability of the aircraft, before deciding to assign missions to the different flight leaders. One of these was Capt Ngo Hoang, who was questioned why

Despite the growing efficiency of the VNAF after the weeks of setbacks in March 1975, the VNAF was sadly lacking in reconnaissance assets to assess the results of its attacks. Only a handful of RF-5As were available, including this example photographed at Bien Hoa in April 1975.
(Anthony J. Tambini)

A group of F-5Es, probably from the 542nd Fighter Squadron, ready for a sortie in early April 1975. The aircraft were parked at the end of the runway, undergoing a final inspection prior to take-off. (Anthony J. Tambini)

his flight would include only three aircraft due to the last-minute un-serviceability of an F-5E. However, Hoang would adapt to the circumstances, and now plotted the flight plan to Phan Rang, where the ARVN had requested a strike against a North Vietnamese position.

Adding to Si's sombre mood was the fact that one of his pilots, 1st Lt Nguyen Van Luom, was still not present. He had a house in Saigon, and sometimes came late to the air base due to traffic jams. He was still pondering the situation with Maj Huynh Duy Anh, the number three of the flight, when 1st Lt Nguyen Thanh Trung stepped in.

Considered one of the five best pilots on the squadron, Trung had a reputation as a maverick. At least three times, Trung caused damage to his aircraft while attempting to land on the shortest runway length possible. As a result, he was dressed down by the squadron's CO and his promotion to rank of captain suffered accordingly. Trung was on the reserve list this morning and volunteered to replace Luom. The flight leader concurred and the three F-5Es departed on schedule. The three aircraft lined up on the runway, ready to take-off.

Seconds short of releasing his brakes, 1st Lt Trung called the leader to announce some sort of electrical problem. The formation, now reduced to two aircraft, pressed on in full afterburner. A few seconds later, Trung accelerated and took off too, his problem apparently 'solved'. Immediately after tucking in his undercarriage, he quickly dove to an altitude of less than 30m (98ft) causing the ground controller to lose him from the radar screen. The GCI attempted several times to raise Trung on the radio but received no answer: instead of trying to catch up with his wingmen, Trung turned towards downtown Saigon, searching for the Presidential Palace.

Once over his target area, the South Vietnamese pulled his F-5E into a climb, rolled out and then entered a dive, releasing two Mk 81 bombs in the process. The weapons hit near the main building and detonated, but caused only relatively slight damage. Trung therefore decided to make another pass, despite the local air defences, consisting of mounted 0.5in (12.7mm) calibre machine guns and 20mm cannon, which had opened fire on him. This time, his two Mk 81s were on the mark: one went through the roof that also served as a helipad, and exploded in the central staircase. The other was a dud. President Thieu and most of his staff were in a basement bomb shelter at the time of this attack, and only one official was injured.

Meanwhile, Trung dove back down to low altitude, to avoid detection by VNAF radars and any interception attempts, and turned towards the Nha Be embankment on the Mekong River, site of South Vietnam's most important petroleum storage depot. Once there, he strafed several Navy gunboats and fuel storage tanks with his 20mm cannon.

On 8 April 1975, Lt Nguyen Thanh Trung, a long-time Communist sympathiser, decided to bomb South Vietnam's Presidential Palace in downtown Saigon. He was part of a flight of three F-5Es sent to Phan Rang for a CAS mission. At the last moment he announced an abort, and flying at low level to escape radar detection attacked the Palace and damaged it slightly with four 250lb (114kg) bombs. He then appeared over the Nha Be embankment, where he strafed fuel storage tanks. He finally recovered at Song Be airfield, north of Saigon. The base had been in Communist hands since January. Trung is seen here cheered by the North Vietnamese who expected his arrival. (PAVN)

Less than 30 minutes later, Trung circled above Song Be airfield, near Phuoc Long, 220km (137 miles) north of Saigon. Skilfully, he made a crash barrier landing on the bomb-damaged runway, which was less than 1,000m (3,281ft) long. There the North Vietnamese greeted him: his F-5E was immediately concealed beside the wreck of one of two VNAF C-130As that had been destroyed there in early January. Later, the Tiger II was dragged further outside the airfield perimeter and camouflaged again.

Back at Saigon, rumours of a new coup soon spread, some even suggesting that the VNAF was behind the plot. President Thieu summoned its commander, Lt Gen Tran Van Minh. He explained that the Palace attack was apparently a solitary act, and that no other personnel were involved. The two pilots belonging to Trung's flight were arrested on their return to be interrogated by VNAF security officers. Later, more than 600 officers gathered at Bien Hoa, including the 3rd Air Division Commander, Brig Gen Huynh Ba Tinh, to hear the findings of a special enquiry team dispatched by the National Security Agency.

Trung's F-5E was initially hidden beside the wreckage of the C-130A that had been damaged and abandoned there on 21 December 1974 during the Phuoc Long fighting. However, in order to escape destruction should the VNAF decide to search for it, the aircraft was later moved out of the airfield and camouflaged. (VPAF)

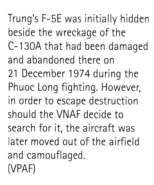

The rapid advance by the North Vietnamese units and the stiffness of ARVN resistance had exhausted the Communist logistic effort. Some units had to suspend their attacks in order to replenish ammunition and fuel. In some pressing situations, the VPAF was mobilised to fly in the required goods. Equipment and ammunition were brought in from North Vietnam in transport aircraft and forwarded to the front lines by helicopters. These Mi-6 (left) and Mi-8 (right) helicopters were bringing in tank gun ammunition as well as AT-3 anti-tank missiles.   (PAVN)

It soon appeared that Trung was an infiltrated Communist agent. Government forces had killed his father, a Viet Cong political commissar, in the early 1960s. Since then, Trung was in constant contact with enemy agents. He joined the VNAF in 1969 with a hidden identity in order to pass through the stringent security check. After graduating in 1971, he became an A-37B pilot, before converting to F-5Es. Throughout these years, he served faithfully as a competent and dedicated officer, waiting for the moment when he could fulfil a 'special mission'. Finally, his Viet Cong handlers got the word to him: sometime between 1 and 10 April 1975, he was to take any available fighter jet and either attack the Presidential Palace or the US Embassy, or both. In order to recover at Song Be, he had to practice short landings. If he couldn't land, he should eject – this was the reason why he had damaged three different F-5s while landing.

Trung's infiltration into the VNAF was indeed a masterstroke by the Communist Intelligence. His bombing certainly lowered the morale of the VNAF. Gen Minh toured his bases trying to rally his men, even as VNAF Security received orders to carefully study the background of its remaining 3,000 pilots. First, strict regulations were issued and any important strikes had to be authorised by the President himself, while each pilot had present a pass. However, these measures were soon dropped due to the mounting enemy pressure against Saigon, and the VNAF was now fully mobilised to try to stop the enemy's advance.

The evacuation of An Loc

The first sector of the Saigon defensive perimeter that came under attack from the North Vietnamese was in the area of Tay Ninh, a town that was soon encircled. The enclave held only thanks to VNAF support. The C-130As flew a series of bombing sorties in front of the city, using 500lb and 750lb bombs. This raised the morale of the defenders as rumours of intervention by USAF B-52s spread rapidly!

The next sector to come under attack was that of Go Dau Ha, on the intersection between Routes 1 and 22, held by the ARVN 25th Division. The assault by a North Vietnamese division was repulsed thanks to very effective air support. The VNAF F-5s and A-37s destroyed 17 tanks but three fighters were brought down in exchange.

On 15 April 1975, North Vietnamese tanks broke through into Phan Rang AB. Here they made prisoner Brig Gen Pham Ngoc Sang, the stubborn commander of the 6th Air Division who stayed until the end in order to supervise the operations and the evacuations of his squadrons. These North Vietnamese soldiers are passing by a damaged C-119G abandoned at the base. (PAVN)

The venerable Skyraider remained a potent strike platform, capable of carrying a hefty payload. This A-1H from the Bien Hoa-based 518th FS was photographed while carrying no less than 10 Mk 82 bombs. (USAF)

By early April 1975, ARVN resistance had stiffened everywhere in the III Corps area as the South Vietnamese consolidated two front lines covering the northern and northwest approaches to Saigon. The VNAF continued to provide outstanding support to the ground unit, supporting the enclaves of An Loc and Chon Thanh. This F-5A from the 63rd Wing of Bien Hoa banks away after a bombing sortie. (Pham Quang Khiem Collection)

While the northwest sector of Saigon was temporarily quiet, the ARVN situation in the northern sector was more than serious. The enclaves of An Loc and Chon Thanh, along Route 13, came under increasing pressure and became difficult and costly to defend. The III Corps commander asked for permission to evacuate these exposed positions, but President Thieu became extremely cautious after the disastrous withdrawals in MR I and MR II: these positions were under constant pressure and any withdrawal from them could lead to a total collapse of the front lines near the capital. Eventually, Thieu gave up, however, and the withdrawal from An Loc began on 18 March, when elements of the 5th Division pulled out in direction of Chon Than, down Route 13. For seven days, the evacuation proceeded according to a plan, and VNAF helicopters of the 43rd Wing even managed to fly out 12 105mm (4.13in) howitzers, even though five other pieces of 155mm (6.10in) artillery had to be abandoned due to the lack of heavy-lift capability,

This had the effect of catching the North Vietnamese by surprise and it was days before they realised what was going on. Furthermore, when the Communists launched a full-scale attack by two divisions, this was stopped cold with VNAF support. The second North Vietnamese attack on Chon Than, launched on 31 March, was stopped as well, after F-5Es from Bien Hoa destroyed several tanks.

The last defenders now received the order to evacuate their positions. During the early hours of 1 April, the VNAF flew 52 strike sorties against the assembly areas of the badly mauled North Vietnamese 341st Division. Under air cover, helicopters flew

Despite the enemy closing on Phan Rang AB, the three A-37B squadrons of the local 92nd Wing under Col Le Van Thao flew an all-out effort. They helped the ARVN hold the front for two weeks, flying numerous missions, with brief stops to refuel and rearm.
(USAF)

By the second week of April 1975, the ARVN defences around Phan Rang began to crumble, attacked by three North Vietnamese divisions and tanks. The air base was left isolated, forcing the VNAF mechanics to fight as soldiers to defend it. The pilots helped to load their aircraft with bombs and flew repeated missions at the gates of their base, destroying half a dozen tanks up until the last moment. In so doing, the pilots of the local 534th Fighter Squadron arguably put up the best fight of the war.
(Do Van Phu)

out the 32nd Ranger Group. In fact, of all the ARVN withdrawal operations carried out, the evacuation of the northern sector of III Corps was the best executed. The South Vietnamese also had the upper hand throughout MR IV, where the enemy stepped up its guerrilla attacks. Most of these attacks were aimed at Route 4, the vital 'Rice Road' that linked Saigon to Can Tho. But the ARVN IV Corps reacted vigorously, supported by the 4th Air Division of Binh Thuy. Until the final collapse, no cities or important towns were taken by the Communists in the Mekong Delta area.

Last stand at Xuan Loc

At the beginning of April the pace of the PAVN advance slowed down, offering the South Vietnamese much-needed respite. The provisional pause was exploited for the redeployment and concentration of some four army corps against the ARVN III Corps. The latter had now to face the enemy advance from the northeast part of its perimeter in the

The North Vietnamese captured a total of two A-37Bs, two C-119Gs and two AC-119Ks at Phan Rang. The VPAF's 919th Transport Brigade soon put one of the C-119Gs back into service.
(PAVN)

A closer view of the one of the C-119Gs of the 720th transport Squadron and one of the AC-119Ks of the 821st Attack Squadron captured at Phan Rang. In the case of the AC-119K, it was the first time that the North Vietnamese had got their hands on such a sophisticated aircraft. The aircraft in the foreground was probably that turned over for immediate VPAF use.
(PAVN)

Long Khanh Province and against the regional capital of Xuan Loc, held by the ARVN 18th Division. Xuan Loc also assured the defence of the huge Long Binh logistics complex, Bien Hoa AB, and the Thu Duc military installations on the outskirts of the capital.

The first enemy assault took place on 17 March on the northern and eastern sides of the town, and involved two divisions. Most of the ARVN positions north of Route 20 were lost, but the North Vietnamese had suffered heavy casualties and were forced to suspend the attack. Two days later, the ARVN counterattacked, but proved unable to advance much. During the next three weeks, only probing actions took place as each side reinforced their positions.

On 9 April three North Vietnamese divisions attacked again. Furious street-fighting ensued but the enemy was repulsed. However, the Communists succeeded in cutting Route 20, isolating the town. After a week-long battle, Route 20 remained blocked. As a result, III Corps had to request reinforcements. The 1st Airborne Brigade was inserted into Xuan Loc on 10 April by the CH-47As from the 237th Helicopter Squadron, using a landing zone south of the city. The sector was then heavily supported by A-1s and A-37s, which helped the paratroopers repulse several counterattacks. On 11 April, an ARVN armoured Task Force tried to reduce the roadblock but ran across dug-in positions reinforced by tanks. Despite intensive artillery and VNAF pounding of the target, the attack was stopped. During this second phase of the battle, the North Vietnamese

The 919th Transport Brigade regrouped all VPAF transport assets. It consisted of 66 transport aircraft and 44 helicopters that were fully mobilised to deliver supplies to the North Vietnamese divisions involved in the invasion of South Vietnam. Here, the crew of a Lisunov Li-2, a Soviet-built version of the C-47, checks the map before their next sortie. (VPAF)

losses amounted to over 2,000 casualties and 11 T-54s recovered on the field by the South Vietnamese. Xuan Loc had developed into one of the toughest battles of the war.

Throughout the battle, the VNAF provided outstanding support. Fighter-bombers pounded the North Vietnamese positions with an average of 70 daily sorties, while helicopters flew in supplies and evacuated the wounded. On 12 April the VNAF CH-47s brought in 93 tons of artillery ammunition, followed by 100 tons the next day. On 13 April, a new assault took place involving seven out of nine regiments of three North Vietnamese divisions, lasting from 04.50 until 09.30. The ARVN positions held firm. Another assault took place at noon, the defenders again repulsing the North Vietnamese by 15.00.

The VNAF fighter-bombers and gunships flew strike after strike, laying a curtain of fire in front of the ARVN troops. Two batteries of 130mm (5.12in) guns located by O-1s northwest of Xuan Loc were also bombed. The South Vietnamese pilots made great use of CBU-55 FAE bombs, with devastating effect on enemy infantry. The C-130As attacked with the huge BLU-82s, the first 'big bomb' being dropped 6km (3.7 miles) northwest of Xuan Loc. The entire provincial city shook as if rocked by an earthquake. Another strike was directed against an enemy concentration east of Xuan Loc. Electronic intelligence intercepts by an EC-47 indicated that the detonation killed over 500 Communist troops. Later, refugees that had crossed the area also reported seeing hundreds of corpses of North Vietnamese soldiers. Another strike hit a newly established SA-2 site.

Eventually, the North Vietnamese losses during these few days of fighting exceeded 5,000 killed and 37 tanks knocked out. The VNAF flew 600 strike sorties in this last phase of the battle despite heavy flak opposition that shot down a dozen aircraft and helicopters. The ARVN highly praised the VNAF support, considering it 'excellent'.[6] But now the enemy began to outflank the ARVN positions at Xuan Loc and positioned artillery to hit Bien Hoa AB. On 15 April, intermittent rocket attacks had forced a partial suspension of the operations on the airfield. Worst, the next day, the Communists pounded the base more accurately with 122mm (4.80in) guns, destroying six F-5s and 14 A-37s. A ground drive by the ARVN and intensive VNAF efforts temporarily alleviated the threat to the air base.

The enemy pressure against Xuan Loc continued to grow with the arrival of fresh troops. By 20 April, the defenders now faced six enemy divisions while the VNAF aircraft began to face increasing numbers of radar-directed 57mm (2.24in) and 85mm

These two photographs, extracted from a video, show an A–37B from the 520th Fighter Squadron at Binh Thuy armed with two of CBU–55 FAE weapons. The canisters were dropped at low altitude and released three parachute-retarded submunitions that exploded above the ground, maximising blast effect. (Author's collection)

By 20 April the defenders of Xuan Loc were outflanked by the enemy and a withdrawal operation was considered necessary, to prevent the ARVN 18th Division being completely encircled and destroyed. This required a coordinated move between the ground units and the VNAF. Meanwhile, the Chinooks continued to bring in supplies and evacuate the wounded and the refugees. (US Army)

(3.35in) guns as well as SA-2s. The ARVN decided to abandon Xuan Loc now that superior enemy forces had outflanked the city to move closer to Saigon. The 18th Division had fought splendidly during one of the toughest battles of the war, but the North Vietnamese High Command used this battle as a 'meat grinder', sacrificing its own units to destroy irreplaceable ARVN forces.

Eventually, the defenders of Xuan Loc concluded that they had to break through the enemy lines even though the retreat could possibly turn into another rout. A close ARVN-VNAF cooperation was considered essential for the scheme. The pull-out began late in the night of 23 April. The start signal would be a BLU-82 'Daisy Cutter' strike against the enemy front headquarters at Dinh Quan. It was hoped this would disrupt communications and throw the enemy into confusion. The strike was scheduled for midnight. The bomb-loaded C-130A took off from Tan Son Nhut but returned to land after 20 minutes in the air. The officers at Air Force Headquarters and JGS were gripped with suspense, but the aircraft landed safely. It was only a minor technical failure, and the Hercules took off again half an hour later.

At 01.00 Maj Nguyen Tan Minh dropped the bomb. The enemy radio station abruptly stopped transmitting; the command post was struck and wiped out. Later, electronic intelligence intercepts by an EC-47 disclosed that several high-ranking North Vietnamese officers had been killed. Another C-130A followed soon after and dropped a second BLU-82 at the Dau Giay Crossroads to clear the passage. Now the South Vietnamese broke out, supported by VNAF fighter-bombers and AC-119s. For three days, the Xuan Loc defenders fought rear-guard actions, closely supported by the VNAF. The withdrawal was completed successfully and the column arrived as a cohesive unit at Long Binh.

Throughout the battle of Xuan Loc, ARVN forces were supplied by helicopters, which also flew out wounded and civilian refugees. These Chinooks were flying in artillery ammunition. The family of civilians had just been disembarked, while reinforcement troops boarded the helicopters.   (US Army)

The VNAF flew 600 strike sorties in the last phase of the battle for Xuan Loc, despite heavy flak opposition. The fighter-bombers were greatly helped by the C-130As used as bombers. Here, a pilot from the 63rd Wing at Bien Hoa races towards his armed F-5A for another sortie. (USAF)

This VNAF C-130A of the 435th Transport Squadron was used in the bombing missions that preceded the withdrawal from Xuan Loc on the night of 23 April.
(Pham Quang Khiem Collection)

1   Buu Vien, the Assistant South Vietnamese Minister of Defence for manpower stated that: 'The faith of the Vietnamese people in the United States was so strong that even when the Communists had occupied all the provinces in MR I and II and closed in around Saigon, there were people, including senior officials in the government, who still believed that the US would soon react to drive back the Communists to save Vietnam. They believed that the Americans were being up to something, maybe to lure the Communists into a trap to destroy once and for all their forces. It sound naïve, but it shows how strong the Vietnamese people's confidence was in the U.S.' See the quotation from The Fall of South Vietnam; Statements by Vietnamese Military and Civilian leaders. Crane, Russack & Company, Inc, New York 1980, p235.

2   'The Vietnamese Air Force, 1951–1975, An analysis of its role in combat and fourteen hours at Koh Tang'. USAF Southeast Asia Monograph Series, Volume III, Monographs 4 and 5, p80. The USAF also resumed its reconnaissance missions over South Vietnam, flying 20 sorties of U-2s and RF-4Cs during the same period from its bases in Thailand, in order to assess the military situation there.

3   Ibid., p78.

4   Lich Su Khong Quan Nhan Dan Viet Nam (1955–1977), Nha Xuat Ban Quan Doi Nhan Dan, Hanoi 1993, p301.

5   Dr Joe F. Leeker. The History of Air America in Vietnam; The collapse E-book, University of Texas, McDermott Library, p14.

6   'The Vietnamese Air Force, 1951–1975, An analysis of its role in combat and fourteen hours at Koh Tang'. USAF Southeast Asia Monograph Series, Volume III, Monographs 4 and 5, p78.

Chapter 9

LAST WEEK OF WAR

On 21 April, under intense political pressure, President Thieu resigned. It was hoped that he could hand the reins of power to Gen Duong Van Minh, a long-time opponent with a leftist-neutralist staff. A coalition government led by Minh, it was contended, stood a good chance of being accepted by the Communists in Hanoi. While waiting for Minh to accept the offer, Thieu transferred the presidency to Vice-President Tran Van Huong and then flew into exile aboard a USAF Douglas C-118 Liftmaster, on 27 April.

The political confusion only increased the breakdown in ARVN morale. While awaiting the establishment of a new government, the JGS drafted a contingency plan to withdraw from Saigon and move the capital to Can Tho in the Mekong Delta. The theory was that the government could consolidate in Military Region IV, which had so far successfully resisted enemy pressure. The swampy nature of the terrain would also offset the PAVN superiority in armour. All that was left was a hope that a last-ditch defence lasting several months, supported by what was left of the VNAF concentrated at Binh Thuy AB, may force Washington to change its policy.

In fact, all of this proved to be wishful thinking. The only military help that arrived from the US was a shipment of 17 105mm (4.13in) howitzers delivered in early April by C-5As. In return, the transports brought out unserviceable South Vietnamese military equipment, including 40 M113 APCs and M41 tanks. Perhaps far more important was the evacuation of thousands of orphans under Operation Babylift. However, tragedy

The North Vietnamese advance on Saigon was temporarily checked thanks to continuing VNAF attacks. Here, a Skyraider from the 23rd Wing at Bien Hoa drops napalm tanks on the front line. (ARVN)

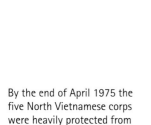

By the end of April 1975 the five North Vietnamese corps were heavily protected from air attack by hundreds of anti-aircraft guns, including a battalion of the new ZSU-23-4 self-propelled guns. (PAVN)

struck on 4 April when a C-5A crashed on take-off at Tan Son Nhut, killing many of the 250 children onboard.

Other humanitarian relief came from friendly nations: Australia dispatched seven C-130s while the Royal New Zealand Air Force sent three Bristol 170s to help move refugees from various assembly camps throughout the country. The US also began to evacuate its 6,000 citizens living in the country as well as some South Vietnamese, using C-130s and C-141s. By 21 April, the pace of the evacuation had increased significantly, with 41 C-130 and 33 C-141 sorties during the next two days. Sixteen additional C-130Es were then dispatched from the US to participate in the evacuation (Operation Talon Vise) now that the North Vietnamese were preparing for the final push against Saigon.

The capital of South Vietnam was now facing five enemy corps, totalling 270,000 troops, supported by over 400 armoured vehicles. Some 27 anti-aircraft artillery regiments with 2,800 guns – including a battalion of the new ZSU-23-4 self-propelled guns that had wrought havoc on Israeli aircraft during the recent Yum Kippur War – had been deployed into South Vietnam as well. There were also three SA-2 missile regiments.

In comparison, the ARVN III Corps had less than three depleted divisions and some Ranger groups and regional units, some 40,000 troops in total, to counter them. These were organised into five major resistance centres. These centres were to extend their

A ground drive by the ARVN and intensive VNAF efforts bought some time for Bien Hoa AB, but its days as an operational base were numbered. These two F-5As are being readied for an air interception mission, the wingtip fuel tanks being removed and replaced with Sidewinder launch rails. (Anthony J. Tambini)

defence areas outwards beyond the effective range of enemy 130mm (5.12in) guns; they were tantamount to five different fronts connected to form an arc enveloping the entire area west, north and east of Saigon.

Orderly evacuation of Bien Hoa

After the battle for Xuan Loc, the VNAF still possessed 169 A-37s and 109 F-5s. However, only 92 A-37s and 93 F-5s were operational. There were also around 35 A-1s on hand.[1]

On 22 April, in the northeast sector of the front, the Communists had pushed back the ARVN far enough to position long-range 122mm and 130mm guns to harass Bien Hoa AB. This time, counterattacks failed to lessen the threat. Two days later, the shelling increased significantly, destroying a dozen aircraft and setting fire to several buildings.[2]

It was time to evacuate Bien Hoa, the most important fighter base of the VNAF. The aircraft evacuation took place in good order, from 24 to 26 April, despite the shelling. The fixed-wing aircraft departed quickly in groups between two artillery bombardments, taking off from runways, taxiways or any other stretch of flat concrete, tarmac of even packed earth. Miraculously, only an A-1H from the 518th Fighter Squadron was lost. Flown by 1st Lt Pham Huu Loc, the Skyraider crashed on take-off from a taxiway, on 24 April. The pilot attempted to eject but the rocket motor of his 'Yankee Seat' failed. Amazingly, he survived the crash on a rice field, paid for a ride on a Honda motorcycle and joined his squadron that same afternoon at Tan Son Nhut!

Most of the aircraft were regrouped at Tan Son Nhut and Binh Thuy. Trucks evacuated the ammunition depot, as well as some ground support equipment and spare parts.

Meanwhile, the US DAO had also discreetly informed the VNAF that it was willing to evacuate some 'unserviceable assets' from Bien Hoa. A special team of USAF technicians, headed by no less than Assistant Secretary for Defense Eric von Mar-

A mix of differently camouflaged F-5As on the flight line at Bien Hoa. The air base was the main hub for fighter-bomber operations since the loss of air bases in the northern part of the country. In addition to the locally based 23rd and 63rd Wings, the base became home to evacuated units. (Anthony J. Tambini)

The evacuation of Bien Hoa AB took place from 24 to 26 April. Part of the technical support equipment as well as the ammunition stock was driven out on trucks along the refugee-clogged Highway 1.
(ARVN)

bod, arrived at the base on 26 April. They helped to load a number of jet engines and electronic equipment waiting for repair aboard several Bird Air C-130Es, which were operated on behalf of the CIA. They also helped to destroy the remaining facilities, in particular the overhaul shop, the computer installations for the logistics system, the calibration shop, and several storage depots. A Bird Air Hercules that landed among intermittent artillery shelling extracted the team on 29 April.[3]

The VNAF attempted to maintain helicopter operations from Bien Hoa until the night of 27 April. Hundreds of helicopter crews were then ordered to disperse elsewhere, most of them to Tan Son Nhut and Binh Thuy. Witnesses reported that gaggles of 'Hueys', with their lights turned on, resembled a 'group of fireflies leaving Bien Hoa forever'.

Despite these new relocations, the VNAF quickly resumed operations from its last two remaining major bases. North Vietnamese sources indicated that their troops had to face 529 fighter-bomber sorties alone around Saigon during the last four days of the war, with an average of 106 daily sorties. These figures did not take into account other sorties flown in the IV Corps area, or those of the AC-119s, the C-130 bombing missions, and the helicopter gunships.[4]

The VNAF fighter-bomber force was now a mix of squadrons operating from their remaining bases in both MR III and IV and strengthened by the units that had been evacuated from the northern part of the country. This A-37B of the former 92nd Wing at Phan Rang now operated from Binh Thuy, where it was incorporated in the local 74th Wing.
(USAF)

Fighting against time

However, even if the majority of VNAF aircrews continued to do their duty, rumours of defections began to spread. The Communist broadcasting now openly called for the defection of South Vietnamese pilots, indicating specific procedures to follow and radio codes to use when landing at enemy-controlled airfields. The VNAF security was tightened and transport aircraft were ordered to be loaded with only enough fuel to accomplish their missions.

It was in this deleterious atmosphere that a first defection took place, on 24 April. A C-130A from the 435th Transport Squadron, flown by Maj Nguyen Huu Canh and 1st Lt Pham Quang Khiem, intended to conduct a food re-supply mission to Phan Rang, left the country. Canh first landed 'his' Hercules at the disused airfield of Long Thanh, 30km (18.6 miles) southeast of Saigon, to quickly embark 56 members of his and the families of his crew. Subsequently, he took off safely and flew at low level outside South Vietnamese airspace. The Hercules landed in Singapore where it was interned. After this event, more stringent measures were put in place. The flight lines were guarded and batteries removed from aircraft that were not intended to be used operationally. The new government also announced that anyone leaving the country without authorisation would see their citizenship stripped and their properties confiscated.

The North Vietnamese offensive resumed on 25 April, in five directions. The first assault took place against the northwest sector defended by the ARVN 25th Division, which stopped the enemy advance at Khiem Hanh. The VNAF flew 20 attack sorties in support, while simultaneously reinforcing the 25th Division by extracting its 46th Regiment from the encircled town of Tay Ninh by helicopter. Despite a heavy deployment of enemy flak near the pick-up point, no 'Hueys' were brought down. The defence of Tay Ninh was now left to local regional troops and Rangers. The enclave held until the final capitulation order, supported by VNAF airdrops and close air support sorties.

The next day, the main thrust was directed against the Bien Hoa sector but the ARVN 3rd Armoured Brigade repulsed the assault. In fact, the South Vietnamese tankers succeeded not only in stopping this attack but also in protecting the now aban-

The 'Hueys' continued to support the ARVN by deploying troops and bringing in supplies despite the increasing threat of anti-aircraft fire. The pilots often had to adopt evasive measures, including low flying in some areas to mask them from enemy gunners. This command and control variant, with additional radios, is making a low pass over refugees that jammed a portion of Route 1 north of Saigon. (US Army)

On 24 April 1975, Maj Nguyen Huu Canh flew out of South Vietnam in a C-130A from the 435th Transport Squadron and landed with 56 refugees in Singapore, where they were interned. It was the first VNAF aircraft to escape the Communist advance. Canh's co-pilot was 1st Lt Pham Quang Khiem, posing here for a photo with his son.
(Pham Quang Khiem Collection)

The VNAF supported the 25th Division's operation at Go Dau Ha between Routes 1 and 22 intensivelly. The involved F-5s and A-37s lost three of their own but claimed 17 tanks, repulsing a major North Vietnamese attack. (USAF)

The pilot of an O-1E from the 74th Wing at Binh Thuy prepares for another sortie. In addition to participating to the ongoing battles taking place around Saigon, the unit was also fully committed to the defence of the Mekong Delta area, which remained under South Vietnamese control until the end. (VNAF)

doned air base until the end of South Vietnam. The VNAF also provided heavy support to this part of the front, flying 38 strike sorties against the enemy 304th and 325th Divisions on 26 April. On the 27th, the same sector saw another 109 strike sorties.

On the same date the VNAF flew a total of 225 fighter-bomber sorties throughout the fronts, notably in support of the ARVN 5th Division in the northern sector. On 28 April the VNAF flew an additional 51 sorties in support of ground units fighting in the northeast sector. However, the main area threatened on this day was the southwest sector, where the enemy attempted to sever Route 4, linking Saigon and Can Tho. The VNAF flew 193 strike sorties on this part of the front, in an effort to slow the enemy advance by bombing several bridges. The price of this effort was dear: within only three days, from 26 to 28 April, the North Vietnamese shot down 23 aircraft, including two A-1s, three A-37s, three F-5s, one O-1 and 14 UH-1Hs.[5]

In the meantime, the US evacuation continued from Tan San Nhut. During two days, April 26 and 27, some 12,000 persons were flown out to the Philippines, in 46 C-130 sorties and 28 C-141 sorties.[6] That same day, a Canadian Air Force C-130E evacuated the personnel of the Canadian Embassy, while an Indonesian Air Force C-130B picked up the diplomats from that country as well as those serving with the ICCS. However, the increasing AA fire now encountered – even above 10,000ft (3,048m) – led to the suspension of the use of USAF C-141s. It was now hoped that when the new 'Neutralist' President would take his function, a ceasefire could be concluded allowing a full-scale evacuation to be resumed.

First enemy air strike

While the South Vietnamese politicians were fantasising about a possible 'coalition' with Hanoi, the Communists were preparing to add a new dimension to the conflict by introducing their own air power into the South.

In early April, the Deputy CO VPAF, Col Dao Dinh Luyen, presented a plan to 'gain total air superiority' over the South. For a period of two years, he had developed air support and strike capabilities for his air defence-oriented force. The 923rd Fighter Regiment had moved its MiG-17s to Tho Xuan, with detachments maintained at Vinh and Dong Hoi, in the southern part of North Vietnam. The unit was supported by MiG-21s of the 927th Fighter Regiment. Both units had received ground-attack training and were well poised to strike. However, the North Vietnamese Army C-in-C, Gen Van Tieng Dung, was still pondering the proposal and appears to never have come to a corresponding decision. Eventually, the VPAF flew only one attack mission during the entire war.

Even the Communist Vietnamese sources now available are still not fully clear as to why the VPAF never deployed its fighter-bombers in combat during the final phases of the war in South Vietnam. It is possible that the Army-dominated North Vietnamese armed forces apparatus lacked confidence in an air arm that was fully integrated within a wider Air Defence Command, and which until that period had been used exclusively for defensive purposes. Neither the North Vietnamese Army nor the VPAF had ever developed reliable air-to-ground coordination procedures and thus there was a high risk of fratricide accidents.

The VPAF was also fully aware that its equipment was far from adequate for the required task. None of its aircraft had the payload or the range necessary. Instead, the MiGs could have been better employed for fighter sweeps that could disrupt VNAF air operations. Finally, the defence doctrine of North Vietnam emphasised foremost the employment of fighters as point defence interceptors, closely supervised by ground control. This required surveillance radars and GCI stations that would take time to

By early April 1975 the VPAF was contemplating the forward deployment of its fighters in order to provide air cover for the North Vietnamese forces and to attack South Vietnamese air bases. The purpose was to challenge VNAF air superiority, but the fast-changing ground situation made VPAF employment very difficult. Despite conducting limited training for ground-attack operations, the VPAF felt that it was not yet flexible enough to cope with the changing conditions. Nevertheless, some specific strikes against the last operational VNAF air bases were given serious consideration. One the left, pilots from the 927th Fighter Regiment were planning a sortie beside their MiG-21PF-Vs and MiG-21PFMs. On the right, the pilot of a more advanced MiG-21MF from the 921st Fighter Regiment briefs the maintenance crew of his aircraft. (VPAF)

deploy in a very fluid ground battle situation – accordingly, these were not available in South Vietnam.

However, much more than the various doctrinal and technical considerations, it was probably the political implication of an VPAF intervention that was the main consideration. Hanoi was still apprehensive of Washington's reactions now that a full-scale invasion of South Vietnam was taking place, and was doing whatever possible to present its troops as 'South Vietnamese guerrillas'. A clear and public deployment of the VPAF over South Vietnam could have been considered a step too far by Washington, and provide a pretext for the return of US military forces. Furthermore, now that the US had begun its aerial evacuation operation, the risk was of harming one of their aircraft was too high.

Despite such concerns, after many deliberations Hanoi decided to launch just one, limited strike operation, which was to emphasise psychological and propaganda aspects rather than genuine military value. For the purpose of this mission, the Northerners were to deploy several A-37Bs captured in Da Nang. These could easily be presented as being flown by defecting South Vietnamese pilots, or even by plotters involved in a coup. The purpose of this operation was to spread confusion and further lower the morale of the South Vietnamese.

Nguyen Thanh Trung, the F-5E pilot who had bombed the Presidential Palace, was put in charge of training a group of MiG-17 pilots of the 4th Squadron of the 923rd Regiment. He was helped in his task by two former VNAF 516th Squadron pilots. Together with several mechanics, these latter were forced to cooperate at gunpoint. A hasty conversion syllabus of less than a week was launched on 21 April, and four A-37Bs deployed to Phu Cat on 27 April.

A fifth A-37B was added later to this flight, codenamed 'Determined to Win'. Meanwhile, their pilots and part of the ground personnel were ferried in an An-24 transport. Now the North Vietnamese awaited the latest political developments in Saigon before launching their strike.

For political reasons, the North Vietnamese decided to conduct a strike with captured South Vietnamese aircraft. Lacking technical personnel accustomed to the aircraft, they forced VNAF mechanics made prisoner to work for them at the gunpoint. Some of these 'new comrades' were seen here working on a Dragonfly at Da Nang under the watch of a North Vietnamese guard. (VPAF)

North Vietnamese mechanics prepare one of the five captured A-37Bs of the 'Determined to Win' Flight on the afternoon of 28 April 1975. This particular aircraft had recently been ferried from Da Nang with six external fuel tanks fitted. The aircraft took off from Phu Cat, led by former VNAF pilot Nguyen Thanh Trung. (VPAF)

On the morning of 28 April, the aircraft launched for a re-deployment to Phan Rang, where they were dispersed and armed, each being configured with two wingtip fuel tanks, four underwing fuel tanks, two Mk 82 and two Mk 81 bombs.

Finally, around 16.25, the five A-37Bs were launched. Led by Trung, their target was Tan San Nhut AB. Absolute radio silence had to be observed in order to surprise the enemy.

The aircraft sported a combination of insignia, with North Vietnamese Air Force roundels on the wings and fuselage and the National Liberation Front (Viet Cong) flag painted on the tail. The aircraft turned south, following the coastline at low level from 600 to 900ft (183 to 274m) in order to avoid radar detection. Arriving at the mouth of the Saigon River, they turned on a northwest heading, increasing their speed. Approaching the suburbs of the capital suburbs, they flew a pass under two A-1s that had apparently not spotted them. In the city, the new 'Neutralist' President had just completed his swearing-in ceremony. Approaching Tan Son Nhut, the Dragonflies climbed to 5,500ft (1,676m) before starting their bombing run at 18.15.

A VNAF controller, completely overwhelmed by the intense air traffic, contacted the incoming aircraft, receiving the curious answer, *'These aircraft are American-built machines'*. Trung and his wingman, Tu De, aimed at a group of transport aircraft and dropped two bombs each. They destroyed a CH-47A that was loading troops and damaged several other aircraft. One of the bombs exploded near an USAF C-130E that was in the process of taking off, but did not cause any damage.

Trung then climbed to altitude to cover the attack by the three other A-37Bs. These aimed at the overcrowded main parking area, making only a single pass and dropping all their bombs at once from 2,500ft (762m). They destroyed three AC-119s, four C-47s and three F-5s. Four other aircraft were damaged. The ground defences were taken by surprise and most of their responses were inconclusive or too late. Now, both Trung and his wingman turned for a second low-level pass. Some South Vietnamese 20mm Vulcan AA guns began to open fire and likely distracted the raiders from their near-

A small group of experienced pilots from the VPAF's 923rd Fighter Regiment, well trained in ground-attack missions, were dispatched to Da Nang to convert onto the A-37B. Former VNAF Lt Nguyen Thanh Trung, the pilot who had defected and bombed Saigon's Presidential Palace, held the conversion course. He was immediately incorporated into the VPAF with the rank of captain. Trung is seen here, with his moustache shaved, in the cockpit of a Dragonfly, instructing a North Vietnamese pilot on its use. (VPAF)

This poor but interesting view shows part of the parking area just hours before the strike. Six C-130As, two C-119Gs and one CH-47A from the VNAF can be counted, together with three DC-4s and a DC-3 from Air Vietnam. (USAF)

The air strike of 28 April destroyed three AC-119s, four C-47s, three F-5s and a CH-47A and damaged a dozen more aircraft. It was followed by artillery shelling the same night that brought additional destruction and chaos. These pictures were taken during a brief respite at dawn on 29 April. Smoke was still rising from aircraft set on fire and only the charred tail of a destroyed USAF Hercules could be seen. This was one of three C-130Es that had just delivered two additional BLU-82 bombs for the VNAF.   (USAF)

horizontal bombing pass. Only Trung dropped his bombs, causing only slight damages. Tu De could not drop his bombs due to a mechanical fault. He later jettisoned his weapons, and these exploded in an open field near the Trieu Bridge.[7]

A pair of F-5As from the alert section took off immediately, but could not make contact. The American C-130E that had been taking off reported that it was being chased by one of the attacking A-37Bs. The pilot was forced to dive to 500ft (152m) and maintain a speed of 280kt to try to elude the pursuer, which made two simulated attacking passes from the six o'clock and eight o'clock positions respectively. However, the North Vietnamese pilot did not open fire. Another C-130E, from the USAF's 374th Tactical Airlift Wing and piloted by Capt Ken Rice, also took off just after the air attack and veered to the west, where it was fired on by Communist 37mm and 57mm AA guns. Rice then turned back towards Tan Son Nhut, where South Vietnamese gunners then fired upon him! On their side, the Communist A-37Bs were also greeted by their own

Nguyen Thanh Trung's conversion training gained momentum and at the end of April 1975 he had qualified five North Vietnamese pilots on the Dragonfly. He is seen here, at far left, returning from a training mission at Da Nang. It is interesting to note that the A-37Bs still wear their South Vietnamese markings. (VPAF)

The attacking A-37 force returned safely from its strike and recovered at Phan Rang for a refuelling stop. They then continued towards Da Nang, their main operating base. The pilots involved pose here with the VPAF Deputy Commander, Col Dao Dinh Luyen, who appeared to greet them personally. Former VNAF pilot Nguyen Thanh Trung is seen on his right.
(VPAF)

AA fire over Phan Thiet during their return journey. The aircraft safely recovered at nightfall at Phan Rang.

Back at Tan Son Nhut, confusion and chaos reigned in the wake of this first enemy air attack. The fires at the base were extinguished and the debris cleared. Only 18 of the 58 USAF C-130 sorties scheduled for 28 April could be flown due to the disruption caused by the strike. A mere 3,500 persons were evacuated.

At nightfall, two VNAF C-47s defected, one being flown to Thailand and another landing at Clark AB in the Philippines. Intelligence reports warned of a possible second raid at 21.00, but the radar warning system was inoperative following the destruction of Bien Hoa AB. Several flights of F-5As and F-5Es were nevertheless launched to maintain CAP orbits over the base, before returning when night fell.

In retaliation, a BLU-82 sortie was directed against Phan Rang AB, where the A-37s had in all probability made their refuelling stopover before continuing towards Da Nang. However, the poor weather and the lack of BOBS guidance forced the C-130A pilot to make a blind reckoning night bombing of the base, without being able to ascertain the extent of the damage caused by his attack.

Although no other air raid took place at Tan Son Nhut, the respite was only short-lived, and from 04.00 enemy artillery opened fire against the air base with guns and multiple rocket launchers. The JGS compound and the Navy Headquarters at Bach Dang Quay were also sporadically harassed. Some rockets also hit the DAO building, killing two US Marines. Three USAF C-130Es were caught on the ground when the bombardment began. They had just delivered two additional BLU-82 bombs, and each intended to pick up refugees. Fortunately, the huge bombs had just been discharged to be stored inside concrete pits. However, they could not be used thereafter since they lacked fuses. The detonations quickly destroyed a C-130E, as well as a VNAF C-130A. The US crews scrambled to take shelter and left shortly afterwards aboard one of the other aircraft.

In coordination with the shelling, enemy sappers tried to infiltrate the base's perimeter but were repulsed thanks in part to an AC-119K of the 821st Attack Squadron, flown by 1st Lt Tran Van Hien, as well as several 'Huey' gunships. By the morning, the shelling had slowed somewhat but the damage was extensive. The parking areas, fuel dumps, and ammunition depots were all hit. A dozen more aircraft were destroyed.

A pair of Sidewinders-armed F-5As took off from their alert pad to try to intercept in vain the escaping North Vietnamese A-37Bs. A VNAF pilot is seen here by an alert F-5A which was a former IIAF aircraft, still in its desert camouflage.
(Can Thep Collection)

Lt Hien landed, refuelled and rearmed, before taking off again at daybreak to resume the fight. He was soon joined by two A-1s of the 514th Fighter Squadron that arrived from Binh Thuy. They circled the air base perimeter at 2,500ft (762m), apparently hoping to unmask enemy gunfire.

At around 07.00, the AC-119K flown by Van Hien was hit by a SA-7 while cruising east of Tan Son Nhut and crashed. Only three parachutes were observed.

The assets of the Air Division at Binh Thuy were fully mobilised in support of ARVN units engaged in the defence of Saigon. This A-37B from the 74th Wing is making a rocket pass against a North Vietnamese position.
(USAF)

The gravity of the situation forced the VNAF to throw its remaining forces into the battle by the end of April 1975. Even the fixed-wing gunships that usually operated by night were ordered to conduct daylight attack operations. This AC-119K from the 821st Attack Squadron was photographed at Tan Son Nhut in this period, returning from one such mission.
(USAF)

Throughout the night of 28 April, until dawn, an AC-119K of the 821st Attack Squadron, flown by Lt Tran Van Hien, circled Tan Son Nhut AB and helped to repulse North Vietnamese sapper infiltrations. At dawn, Hien landed, refuelled and rearmed, before taking off again to resume the fight. He was soon joined by two A-1s, but at around 07.00, the AC-119K was hit by an SA-7 while cruising east of Tan Son Nhut and crashed. This exceptional photograph shows the final demise of the gunship: it seems that part of the tail became detached from the main fuselage.
(USAF)

Meanwhile, one of the two Skyraiders of the 518th Squadron that succeeded in taking off on the debris-littered runway was brought down by another SA-7 in the southwest part of Saigon. The A-1 had been piloted by Maj Phung Truong. Thanks to their efforts, between 07.00 and 09.00, the situation was settled enough to launch several flights of A-1s, A-37s and F-5s to fly close support missions. Their pilots received the order to recover at Binh Thuy after their sorties.

The faithful Skyraider remained very active until the last days of the war. Capt Nguyen Van Xe of the 518th Fighter Squadron poses here on his A-1H at Bien Hoa in 1975. He was a former O-1 observation pilot who had been retrained for fighter operations in order to fill the ranks of the squadrons newly established during Operations Enhance and Enhance Plus. (Nguyen Van Xe)

With the North Vietnamese divisions closing on Saigon, the combat aircraft of the nearby Bien Hoa AB required a very rapid turnaround between sorties. Northrop contractor Anthony Tambini is seen here in discussion with a VNAF F-5E pilot. Note that the nose landing gear strut has already been placed in the take-off position. (Anthony J. Tambini)

1   'The Vietnamese Air Force, 1951–1975, An analysis of its role in combat and fourteen hours at Koh Tang'. USAF Southeast Asia Monograph Series, Volume III, Monographs 4 and 5, p79. In spite of the evacuations, artillery shelling and aircraft out of commission for one reason or another, the VNAF still had an operational ready fighter force of approximately 180 aircraft as compared to 392 aircraft at the beginning of the North Vietnamese offensive.

2   During the last days before the evacuation of the Bien Hoa AB, its pilots tried all their best to spot and silence the elusive enemy guns. Many F-5 pilots flew up to eight sorties per day, most of their operating sector being over the Tri Han Forest sector. There, the North Vietnamese M-46 130mm guns constantly moved their batteries after firing salvoes of 12 shells.

3   Warren A. Trest. *Air Commando One, Heinie Aderholt and America's Secret Air Wars*. Smithsonian Institution Press, Washington DC, 2000, p251.

4   Lich Su Khong Quan Nhan Dan Viet Nam (1955–1977), Nha Xuat Ban Quan Doi Nhan Dan, Hanoi 1993, p312.

5   Lich Su Khong Quan Nhan Dan Viet Nam (1955–1977), Nha Xuat Ban Quan Doi Nhan Dan, Hanoi 1993, see pp314–332 for description of the PAVN anti-aircraft units operations during the last four days of the war. In absence of South Vietnamese and/or US data data, the author relied mainly on this Communist source for reconstruction of the final VNAF operations.

6   At the outset of Operation Frequent Wind, the US evacuation by helicopters of Saigon, the passenger loads had been limited to 94 for the USAF C-141As and 75 for the C-130Es. By now, the peacetime rules had been dropped, and standard loads of 180 were being prepared for both aircraft. The Supervisor of Airlift reported loads as high as 316 on a C-141A and 243 on the C-130Es. See for more details on the USAF evacuations in Last Flight from Saigon. USAF Southeast Asia Monograph Series, Volume IV, Monographs 6, p69.

7   Lich Su Khong Quan Nhan Dan Viet Nam (1955–1977), Nha Xuat Ban Quan Doi Nhan Dan, Hanoi 1993, see pages 303 to 307 how the North Vietnamese planned and executed the air strike against Tan Son Nhut.

Chapter 10

THE GREAT ESCAPE

The new 'Neutralist' government in Saigon desperately attempted to negotiate a cease-fire with the Communists, even if their unabated offensive clearly indicated that there was no will for political accommodation – if indeed they ever contemplated this possibility. The new President Minh now instructed the US Ambassador that he had 24 hours to evacuate the DAO *'in order that the question of peace for Vietnam can be settled early'*. Ambassador Graham A. Martin was determined to speed up the evacuation, including the pick-up of the last remaining US military personnel. He insisted that the C-130 air bridge would resume as soon as possible despite the situation at Tan Son Nhut remaining precarious. The USAF stream of C-130s began arriving at dawn. Sixty sorties were scheduled for 29 April, to be covered by aircraft from US Navy carriers. However, these were met by AA fire up to 20,000ft (6,096m), and several SA-7s. Reluctantly, the US Ambassador accepted the necessity to switch to a helicopter evacuation – Operation Frequent Wind.

The new government was unable to give clear indications of its intended action, apart from ordering the armed forces 'to gain time' in order to reach a peaceful solution. The new president also replaced some top military leaders, including the Chairman of the JGS. For many elements of the South Vietnamese military, the end was now near. Many continued to fight, but others did not want to be aligned with a coalition government that included the Communists. For many, defeat was imminent and

From 29 April on, the Americans were forced to accelerate the pace of the refugees' evacuation by resorting to the use of helicopters. They initially used two main landing zones at the US Embassy and at the DAO compound, within the Tan Son Nhut AB perimeter. However, due to increasing artillery shelling, this last location was soon closed. This aerial view shows the abandoned and sabotaged DAO buildings after the evacuation. (USAF)

By early April 1975 the US had begun evacuating its citizens from South Vietnam via an air bridge, using C-130s, C-141s and C-5s. This Galaxy is being directing towards a parking area at Tan Son Nhut AB, passing VNAF AC-119Ks and C-130As. (USAF)

they did not want to be left trapped when the North Vietnamese took over the whole country. Many top leaders, including the VNAF commanders, were disillusioned and distressed. The Presidency was unable to give clear indications as to whether Tan Son Nhut was to be evacuated or not. The VNAF Commander, Lt Gen Tran Van Minh, was then approached by DAO officials who asked him to evacuate the maximum possible number of aircraft and personnel towards Thailand. A special emphasis was put on the

On 29 April, in one of his last orders as VNAF Commander, Gen Tran Van Minh called upon his wings and squadron commanders, and especially the F-5 units, to fly out of the country. The pilots took off and selected economic cruise, in order to reach U Tapao in Thailand. (USAF)

The two squadrons of C-130As saw much use during the last week of the war, continuing to bring in supplies to ARVN units or sustaining besieged South Vietnamese cities. However, most missions were now devoted to BOBS-directed bombing operations. (Pham Quang Khiem Collection)

While Tan Son Nhut AB, on the outskirts of Saigon, was the VNAF transport and fixed-wing gunship hub, it also became an important fighter-bomber base during the last weeks of the war. This A-37B from an unidentified squadron was seen departing for another sortie at the end of April 1975. (USAF)

After a short pause, the North Vietnamese artillery harassment continued against Tan Son Nhut, despite the efforts of VNAF aircraft to silence the batteries. This forced the Americans to cancel their fixed-wing operations and launch a helicopter evacuation. These pictures show the extent of the destruction suffered by the VNAF at the base. The destruction included AC-119Gs from the 819th Attack Squadron, as well as C-130As and C-7As. (USAF)

evacuation of the brand-new F-5Es. On the other hand, Minh had to continue supporting the ongoing battle and obey a government that he utterly disapproved of.

While the VNAF leadership was still debating their future course of action, events around them accelerated. At 09.00, Tan Son Nhut AB came under intense shelling for the second time. Damage was heavy: a number of aircraft parked on the apron – including several A-37Bs and four C-130As already loaded with 250kg (551lb) bombs – were hit and exploded. Fires spread rapidly across the main transport parking area. The air base was put completely out of operation. Over 3,000 people who had been waiting in the area behind the DAO compound since the previous day for US evacuation aircraft became terrified and frantically fled the base. By 10.00 the VNAF Headquarters had also been heavily hit, and was no longer in control of its personnel.

Exodus from Tan Son Nhut

In the air, waves of US helicopters, operated by the military and Air America, swirled and hovered, evacuating US personnel and refugees. While the US military helicopters operated from helipads at the DAO compound and the US Embassy, some 30 Air America 'Hueys' evacuated people from the prepared roofs of 13 buildings. Gen Tran

Despite enemy artillery shelling, the VNAF continued to operate from Tan Son Nhut until the last moment, attempting to keep the base open for offensive operations or for evacuation missions. In addition to the exploding shells, the pilots had to avoid the numerous debris that littered the runways and parking areas, as seen in this view of the part of the base that accommodated the EC-47Ps. (USAF)

Van Minh moved into the DAO with his staff and was evacuated by the Americans.[1] One of his last orders called upon his wings and squadron commanders to fly out of the country; special emphasis as placed on the evacuation of the F-5 units. However, due to the generally chaotic conditions, these informal orders did not reach all of the units. In fact, most VNAF pilots were left leaderless and acted according to their own conscience and sense of duty. Many tried to extricate themselves and their families from the enemy's advance. When the artillery shelling diminished at around 11.00, many aircraft, mostly transports, took their chance and took off. Most of them were overloaded with VNAF personnel and their families.

One of the VNAF escapees that morning was 1st Lt Nguyen Van Chuyen of the 518th Fighter Squadron. In common with several of his squadron mates, he had flown a last mission in the early morning, taking his A-1 over the northwest sector of the front. Now he boarded a C-119G with his wife and his two boys, aged five years and two months, respectively.

2nd Lt Le Hung had woken that morning to the sound of exploding rockets. He usually operated from Binh Thy but had landed his A-37B for overnight refuelling and servicing at Tan Son Nhut. Now, riding a Honda motorcycle, he tried to reach the flight line but was arrested by security guards who ordered him to take cover in a shelter. Together with other pilots, he planned what to do next. Some had received the word to fly out to Thailand, while others wanted to continue to fight. A final option was to simply take off and eject wherever the fuel ran out.

When there was a lull in the shelling, Le and other fighter pilots ran to check the aircraft. Le found a serviceable Dragonfly and he, together with a pilot friend and a maintenance crewman, crammed themselves into the two-seater. This eliminated the option of Le's friend and the mechanic using the ejection seat. Le promised them that whatever happened, he would remain with them in the aircraft. Fortunately, he could climb to altitude without mishap and after setting the power for an economic cruise, he succeeded in reaching U Tapao in Thailand.[2]

The exodus continued in a frenzied atmosphere, regularly interrupted by enemy shelling and attempts by ARVN and refugees to board any aircraft by force. During a renewal of shelling, a pilot abandoned his F-5 at the entrance to a taxiway, blocking access to one of the loading areas.

The US military at the DAO compound witnessed the scenes of chaos. People were fighting to get aboard the transport aircraft while a C-130A took off on a parallel taxiway. Another Hercules took off on the old north-south runway and barely cleared the old airfield control tower on its climb out. A C-7A tried to take off on one engine before spinning off the runway into the grass and burning.

On one occasion around 40 vehicles and several hundred people occupied the runway area in an attempt to board two VNAF C-130As that were trying to launch.[3]

Another C-130A, piloted by Maj Phuong, rolled out of the parking ramp, and was literally assaulted by refugees. The pilot repeatedly increased the power, lumbered forward, and slammed on the brakes. Each time he did this, more people sprinted out to try and board the aircraft. But the pilot wasn't trying to pack more people in – he was trying to avoid the debris on the ramp! The loadmasters were fighting and beating back additional people that tried to climb aboard. Finally, the Hercules lined up and accelerated down the long runway. The pilot couldn't pull the nose up until he got to the end of the 1,000ft (305m) overrun. He then struggled to gain altitude. The transport remained in ground effect for more than 24km (15 miles) before gaining height. In his haste, the pilot then discovered that he had no maps, and simply pointed the nose westwards towards Thailand. After more than half an hour over the sea, he realised that he had become lost, and was heading in the wrong direction. He reversed its course, and returned to Saigon.

A C-7 pilot managed to work his way through the crowd and into the co-pilot seat of the Hercules. Fortunately, he had a map, and began navigating. On their arrival in Thailand, a record 452 persons climbed out, including 32 who had crammed into the crew compartment!

The arrival of another overloaded Hercules revealed another drama. When the aircraft was preparing to depart, rockets began to fall again, provoking panic among the many people trying to climb aboard. The wife of the co-pilot leaned outside, helping to

This F-5A from the 63rd Wing landed at U Tapao with no fewer than two pilots on board! One of the men was sat on the lap of his friend for the duration of the 350-mile (563km) flight. (USAF)

Nine C-130As reached Thailand before the fall of South Vietnam, while a tenth landed in Singapore. The North Vietnamese captured 14 others. This Hercules had just stopped at the parking area at U Tapao when the crew opened the rear ramp to reveal just how cramped it was inside the fuselage. The occupants had been standing throughout the flight. (USAF)

Forty transports and fixed-wing gunships landed in Thailand. The Communists captured some 170 others. These EC-47Ps from the 718th Reconnaissance Squadron were photographed at U Tapao, where at least three were taken over by the RTAF.
(Dave Quigley)

embark more people. As the transport lurched forward, she fell. The left main under-carriage rolled over her, crushing her. No one told the co-pilot until the Hercules had reached Thailand.

The VNAF transports were accompanied in their exodus by several Air America aircraft. These included two C-46s, four C-47s and one Volpar. One of the C-47s developed an engine problem and landed at Co Son Island to repair before taking off again. A Caribou that had landed there the previous day with an oil leak was abandoned. Another Air America C-47 crash-landed at U Tapao, as did two VNAF C-47s with main landing gear failures – fortunately without any injuries. From one of the C-47s, which temporarily blocked the runway, emerged over 100 passengers.[4]

However, a semblance of order could be reinstated in the afternoon at Tan Son Nhut AB. The operation resumed and continued sporadically until the next morning and the final capitulation.

Some fighters, mostly F-5, took off and flew directly to Thailand. At U Tapao, some 350 miles (563km) to the northwest of Saigon, the USAF had put the base on alert to recover the fleeing aircraft that arrived on their last fuel drops, and amid great disorder. The personnel already had plenty of experience of this kind of operation, since two weeks previously they had recovered several dozen Cambodian aircraft fleeing the Khmer Rouge.

In the early afternoon, a first group of 26 F-5s arrived in quick succession. Many could not contact the ground approach control and landed without instructions. On one occasion two F-5Es landed side-by-side in the correct direction when suddenly a

During the last two days of the war, a total of 21 F-5Es landed in Thailand from a total delivery of 54 airframes. The North Vietnamese captured 27 F-5Es that they pressed into service for operations in Cambodia against the Khmer Rouge. Here, USAF armourers remove 20mm ammunition from the aircraft just after landing.   (USAF)

A view of the parking area at U Tapao on 30 April 1975 shows some of the F-5Es that reached Thailand. Note that one aircraft still has four rocket pods on the underwing pylons. The F-5Es would later serve in USAF Aggressor squadrons. (Pham Quang Khiem Collection)

Another view of the parking area at U Tapao shows some of the 27 A-37Bs and 14 U-17s that escaped to Thailand. Some Dragonflies landed with three or even four people in their cockpits. Note that the South Vietnamese markings had already been painted over on the demand of the Thai authorities. (Jem Aviation)

third appeared and landed in the opposite direction! One F-5A landed with two pilots on board, another with the pilot, his wife and three children, all inside the cockpit. To accomplish this, the ejection seat had been removed and the pilot was seated on a box.

While many pilots elected to fly to Thailand, others continued to fly combat missions from Tan Son Nhut, recovering at Binh Thuy. All these missions were carried out on the own initiative of the pilots, without coordination with the ground forces. The pilots took off, patrolled an assigned front sector and attacked targets of opportunity. Sometimes they were contacted by a FAC that guided them towards an objective. The situation was so desperate that some AC-119s were now launched in full daylight to attack the enemy. These had to pay a heavy price, with two AC-119s brought down in the area of Phu Lam.

The A-37Bs were regrouped at Tan Son Nhut and Binh Thuy while Bien Hoa remained the main operating base for VNAF A-1s and F-5s. However, due to increasing pressure from the North Vietnamese forces, the ARVN was forced to pull back under intermittent artillery fire. Operations continued for two days in these difficult circumstances, before the VNAF resigned to a definitive evacuation. (Pham Quang Khiem Collection)

Chaos within the VNAF

Vice Air Marshal Nguyen Cao Ky, who had politically opposed the constitution of a 'Neutralist' government during these last days, recounted how disorganised the VNAF's last missions were. On the morning of 29 April, Ky left his villa in the compound reserved for VNAF officers near Tan Son Nhut AB and headed for one of the 'Huey' helicopters reserved for his use. He was accompanied by a couple of other pilots and a navigator and decided to look at the situation for himself.

Ky first encountered four A-1s coming from Binh Thuy, loaded with a mix of M117 and Mk 82 bombs. Acting as an improvised FAC, he contacted them. Codenames were pointless by this stage. *'This is Marshal Ky. The biggest rocket-launching position is over at Phu Lam, near the radio transmitter. Go in and destroy it.'* He guided the A-1s to two other positions on Route 1. Ky was now getting low on fuel. He set down at Nha Be Petroleum Port, outside the city, where there was a small airfield near a huge Shell aviation-fuel depot. Dozens of helicopters and O-1s were lined up for refuelling. Most of the pilots had lost contact with their commands and looked to Ky for guidance. He crouched, with the young officers forming a semicircle before him. He told those who had run out of ammunition to refuel and fly back to Binh Thuy. Those who were still armed should expend their rockets and ammunition on the enemy and then they too should head to the Mekong Delta.[5]

At the adjacent Vietnamese Navy base, what was left of the 221st Helicopter Squadron from Bien Hoa had been forced to vacate its base on 27 April and resettle at Tan Son Nhut. After a day there, the unit was re-deployed to a small landing zone nearby, barely large enough to accommodate the remaining 12 'Hueys'. The squadron CO, Lt Col Nguyen Van Trong, made great efforts to keep his unit together. When he was ordered to move one more time, he forced a number of VNAF technicians at gunpoint to load his helicopter with crates of spare parts. Now, he was overwhelmed by dismay when the order came to disband the squadron. He gathered the pilots to wish them goodbye and ordered them to escape by any means necessary. He then hired a Lambretta taxicab to return to Saigon to take care of his family. He would later die in a Communist re-education camp.[6]

With a dozen VNAF and ARVN officers as his entourage, Vice Air Marshal Nguyen Cao Ky took off in 'Huey' serial number 15365 for the carrier USS *Midway*. Curiously, the aircraft also had a civilian registration (XV-GCU) that was claimed to be an Air America helicopter. The UH-1H was later transferred to this company. (US Navy)

With Tan Son Nhut under artillery fire, the VNAF operated primarily from its last remaining main base at Binh Thuy. Situated near Can Tho City, in the Mekong Delta, the location saw a concentration of the last South Vietnamese fighters that continued to give support to the ARVN. This is an A-37B from one of the local fighter squadrons.
(Pham Quang Khiem Collection)

Since midday, ARVN III Corps had not received any direct air support. The JGS tried to coordinate the air operations, but without much success. It then tried to retrieve a Ranger battalion from Route 5A in order to protect Saigon. But there was no chance of assembling enough helicopters for the task. In fact, around Saigon on 29 April the North Vietnamese shot down an additional F-5, two O-1s, two UH-1Hs and one CH-47A. Even so, it must be observed that North Vietnamese AAA units were restrained in their operations for fear of hitting one of the many US aircraft still engaged in the evacuation operations.

North Vietnamese transports and helicopters had also flown 48 sorties in this last stage of the campaign in the Saigon area itself, bringing in supplies and even dropping leaflets urging the isolated ARVN units to surrender.

The end of Frequent Wind

Throughout the day and until the early hours of 30 April, the US helicopter evacuation operation continued, protected by USAF fighters and AC-130s from Thailand, and supported by the carriers USS *Midway* and *Hancock*, as well as the helicopter carrier USS *Okinawa*, forming Carrier Task Force 76. The Marines employed 28 Boeing Vertol CH-46 Sea Knights and 40 Sikorsky CH-53 Sea Stallions for the task, alongside 12 USAF HH-53Cs. The USAF pilots were flying for the first time from carrier decks. Top cover was provided by US Navy F-4s from the carrier USS *Coral Sea* as well as two squadrons of the new Grumman F-14A Tomcats operating from the USS *Enterprise*, both of which were assigned to Task Force 77.

The 9th Marine Amphibious Brigade deployed some 850 men to secure the different landing zones within Saigon. Quickly it turned out that only the US Embassy, surrounded by some 10,000 refugees, was the safest of the pick-up points. The US State Department had first got a message from the Soviets that North Vietnamese troops had received orders to refrain from opening fire on US aircraft. Two air routes were then defined for helicopters operations. However, on some occasions Communist AA batteries fired at the US aircraft – even though no aircraft were hit. USAF EF-4C 'Wild Weasels' operating out of bases in Thailand kept a constant watch over a new SA-2 battery set up in the vicinity of Bien Hoa.

This An-24 of the VPAF's 919th Transport Brigade was embarking reinforcement troops for the South. These men were almost certainly specialist personnel needed for the maintenance of the North Vietnamese motorised divisions that were now poised to attack Saigon before the monsoonal season. Note that the aircraft was repainted with Viet Cong insignia instead of the usual North Vietnamese markings. This was for propaganda purposes, maintaining the myth that the Communist forces comprised local insurgents.
(VPAF)

On 29 April 1975 the Americans implemented Operation Frequent Wind, the final evacuation of Saigon by helicopters operating from the USS *Midway*, *Hancock* and *Okinawa* of Carrier Task Force 76. Operating alongside Marine helicopters were 12 USAF HH-53Cs, as seen here.
(US Navy)

At 07.53 on 30 April, the last helicopter left the Embassy roof. The USAF and USMC helicopters had flown 638 sorties that evacuated 7,815 people and 989 personnel of the Marine security forces. This was achieved with only minimal losses – one A-7E and two helicopters (one AH-1J and one CH-46F), all lost due to accidents. The Air America 'Hueys' also transported around 1,000 people from pick-up points to the main helicopter landing zones or directly towards the ships. Three such helicopters, two UH-1Hs and one Bell 204B, were damaged or destroyed.

The Grumman F-14A Tomcat interceptors of the USN flew their first combat sorties while protecting the ongoing helicopter evacuation operations. This Tomcat from the VF-1 'Wolfpack' is readied to be launched from the waist catapult No. 3 of USS *Enterprise* (CVN-65).
(US Navy)

Air America played a vital role during the evacuation of Saigon, the CIA contracted pilots performing heroically under difficult circumstances and without protection. Three helicopters were lost in the process.
(US Navy)

The escape of the helicopters

While the US helicopters were departing, those of the VNAF increasingly joined them. As early as the afternoon of 29 April, some of them had followed the American helicopters, operating mostly from Binh Thuy or Con Son Island off the southeast coast

The first VNAF helicopters began to land on US ships on the afternoon of 29 April, following the stream of American helicopters that shuttled between Saigon's landing zones and the carriers. This 'Huey' brought in Lt Gen Nguyen Van Toan, commander of the ARVN III Corps that defended South Vietnam's capital.
(US Navy)

The pilot of this UH-1H deliberately ditched near the *Blue Ridge* when landing space was not available on its deck. One of the ship's boats stands by to pick up those on board. Not all South Vietnamese crews had the chance to reach an American ship, however. According to US Navy reports, some 18 additional VNAF helicopters were counted as having crashed at sea, most of them due to fuel starvation. (US Navy)

of South Vietnam. This latter group included many of the helicopters that fled Saigon that morning. Most of these recovered on small ships, such as the command ship USS *Blue Ridge*, discharged their passengers, and were then ordered to ditch in the South China Sea. Several others recovered on the USS *Midway*. Most of these aircraft were retained aboard the aircraft carrier, including 12 UH-1Hs and some Air America 'Hueys' stolen by VNAF crews. In fact, some five UH-1Hs, supporting the ICCS, as well as a Bell 204B, were taken over by South Vietnamese airmen at Tan Son Nhut. One UH-1H crashed soon after take-off, the others succeeding in reaching the US Navy ships. Another UH-1H damaged the *Blue Ridge* when it was ordered to ditch nearby.

However, when the number of arriving VNAF helicopters was such that they began to disturb US helicopter operations from the carriers, they too were ordered to be

USS *Blue Ridge* was the flagship of Task Force 76 and was chosen as a landing place by at least a dozen VNAF helicopters. It also served as a refuelling stop for Air America 'Hueys' that made shuttles between Saigon and the ships. There were so many helicopters that many were simply tossed overboard or their pilots ordered to ditch beside the ship. During one such manoeuvre, a UH-1H crashed into the side of the command ship, damaging it as well as an Air America 'Huey'. (US Navy)

When unconditional surrender was ordered on the morning of 30 April, many helicopter crews based in the Mekong Delta tried to catch up with the departing US evacuation fleet. A group of 32 aircraft, mostly taking off from Binh Thuy, but also from Con Son Island, succeeded in reaching USS *Midway*. The deck crew made a superb effort to accommodate all of them. This 'Huey' gunship, probably from the 217th Helicopter Squadron, had just landed, fully loaded with families of the crew. (US Navy)

dumped overboard. When there was no more room or the helicopters were denied permission to land, some pilots chose to ditch close to a ship, hoping to be rescued. Others leapt from the helicopters, hoping the sea below would cushion their fall. At least 45 VNAF helicopters were dumped in the sea.

Among the 'Hueys' that had landed was the helicopter flown by Vice Marshal Nguyen Cao Ky. Throughout the morning Ky had acted as a FAC around Saigon, before settling into the VNAF Headquarters, and then the JGS compounds to discuss the situation with the commanders. Finding the situation desperate, he resigned to leave. Together with a dozen VNAF and ARVN officers, he took off and followed the US helicopters to the carriers. Ky was awaited by Admiral Harris, but could say nothing. The Admiral

Some 45 VNAF helicopters were dumped into the sea to make room for the other aircraft that continued to arrive. Pictures showing the fate of these machines symbolised for many the failure of US policy in Vietnam. (Pham Quang Khiem Collection)

Maj Ly Bung of the 114th Observation Squadron appeared over the USS *Midway* in a 'borrowed' O-1E from the 124th Observation Squadron. The South Vietnamese pilot made a perfect landing on the carrier, sans tail hook, with room to spare. Maj Bung's aircraft, still in its VNAF markings, is now displayed in the Naval Aviation Museum in Pensacola, Florida.   (US Navy)

took him to his quarters and left him alone for 20 minutes when it became apparent that he was struggling to hold back his tears.[7]

Around mid-morning, CH-53s and HH-53s began cross-decking processed evacuees from the *Midway* to the Military Sealift Command ships scattered around the ocean nearby. During this operation, a VNAF O-1 appeared overhead and set up a holding pattern around the carrier. The deck was full of helicopters working on the transfer. The initial decision was to deny landing and the carrier zigzagged to prevent an approach. When this failed to discourage the pilot, Maj Ly Bung of the 114th Observation Squadron, an attempt was made to convince him to ditch near the carrier and a smoke bomb was dropped in the water while a US Navy rescue helicopter hovered overhead. Again unconvinced, the VNAF pilot tried to drop a message on the deck, failed, and then succeeded with a second. The message was clear; he was low on fuel and had his wife and four young children aboard! He was going to land, even if the helicopters were in the way. The deck was cleared, the carrier's course straightened, and the speed increased to 30kt. The aircraft made an excellent landing, while the deck crew applauded.

On the morning of 30 April, among the pilots who were still questioning their course of action was a group from the 215th and 243rd Helicopter Squadrons. Since their evacuation from Military Region II, they had been grouped into a provisional unit at Tan

Among the 'Hueys' that landed on the USS *Midway* was this UH-1H used for the transportation of ICCS members. The VNAF operated some 30 of these aircraft that flew with a 'neutral' status, with recognition bands painted on the fuselage and tail. This machine was dumped overboard in order to make space on the deck. (US Navy)

Some VNAF helicopter pilots decided to leave their country in its last hours of existence by flying out to the sea, hoping to catch an American ship. They also tried to pick up their families from their homes or at a prearranged landing spot. This 'Huey' was seen departing the courtyard of a house in downtown Saigon on the morning of 30 April 1975. (VNA)

Son Nhut and were commanded by Lt Col Khun Van Phat. The unit had planned to launch three gunships for an attack mission, but now their crews were seriously considering escaping. They checked the flight line and found some serviceable 'slicks'. They asked the driver of their vehicle to return to the Operations Room to bring back those who now elected to follow them. While waiting, two other pilots unknown to them rushed into one of the helicopters and asked them to take off immediately, as the North Vietnamese troops were nearby. After scrutinising the perimeter they saw nothing and ordered the interlopers to find another helicopter.

Suddenly, artillery rounds exploded around the parking area. They decided to depart and hover nearby. They then observed that another 'Huey' had also taken off but soon crashed when its tail became caught on barbed wire. It was flown by the two pilots that they had just spoken with, and who miraculously escaped the mishap uninjured. They rejoined them soon after when two Dodge trucks brought back around 40 additional pilots. Among them was the squadron commander as well as Lt Col Luong and Hanh, respectively the commander of Detachment C of the 259th SAR Helicopter Squadron, and the former Operations Officer of Phan Rang AB. They now settled in

Maj Ngyen Van Ba, pilot of this CH-47A of the 237th Helicopter Squadron, managed to disembark his passengers (including his wife and three children) aboard USS *Kirk* (FF-1087). He then distanced and jumped out of the cockpit from around 200ft (61m) above the sea surface. Miraculously, he survived the fall of the crashing machine and was warmly welcomed on board of the US frigate. (US Navy)

This 'Huey' that landed on the roof of a building had its rotor blades become entangled in the TV antennae, destroying the engine.
(VNA)

Another 'Huey' fell from the rooftop of the building where it attempted to land and crashed onto the adjacent street.
(VNA)

North Vietnamese soldiers overrun the helicopter parking area at Tan Son Nhut AB. The Communists captured no fewer than 434 UH-1Hs, some of which are still flown today.
(PAVN)

three 'Hueys' and decided to fly to Con Son Island where their families had been evacuated by a C-130A the previous day. Lt Col Phat flew as leader as they followed the last US helicopters evacuating refugees towards the aircraft carriers. They were tempted to push forward and catch up with the American ships, but instead stuck to their idea of joining their loved ones at Con Son Island. They now veered to Radial 130 and left the departing US Navy Task Force behind them. It was calculated that from Tan Son Nhut to their destination would require only 1.5 hours of flight. But after the elapsed time, nothing was in view.

Lt Col Luong, in the third helicopter, replaced the co-pilot with a navigation map and now indicated the correct course to the formation. Then the warning lamp began to flash in the cockpits, indicating less than 20 minutes' of fuel left. They pressed on and after 15 more minutes, the island finally appeared. They landed on their last drops of fuel. In fact, Con Son Island had been chosen by the Vietnamese Navy as a regrouping point for ships leaving the estuaries of the Mekong and Saigon Rivers. Many VNAF personnel elected to evacuate there to join the sailors. After the fall of Saigon, the ships, now laden with refugees, regrouped in convoy and sailed for the Philippines, escorted by US Navy destroyers.[8]

North Vietnamese move into the parking area of the 819th Attack Squadron at Tan Son Nhut. The unit was badly hit, having several of its AC-119Gs destroyed or damaged by artillery shelling as well as the attack carried out by captured A-37Bs. (PAVN)

A K-63 APC of the North Vietnamese 10th Division drives down one of the flight lines at Tan Son Nhut. The air base had suffered extensive damage due to artillery shelling. The armoured vehicle is passing a number of EC-47Ps of the 718th Reconnaissance Squadron. US Intelligence indicated that some of these highly specialised aircraft were later employed by the Communists, who also adapted some of the ELINT equipment for their own An-26s. (PAVN)

Two North Vietnamese officers walk down the debris-littered parking area of the 431st Transport Squadron at Tan Son Nhut. The C-7As display the 'G' tail code of the unit. Note, however, that the last aircraft on the far right carried the 'Y' tail code of the 427th Transport Squadron. This unit was initially based at Da Nang, but operated as part of the 33rd Wing during the final days of the war. With the exception of two aircraft, the latter unit fell almost entirely into Communist hands. (PAVN)

North Vietnamese soldiers walk alongside captured U-6s from the 716th Reconnaissance Squadron at Tan Son Nhut. This unit had a mixed role of transport, photo-reconnaissance and ELINT gathering. It therefore operated a variety of equipment including C-47s, RC-47s, EC-47s and U-6s. Note in the background the C-7As from the 429th Transport Squadron ('P' tail codes). (PAVN)

The North Vietnamese captured 32 CH-47As intact. This Chinook was found abandoned on a debris-littered parking area at Tan Son Nhut. The machine probably belonged to the 237th Helicopter Squadron that had been evacuated from Bien Hoa. (PAVN)

A close-up view of the previous photograph shows the remains of an A-37B. The aircraft was probably hit by a direct artillery shell, leaving only the forward fuselage and part of a wing discernible.
(PAVN)

Triumphant North Vietnamese raise the Viet Cong flag over the control tower of Tan Son Nhut AB on 30 April 1975. Some intact AC-119Gs and C-7As can be seen below. The Communists received immense war booty, including more than 1,100 aircraft according to US Intelligence.
(PAVN)

The first VPAF aircraft to land at Tan Son Nhut AB was this Mi-6 from the 919th Transport Brigade on the afternoon of 30 April 1975. It was cheered by the jubilant North Vietnamese troops. The legendary Gen Vo Nguyen Giap would soon follow in a Mi-8, while other members of the Politburo would land for May Day Celebrations in a specially chartered Il-18.
(VPAF)

In the name of honour

During these last hours of agony many ARVN units continued to fight. The dislocated 25th Division fought until the end, trapped and attacked by the 320th and 316th Divisions at Cu Chi. It was then bypassed by the enemy 10th Division that continued towards the northern perimeter of Tan Son Nhut AB. The northern front was also collapsing under the repeated assaults of the enemy 1st Army Corps. The most intense combats took place on the Bien Hoa sector, which was attacked by the North Vietnamese 2nd and 4th Armies Corps.

The VNAF continued to fly sporadic attack sorties during the night of 29 April as well as on the morning of the 30th. Nearly all the missions were now flown from Binh Thuy, the last major air base in the hands of the South Vietnamese.

During the night of 29 April, two Communist divisions attacked the Can Tho Perimeter, which included Binh Thuy. However, the ARVN 21st Division defended vigorously, supported by several flights of helicopter gunships. Those of the 221st, 225th and 255th Helicopter Squadrons fought particularly gallantly, launching night-time attack sorties from advanced airstrips including Fire Support Bases 31 and 40 around Can Tho.

During the last two days of the war, 29 and 30 April 1975, the VNAF continued to fly sporadic attack sorties. This A-37B from the 74th Wing at Binh Thuy is seen en route for another attack sortie.
(Pham Quang Khiem Collection)

Many troops continued to fight, despite the unconditional surrender, including some VNAF pilots. This UH-1H (left) was damaged during a mission on the morning of 30 April and was forced to make a crash-landing in a rice field south of Saigon. The O-1E (right) was shot down and crashed at the same time, coming down on Nguyen Hoang Street in 5th Quarter of the capital.   (VNA)

At dawn on 30 April, the local 4th Air Division continued to launch attack sorties for the battle for Saigon, as well as in support of forces fighting elsewhere in the Mekong Delta. The VNAF also launched an unknown number of air strikes against North Vietnamese armoured columns entering Saigon. The A-37Bs destroyed several tanks inside the city limits, including five T-55s at the gates of Tan Son Nhut AB.

In the western sector, the A-37Bs inflicted heavy casualties on an enemy convoy at the Bay Hien intersection. A battalion of Rangers resisted at Newport Bridge for several hours, with the help of UH-1H gunships and a flight of A-37Bs. At 10.24 on 30 April President Minh ordered the unconditional surrender of all the South Vietnamese forces on National Radio. For many in the broadly intact 4th Military Region, the news came as a shock. For example, the general commanding the 21st Division, at first light, had boarded a command and control UH-1H to lead a successful counterattack against the enemy and had personally directed air support when he was ordered to land immediately to supervise the disbandment of his troops! Other high-ranking officers were determined to take their lives rather than surrender. The IV Corps Commander, Lt Gen Nguyen Khoa Nam, committed suicide soon after.

The remaining pilots at Binh Thuy refuelled, stripped down their A-37s and flew to Thailand, recovering at U Tapao, where many aircraft from Tan Son Nhut had already been evacuated the previous day. Most aircraft carried three pilots, some even four. Others were unable to reach Thai airfields and had to land in fields and on roads. Reports from officials at U Tapao indicated that several fighters, including at least one F-5, landed on highways in eastern Thailand and were eventually recovered. Another F-5 that tried to land on a road not far from U Tapao crashed and exploded.

Some FAC pilots also took their chance, including Capt Huynh Thu Thoai of the 116th Observation Squadron, who flew an O-1 carrying his wife, his two-years-old child, and – inside the fuselage – another pilot from his squadron. He followed the coast of Cambodia, now in the hands of the Khmer Rouge, until he was not sure where he was. His wife remarked that it was curious that the vehicles below were driving 'like in England'. That confirmed to him that he was at least in Thailand. Low on fuel, he landed on a highway.

Even after the capitulation order, the squadrons at Binh Thuy continued to launch attack sorties in support of the ARVN 21st Division, which fought off an enemy offensive against the city of Can Tho. Some A-37B pilots, like these from the 526th Fighter Squadron of the 74th Wing, also destroyed North Vietnamese tanks on the outskirt of Saigon.
(Can Thep Collection)

A few helicopters also reached Thai territory, though some ran out of fuel and were forced to land in Cambodia. The Khmer Rouge promptly executed the unfortunate passengers. The Americans had nevertheless hastily prepared a field just inside Thailand, immediately across Cambodia's Trat Peninsula, as a recovery point for VNAF helicopters attempting to cross the Gulf of Siam. Apparently, some pilots had been informally briefed about this facility by DAO personnel, notably those who had redeployed to Con Son Island. Some helicopters were picked up on their way in by pre-positioned USMC AH-1Js and escorted towards Thailand. A USAF advisor to the Thais, Capt Roger L. Youngblood, also boarded an RTAF AU-23A and circled the area with a VNAF co-pilot that had just landed. The South Vietnamese stayed on the radio, giving indications to his countrymen and the tower frequency at U Tapao.

However, fully aware that they lacked the range to reach Thailand, many of the helicopter crews at Binh Thuy decided to ride their luck by heading east instead, hoping to catch the departing US Navy Task Force 76. They loaded their aircraft with their families and took off in a group, scanning the sea for American ships.

Shortly after noon on 30 April, another amazing drama occurred. Most of the US military evacuees were on deck of USS *Midway* watching the cross-decking operation or touring the carrier. Suddenly from the west came an armada of 32 VNAF aircraft comprising 29 UH-1Hs, two CH-47As, and an O-1. The recovery task seemed impossible, as the aircraft set up wide holding patterns, in opposite directions, around the ship. Feverishly the ship's crew cleared the deck in one hour. Working with absolute precision, all the aircraft and passengers were recovered safely. At one time, there were seven helicopters sitting on the deck of the carrier with rotors turning. Only one aircraft, the second O-1, which landed safely, was tossed overboard during the recovery.

Throughout these two days of air evacuation, not all South Vietnamese aircraft succeeded in their escape attempts. The US Navy reported that at least 18 VNAF helicopters were counted as having crashed at sea, most of them due to fuel starvation. All told, some 130,000 people, had been evacuated from South Vietnam since early April. Of these 54 per cent were evacuated by air, the balance by sea.

North Vietnamese troops stormed Tan Son Nhut AB at around 10.00 on 30 April 1975. The base was bitterly defended by ARVN Paratroopers, supported by VNAF air strikes until the last moment. These soldiers are passing abandoned C-7As from the 429th Transport Squadron and C-47s from the 716th Reconnaissance Squadron. (PAVN)

At Can Tho, even after the capitulation order had been proclaimed, the 21st ARVN Division continued to resist the enemy advance throughout 30 April. At the end of the morning, the 255th Helicopter Squadron made an air assault, with 'slicks' covered by gunships to bring in reinforcements to the encircled 32nd Regiment on the outskirts of the city. By early afternoon, the North Vietnamese had broken through into Binh Thuy AB, capturing 113 aircraft. The last VNAF stronghold had fallen. Minutes earlier, 1st Lt Nguyen Manh Dung of the 516th Squadron, evacuated from Da Nang, and now attached to the local 526th Fighter Squadron, took off in his A-37B and went to attack the enemy columns en route towards Can Tho. He was brought down – probably the last South Vietnamese airman to be killed in action after the official surrender of his country.

The North Vietnamese also captured this Air America Caribou at Con Son Island. The aircraft had been positioned there as a back-up for the evacuation missions to extract CIA agents operating in the Mekong Delta area. It then developed an oil leak and was consequently abandoned. Ironically, this particular airframe, lost on the last day of the Vietnam War, was also the first Caribou put into service with Air America. (PAVN)

The North Vietnamese occupied Con Son Island by early May 1975. The location served as a regrouping point for South Vietnamese Navy ships before they set sail in convoy for the Philippines. The Communists discovered these abandoned VNAF aircraft at the local airfield, including two C-119Gs, one U-6A and one O-1E. (PAVN)

Another view of Con Son Island airfield shows additional abandoned VNAF aircraft. These North Vietnamese troops from the 126th Marine Brigade had just landed and are passing by a 'Huey' gunship. Two other UH-1Hs and a CH-47A can be seen in the background. (PAVN)

1 An incident occurred at the same time at the USAF 'Tiger Operation' Room that supervised the American air bridge from Tan Son Nhut AB. A group of around 40 South Vietnamese officers, including some from the VNAF, burst into the compound heavily armed. They appeared both dismayed and angered that the Americans were leaving and pointed their guns towards them. They finally left the Americans to move out toward the DAO building when these last ones had promised to return to pick them up when they would be evacuated.

2 Le Hung electronic posting about his escape from South Vietnam. Can Thep, translated from the Vietnamese.

3 Last Flight from Saigon. USAF Southeast Asia Monograph Series, Volume IV, Monographs 6, p81.

4 The Air America C-47 that crash-landed was flown by Art Kenyon who already experienced problems while still at Saigon. It had difficulties to start the right-hand engine and during the flight the hydraulic system blew up, resulting in the loss of the landing gear and brakes.

5 Nguyen Cao Ky, *Twenty years and twenty days.* Stein and Day Publishers, New York, 1976, p227.

6 Can Thep, narrative about the last days of the 221st Helicopter Squadron VNAF, on the Quan Su Khong Viet Nam website (in Vietnamese).

7 Most of the VNAF pilots who landed on the American ships were emotionally in shock state and feel despair and humiliation until this very day, not the least due to the often rude way they had been unceremoniously searched by the US Marines. Vice Air Marshal Nguyen Cao Ky recalled a discussion he had with a US Colonel who had searched the high ranking officers who came with him: 'I understand that you might be suspicious, but after all, we have all sacrificed everything in this war. We may have lost, but we are not the only loser. You Americans have lost, too. What I can't understand is why did you have to treat the officers who were with me the way you did? After all, we have been comrades in arms. We are not Communists, you know.'

8 Can Thep, narrative on the last days of the 215th Helicopter Squadron VNAF, on the Quan Su Khong Viet Nam website (in Vietnamese).

Chapter 11

POSTSCRIPT

In retrospect, there is one question left unanswered: was the South Vietnam defeat inevitable or could the VNAF have decisively offset the situation?

It is clear that US military aid cuts gravely undermined the survival prospects of an independent South Vietnam. However, without President Thieu's decision to abandon half of his country to the enemy, the end would surely have taken longer to arrive, and would probably have been bloodier for both sides. Thieu played his hand, and lost.

But Thieu was probably well aware of the limits imposed on the VNAF, and in this desperate decision he tried to enforce the United States to implement their promised air support. Poorly organised and equipped to face a low-level guerrilla campaign, and with a great emphasis placed on helicopters, the 'fourth largest air force in the world' was woefully inadequate to cope with the threat of North Vietnamese motorised divisions, covered as they were by an impressive array of air defences. A smaller force of higher-performance fighter bombers, such as F-4s or A-7s, would surely have done better, but by the end even equipment of this calibre would surely not have changed the course of the war. This destiny had been established since the termination of US backing for the Saigon regime.

A strong, centralised leadership was also lacking the ability to fully exploit the available VNAF assets. However, the VNAF displayed courage and daring right until the end, particularly so at Phan Rang or Xuan Loc, and as a whole fought better than any other elements of the military.

The fate of the VNAF

US sources indicated that 132 VNAF aircraft were flown to U Tapao, while the Thai authorities claimed that 142 South Vietnamese aircraft had recovered on its territory. The discrepancy between the two figures can be explained by the fact that the Thais also reported cases of aircraft that had landed on other bases, or elsewhere in the countryside and on roads.

The massive arrival of South Vietnamese aircraft put the Thais in an awkward position. For months, the new civilian government had advocated the departure of the last US forces from its territory, pleading for a new, neutral policy in Southeast Asia. The Thais firstly wanted the US to pick up the South Vietnamese refugees as soon as possible. This was completed quickly, USAF C-141s bringing them to Guam.

A small group of refugees, under the leadership of VNAF 2nd Lt Cao Van Li, protested and wanted to return to Vietnam. They were not aware when they boarded a

A general view of the parking area at U Tapao AB in Thailand in early May 1975 shows that it was fully occupied by former VNAF aircraft that had sought refuge there.
(Pham Quang Khiem Collection)

The Americans turned over 72 former VNAF as well as 97 Cambodian aircraft to the Thais. In exchange, the Americans took away 109 machines. The fighter-bombers and the helicopters were loaded aboard the USS *Midway*.
(US Navy)

C-130 that it was flying to Thailand. Li protested. *'I'm not a Communist'*, he said, *'but I want to go home. My family is there. They need me'*. The group was eventually talked out of this by Military Police and brought to Guam. The event made headlines, provoking an international incident. More problematically, a dispute soon emerged over the rightful ownership of the former VNAF aircraft. The victors in Vietnam claimed ownership, while the United Sates expressed their right of ownership, since the aircraft were leased through the Military Assistance Program to the South Vietnamese Government, which no longer existed.

The Thais at first resisted the removal of these aircraft. While waiting a resolution, the South Vietnamese markings were painted over within hours of their arrival.

It took much diplomacy to settle the problem, thanks in no small part to the commander of the American Joint Advisory Forces, USAF Brig Gen Heinie Aderholt. The legendary Air Commando, who had spent most of his career in Thailand in numerous clandestine or 'low profile' air operations, had developed particularly good relationships with the Thai military and sort to find a compromise.

A portion of the VNAF aircraft and nearly all of the 97 Cambodian aircraft could be turned over to the Royal Thai Air Force if Washington could bring back the remaining South Vietnamese aircraft. The Americans turned over to the Thais 72 aircraft, comprising 16 C-47s, three EC-47s, 11 A-1E/H Skyraiders, two F-5As, one RF-5A, one F-5B, six C-7As, three AC-119s, three C-119Gs, 14 U-17s, three O-1s and nine UH-1Hs.[1]

Not all of them would be taken into service, and some were immediately dumped.

The remaining aircraft were loaded onto the USS *Midway*. Seven F-5Es were airlifted by CH-53 helicopter to the carrier when one of them dropped into the ocean. The remainder of the aircraft were thereafter loaded aboard barges. In all, the Americans recovered 21 F-5Es, one F-5A, 27 A-37Bs, nine C-130As, 46 UH-1Hs, three CH-47As and one O-1E.

Among the impounded aircraft at U Tapao were these C-47s. The South Vietnamese markings had been painted over within hours of their arrival.
(USAF)

Postscript

Eleven A-1s escaped to Thailand, including one that landed on a highway. The A-1Es sometimes landed with up to a dozen passengers onboard. The Skyraiders were officially handed over to the RTAF but were never pressed into service by the Thais. At least four or five were later transferred to the US. (USAF)

Ownership of the former VNAF aircraft was finally settled when Washington claimed a proportion of the airframes since they had been US-financed and officially 'leased' to the South Vietnamese. In exchange, Bangkok would be given 72 aircraft.
(Dave Quigley)

US Intelligence estimated that more than 1,100 aircraft had fallen into the hands of the North Vietnamese. Based on Communist sources, Hanoi claimed that its forces had captured 877 intact aircraft.[2] Included in this number were 87 F-5s, of which 27 were the newer F-5Es, as well as 95 A-37Bs and 26 A-1s. Air America also lost one Caribou, 1 Volpar, 11 PC-6s and two UH-1Hs to the Communists.

It was reported that at least one F-5E, one A-37B, one CH-47A and one UH-1H were disassembled and shipped to the Soviet Union for evaluation purposes, while an A-37B was tested in Poland, and an F-5E was tested in Czechoslovakia.

The Russians also brought back for analysis the electronic and optronic equipment of the AC-119s. A large number of transport aircraft were also abandoned and these included 38 C-47s and EC-47s, 33 C-7s, 45 AC-119s and C-119s, and 14 C-130As. The

The USS *Midway* repatriated 46 UH-1H and three CH-47A helicopters. Nine other 'Hueys' were donated to the Thais. The aircraft carrier also brought back 23 Bell 204s and Bell 205s from Air America – including six stolen by VNAF pilots. (US Navy)

217

An aerial view of the USS *Midway* departing Thailand with the 109 VNAF aircraft on board. More than half of the aircraft are arranged on the flight deck. Two US Navy Sikorsky SH-3 Sea Kings can also be seen.
(US Navy)

Another view of the forward part of the USS *Midway* shows some of the repatriated aircraft, including 12 F-5Es, 14 A-37Bs and the O-1E of Maj Ly Bung. Note that the aircraft received only minimum sealing protection measures in order to prevent damage by the salty environment.
(US Navy)

The North Vietnamese captured a total of 87 F-5s, including this example seen at Tan Son Nhut. The aircraft is still armed with four rocket pods, a typical configuration for tank-hunting missions. The F-5A in the background is a former Iranian aircraft, and is armed with four M117 bombs.
(PAVN)

The Communists captured 95 intact A-37Bs. They were later put into service with the VPAF and operated until the mid-1980s. These two were based at Tan Son Nhut during the last weeks of the war. They probably belonged to one of the squadrons that had been evacuated from the northern part of the country when their bases were lost to the enemy advance.   (PAVN)

North Vietnamese inspect the heavily damaged Hercules parking area at Tan Son Nhut. The destroyed aircraft carried the 'GZ' tail code of the 437th Transport Squadron. Artillery shells hit some while they were being loaded with bombs for a planned BOBS-guided attack sortie. The Communists captured at least 14 C-130As.   (PAVN)

greatest numbers of lost aircraft comprised 434 Bell UH-1Hs, 32 CH-47As, and 114 Cessna O-1s. There were also 72 miscellaneous types lost, including U-17s, O-2s, T-41s, U-6s and T-37s.[3]

It was clear that from this huge booty, the Communists could not support all of the captured fleet. Many airframes listed above were destroyed or damaged during the final days of the war, while many more were already mothballed by the VNAF prior to the final offensive against the South. Furthermore, many aircraft were short on spare parts, suffered from corrosion or structural failures that needed overhaul, and many technical support installations, notably at Bien Hoa, had been sabotaged. It would be unrealistic to imagine that the small VPAF could absorb such a large force and related infrastructure in a short period, without resorting to the former VNAF personnel. However, by all available accounts, the vast majority of South Vietnamese airmen were quickly rounded up and interned in the vast local Gulag system that was put in place after the North Vietnamese victory.

Nevertheless, and in a surprisingly short period of time, the North Vietnamese moved in to take over the captured air bases' installations and to make flyable a number of aircraft. The VPAF's 919th Transport Brigade immediately took over the assets of the former South Vietnam national carrier, Air Vietnam, with seven DC-3s, five DC-4s, two DC-6s, two Boeing 727s and two Boeing 707s.[4]

North Vietnamese soldiers hoist the Communist flag over a captured C-119G of the 720th Reconnaissance Squadron at Tan Son Nhut. (PAVN)

Due to personnel shortages, those Air Vietnam employees who were deemed politically reliable were asked to return to their work places, while many VNAF mechanics and other technicians were also retained, as prisoners, to return equipment and machines to an operational state. Three months later, the air bases of Phu Bai, Da Nang, Phan Rang, Phu Cat, Pleiku, Bien Hoa, Tan Son Nhut and Binh Thuy were cleared for limited operations. It was from Binh Thuy that the first strike sorties were launched in support of the occupation of contested islands in the Gulf of Siam. This was the first fighting that pitted the Vietnamese Communists against their former Khmer Rouge allies. A group of VNAF helicopter pilots, euphemistically called 'new comrades', were pressed into service to fly UH-1H gunships to support landings made by the Navy. By the end of 1975, all these prisoners were removed from VPAF ranks and sent back to prison camps, where most of them languished for a number of gruelling years.

Most of the VNAF officers, particularly the pilots, would spend an average of eight to 15 years in detention. Some of them, however, were released by the end of 1978; after a political indoctrination course, they were again pressed into service to bolster the ranks of the Communist squadrons for the upcoming operations against Cambodia. However, they were never fully trusted and the experience was discontinued when some of them defected. On 24 November 1979, a Hercules flown by a former South Vietnamese pilot defected to Singapore. It was followed in 1980 by another former VNAF pilot who escaped to Thailand flying his CH-47A. The VPAF was constantly lacking qualified aircrews and throughout the 1980s its ranks were bolstered by Soviet pilots flying An-26 transports during the war in Cambodia.

Some 19 C-47s and EC-47s reached Thailand, laden with refugees. Two of them crash-landed due to main landing gear failures, fortunately without any injuries. This C-47 from the 716th Reconnaissance Squadron had just arrived and was being directing towards the parking area. The crew had opened the doors in order to provide the overcrowded passenger compartment with some fresh air. (Dave Quigley)

In addition to the military aircraft that landed in Thailand were some civilian machines from Air America and Air Vietnam. This DC-3 was from the South Vietnamese national airline.
(Pham Quang Khiem Collection)

The VPAF established the 372nd Air Division equipped with former VNAF aircraft. This consisted of the 917th Regiment with the O-1/U-17 and UH-1/CH-47, the 918th Regiment with the C-47/C-119/C-130, the 935th Regiment with the F-5, and the 937th Regiment with the A-37.

The former VNAF ATC at Nha Trang became part of the VPAF educational system, its extensive installations now serving the North Vietnamese who used a mix of T-41Ds, Chinese-built Nanchang BT-6s and Aero L-29s.[5]

The captured aircraft served their new masters well in the protracted campaign in Cambodia, as well as against anti-Communist guerrillas in Laos and in the Central Highlands of Vietnam. Like the South Vietnamese, the VPAF also turned its C-130As into makeshift bombers, attacking the Khmer Rouge divisions during the invasion of Cambodia in 1979. The VPAF continued to use US-built aircraft until it ran out of spare parts, in the early 1980s. In 1985, marking the 10th anniversary of the fall of Saigon, a flight of F-5Es overflew Ho Chi Minh City, alongside MiG-21s, during a military parade. Hanoi then tried unsuccessfully to sell the remaining airframes when the US warned that they would not provide technical support. Apparently only Iran bought a batch of remaining F-5 spare parts and some ground support equipment in the 1980s. F

Of the hundreds of VNAF pilots who succeeded in escaping in the last hours of the conflict, most were resettled elsewhere in the world, and particularly in the United States and France. Only six fixed-wing pilots found a living in the US by flying for various airlines, as well as six helicopter pilots.

Former Lt Le Hung, who escaped with his friend and a mechanic in an A-37, enlisted into the US Navy and become carrier qualified. He later flew the Lockheed S-3A Viking and participated in the 1991 Gulf War as a Grumman A-6 Intruder pilot.

In France, several former VNAF officers with Skyraider experience were approached by French Intelligence to be hired for the Air Wing of the Presidential Guard of Gabon under President Omar Bongo. This unit was entirely staffed by foreign mercenaries and operated as a parallel counter-coup force alongside the official Gabonese Air Force.

The majority of former VNAF pilots had to find other ways to start an entirely new life. Maintaining the 'esprit de corps' of the VNAF that once prevailed in South Vietnam, former members have joined together in comradeship in exile, in establishing Associations of the Vietnamese Air Force in the US, France, Australia and New Zealand.

Nguyen Thanh Trung, the Communist-infiltrated pilot who bombed the Presidential Palace, continued a distinguished career with the VPAF, flying a number of F-5 sorties over Cambodia. He left the military in 1990 with the rank of colonel, before joining the new national carrier, Vietnam Airlines. In 2005, as co-director of the company, he made a highly symbolic flight by bringing PhanVan Khai to the US, the first ever Vietnamese

Soon after their victory over South Vietnam, the North Vietnamese were involved in the first armed clashes with their former Khmer Rouge allies. The relationship between the two Communist regimes soon deteriorated and then escalated into an open war. One of the first incidents occurred when the Vietnamese landed their troops to occupy an island in a contested area of the Gulf of Siam in 1975. The amphibious operation was covered by captured VNAF aircraft, some flown by South Vietnamese prisoner pilots, forced to do so at gunpoint. After the operation, they were deported to detention camps. These 'Huey' gunships were seen taking off for an attack sortie against the Cambodian Communists, piloted by some of the 'new comrades'. Ironically, they still carried South Vietnamese colours, for in their haste their new owners had not found the time to repaint them. It was probably the last time that an aircraft was flown operationally with such markings. (VPAF)

Prime Minister to visit Washington. Since 1995 both countries have normalised their relations, and since then Vietnam has adopted the market economy and show signs of strong economic recovery.

Vice Air Marshall Nguyen Cao Ky became an active member of the Vietnamese Diaspora, helping many South Vietnamese to resettle in the United States. In January 2004, he was allowed to visit Vietnam, where he called for a healing of the wounds of the past. His visit was not without some controversy and provoked much outcry from many former South Vietnamese military officers living in the US. Clearly, the suffering from a long and bitter civil war had not yet been forgotten. Ky eventually decided to retire in Ho Chi Minh City. It is perfectly possible that he was able to observe the operations of former VNAF UH-1Hs from the nearby Tan Son Nhut AB – one of relatively few lasting legacies left behind by the once proud South Vietnamese Air Force.[6]

1   Of the 11 Skyraiders, seven were from the 514th Fighter Squadron, three from the 518th Fighter Squadron and one from the 530th Fighter Squadron. One A-1E from the 518th Squadron landed with no less than 20 passengers on board! Another A-1E of the same unit reached Thailand with a total of 15 pilots. The aircraft had taken off from Tan Son Nhut on 29 April and flew down South to Binh Thuy but was ordered to wait for the runway there was fully mobilized for some evacuation operations. After circling the area for 40 minutes, the aircraft finally diverted to the Phu Quoc Island in the Siam Gulf. After spending there the night, it took off again this time for U Tapao, Thailand.

2   Lich Su Khong Quan Nhan Dan Viet Nam (1955–1977), Nha Xuat Ban Quan Doi Nhan Dan, Hanoi 1993, p311.

3   The North Vietnamese reported that their forces had captured at Tan Son Nhut Airbase the following aircraft: 41 F-5s, 23 A-37s, five A-1Hs, seven C-130s, 28 C-7s, 36 AC-119s and C-119s, 21 C-47s and EC-47s, five CH-47s, 50 UH-1s, 41 O-1s, 15 U-17s, 18 T-41s, five U-6s, one PL-1 and one AC-10M, this last one being a locally designed and manufactured light liaison aircraft. The North Vietnamese also found no less than 117 different aircraft at Binh Thuy.

4   Lich Su Khong Quan Nhan Dan Viet Nam (1955–1977), Nha Xuat Ban Quan Doi Nhan Dan, Hanoi 1993, p309.

5   In late 1975, the North Vietnamese indicated that they succeeded to put back into service 97 aircraft at Tan Son Nhut, 83 at Bien Hoa, and 39 at Da Nang.

6   Former Vice Air Marshal Nguyen Cao Ky passed away in a hospital in Kuala Lumpur on 23 July 2011 at the age of 80.

APPENDIX I

VNAF order of battle, February 1975

Commander: *Lt Gen Tran Van Minh*

1st Air Division Da Nang
CO Brig Gen Nguyen Duc Khanh

41st Tactical Wing Da Nang *CO Col Thai Ba De*	**110th Observation Squadron** O-2, O-1, U-17 (tail code X) *CO Maj Ly Thanh Ba* O-2s in storage	**120th Observation Squadron** O-1, U-17 *CO Maj Le Cong Tinh*	**427th Transport Squadron** C-7A (tail code Y) Disbanded in November 1974; aircraft in storage

718th Reconnaissance Squadron (Det.) EC-47P (tail code W) ELINT operations	**821st Attack Squadron (Det.)** AC-119K

51st Tactical Wing
Da Nang

213th Helicopter Squadron
UH-1H
CO Maj Cao Quang Khoi

233rd Helicopter Squadron
UH-1H
CO Maj Nguyen Van Thanh

239th Helicopter Squadron
UH-1H
CO Maj Nguyen Anh Toan

247th Helicopter Squadron
CH-47A
CO Maj Nguyen Van Mai

253rd Helicopter Squadron
UH-1H
CO Maj Huynh Van Pho

257th Helicopter Squadron
UH-1H
CO Maj Le Ngoc Binh

61st Tactical Wing
Da Nang

516th Fighter Squadron
A-37B

528th Fighter Squadron
A-37B

536th Fighter Squadron
F-5A (tail code HJ)
CO Maj Dam Thuong Vu
Moved in from Bien Hoa

538th Fighter Squadron
F-5E
CO Maj Pham Dinh Anh

550th Fighter Squadron
A-37B
CO Maj Le Trai

 2nd Air Division Nha Trang and Phan Rang
CO Brig Gen Nguyen Van Luong

62nd Tactical Wing
Nha Trang
CO Col Nguyen Huy Oanh

114th Observation Squadron
O-1, U-17
CO Maj Vo Van Oanh

215th Helicopter Squadron
UH-1H
CO Maj Khuu Van Phat

219th Helicopter Squadron
UH-1H
CO Maj Pham Dang Luan

**259th Helicopter Squadron
(Det. C)**
UH-1H
CO Maj Nguyen Minh Luong
Medevac operations

817th Attack Squadron
AC-47D (tail code K)
Disbanded November 1974;
Aircraft in storage or returned
to cargo configuration

92nd Tactical Wing
Phan Rang
CO Col Le Van Thao

524th Fighter Squadron
A-37B
CO Maj Su Ngoc Ca

534th Fighter Squadron
A-37B
CO Maj Nguyen Van Thi

548th Fighter Squadron
A-37B (tail code A)
CO Maj Tran Manh Khoi

259th Helicopter Squadron (Det. D)
UH-1H
CO Maj To Thanh Nhan
Medevac operations

3rd Air Division Bien Hoa
CO Brig Gen Huynh Ba Tinh

23rd Tactical Wing
Bien Hoa
CO Col Vo Xuan Lanh

112th Observation Squadron
O-1, U-17 (tail code D)
CO Maj Ly Thanh Ba

124th Observation Squadon
O-1, U-17 (tail code FD)
CO Maj Vo Trung Khuong

514th Fighter Squadron
A-1E/H/G (tail code FF)
Out of storage in January 1975

518th Fighter Squadron
A-1E/H/G (tail code KW)
CO Lt Col Nguyen Quang Vinh
Out of storage in January 1975

43rd Tactical Wing
Bien Hoa

221st Helicopter Squadron
UH-1H
CO Lt Col Nguyen Van Trong

223rd Helicopter Squadron
UH-1H
CO Maj Tran Van Luan

231st Helicopter Squadron
UH-1H
CO Maj Nguyen Huu Loc

237th Helicopter Squadron
CH-47A
CO Maj Nguyen Phu Chinh

245th Helicopter Squadron
UH-1H
CO Maj Nguyen Huu Lai

251st Helicopter Squadron
UH-1H
CO Maj Duong Quang Le

**259th Helicopter Squadron
(Det. E)**
UH-1H
CO Maj Huynh Van Du
Medevac operations

63rd Tactical Wing
Bien Hoa
CO Col Nguyen Khoa Phuoc

522nd Fighter Squadron
F-5A/B, RF-5A (tail code HZ)
CO Maj Nguyen Van Tuong

540th Fighter Squadron
F-5A/B (tail code FU)
CO Maj Nguyen Tien Thanh

542nd Fighter Squadron
F-5E (tail code HB)
CO Maj Trinh Buu Quang

544th Fighter Squadron
F-5E (tail code HQ)
CO Maj Vo Vang Si

4th Air Division Binh Thuy and Can Tho
CO Brig Gen Nguyen Huu Tan

64th Tactical Wing
Can Tho

217th Helicopter Squadron
UH-1H
CO Maj Nguyen Van Vong

249th Helicopter Squadron
CH-47A
CO Maj Pham Xuan Viet

255th Helicopter Squadron
UH-1H
CO Maj Nguyen Kim Huon

**259th Helicopter Squadron
(Det. F)**
UH-1H
CO Maj Nguyen Thanh Quoi
Medevac operations

74th Tactical Wing
Binh Thuy

116th Observation Squadron
O-1, U-17 (tail code E)
CO Maj Bui Thanh Su

122nd Observation Squadron
O-1, U-17
CO Maj Tran Trong Khuong

520th Fighter Squadron
A-37B

526th Fighter Squadron
A-37B
CO Maj Huynh Huu Hai

546th Fighter Squadron
A-37B
CO Maj Le Mong Hoan

84th Tactical Wing
Binh Thuy

211th Helicopter Squadron
UH-1H
CO Maj Tran Que Lam

225th Helicopter Squadron
UH-1H
CO Maj Le Van Chau

227th Helicopter Squadron
UH-1H
CO Maj Tran Chau Ret

**259th Helicopter Squadron
(Det. H)**
UH-1H
CO Maj Nguyen Trong Thanh
Medevac operations

5th Air Division Tan Son Nhut
CO Brig Gen Phan Phung Tien

33rd Tactical Wing
Tan Son Nhut
CO Col Bui Duc My

259th Helicopter Squadron (Det. G)
UH-1H
CO Maj Tran Quan Vo
Medevac operations

314th Special Mission Squadron
C-47, VC-47, DC-6, U-17,
Aerocommander 520, UH-1H
(tail code C)
VIP transport

429th Transport Squadron
C-7A (tail code P)
Out of storage in
February 1975

431st Transport Squadron
C-7A (tail code G)
Out of storage
in February 1975

716th Reconnaissance Squadron
RC-47, EC-47D,
U-6, RU-6 (tail code M)
ELINT and photo-
reconnaissance operations

718th Reconnaissance Squadron
EC-47P (tail code T)
CO Lt Col Nguyen Huu Bach
ELINT operations

53rd Tactical Wing
Tan Son Nhut
CO Col Huynh Van Hien

435th Transport Squadron
C-130A (tail code HC)
CO Lt Col Mac Manh Cau

437th Transport Squadron
C-130A (tail code GZ)
CO Lt Col Mac Huu Loc

720th Reconnaissance Squadron
C-119G
Transport role only;
CO Lt Col Ta Pham Bich

819th Attack Squadron
AC-119G
CO Lt Col Nguyen Van Hong

821st Attack Squadron
AC-119K (tail code HR)
CO Lt Col Hoang Nuoi

6th Air Division Pleiku and Phu Cat
CO Brig Gen Pham Ngoc Sang

72nd Tactical Wing
Pleiku

118th Observation Squadron
O-2, O-1, U-17
CO Maj Nguyen Van Duoc
O-2s in storage

229th Helicopter Squadron
UH-1H
CO Maj Doan Van Quang

235th Helicopter Squadron
UH-1H
CO Maj Huynh Hai Ho

**259th Helicopter Squadron
(Det. B)**
UH-1H
CO Capt Trinh Viet Hao
Medevac operations

530th Fighter Squadron
A-1E/H/G
Skyraiders in storage

82nd Tactical Wing
Phu Cat

241st Helicopter Squadron
CH-47A
CO Maj Do Van Hieu

**259th Helicopter Squadron
(Det. A)**
UH-1H
CO Maj Nguyen Huu Nghe
Medevac operations

532nd Fighter Squadron
A-37B
CO Maj Nguyen Van Thi

Air Training Center
Nha Trang
*CO Brig Gen Nguyen
Ngoc Oanh*

918th Air Training Squadron
T-41D
Aircraft in storage

920th Air Training Squadron
T-37C
Aircraft in storage;
based at Phan Rang

APPENDIX II

VNAF squadron activations | July 1971 to February 1973

Date	Squadron	Aircraft	Base	Remarks
3/1971	819th	AC-119G	Tan Son Nhut	Spread among all bases
3/1971	423rd	C-123K	Tan Son Nhut	Deactivated 4/1972
3/1971	425th	C-123K	Tan Son Nhut	Deactivated 4/1972
3/1971	427th	C-7A	Da Nang	
4/1971	243rd	UH-1H	Phu Cat	
4/1971	245th	UH-1H	Bien Hoa	
1/1972	239th	UH-1H	Da Nang	
2/1972	241st	CH-47A	Phu Cat	
2/1972	429th	C-7A	Tan Son Nhut/ Phu Cat	Moved to Tan Son Nhut in 1973
3/1972	431st	C-7A	Tan Son Nhut	
3/1972	124th	O-1/ U-17	Bien Hoa	Initially intended to operate on AU-23A from Pleiku
3/1972	718th	EC-47P	Tan Son Nhut / Da Nang	Squadron split in two and operating from both bases
4/1972	532nd	A-37B	Phu Cat	
4/1972	534th	A-37B	Phan Rang	
4/1972	536th	F-5A	Bien Hoa	
4/1972	435th	C-130A	Tan Son Nhut	
4/1972	437th	C-130A	Tan Son Nhut	
12/1972	720th	C-119G	Tan Son Nhut	Initially intended to operate on RC-119L for maritime patrol operations. Used for transport missions only
1/1973	538th	F-5A	Da Nang	Converted to F-5E in 1974
1/1973	540th	F-5A	Bien Hoa	
1/1973	821st	AC-119K	Tan Son Nhut / Da Nang	Spread among all bases
1/1973	247th	CH-47A	Da Nang	
1/1973	251st	UH-1H	Bien Hoa	
1/1973	255th	UH-1H	Binh Thuy	
1/1973	257th	UH-1H	Da Nang	
1/1973	259th	UH-1H	Bien Hoa	Medevac operations. Brought up to Group status in 1974. Spread among all bases
2/1973	546th	A-37B	Binh Thuy	
2/1973	548th	A-37B	Phan Rang	
2/1973	550th	A-37B	Da Nang	
2/1973	542nd	F-5A	Bien Hoa	Converted to F-5E in 1975
2/1973	544th	F-5A	Bien Hoa	Converted to F-5E in 1975
2/1973	249th	CH-47A	Binh Thuy	
2/1973	253rd	UH-1H	Da Nang	
2/1973	920th	T-37C	Phan Rang	

Aircraft deliveries to the VNAF under Projects Enhance and Enhance Plus (23 October 1972 to 12 December 1972)

Aircraft Type	Project Enhance	Project Enhance Plus	Project Total	Grand Total
A–37B	2 squadrons	3 squadrons	90	249
AC–119K	1 squadron		22	
C–119G	1 squadron			
C–7A	1 squadron			
C–130A		2 squadrons	32 (replacing all C–123s)	
RC–47	12			
EC–47		10	23	33
F–5A/B	5	2 squadrons	118	153
F–5E		3 squadrons		
A–1			28	
O–2A			35 (replacing O–1A on 1:1 basis)	
T–37			24	
UH–1	32	3 squadrons	286	
CH–47	2 squadrons		23	

APPENDIX III

VNAF aircraft 1953–1975

Manufacturer	Aircraft Type	No. Delivered	In Service from/to	Remarks
Aero Commander	L-26	1		Presidential liaison aircraft
Beechcraft	C-45 Expeditor	10	1955–1969	Liaison missions
Bell	OH-13 Sioux		1958–1965	A handful were received for liaison and training missions
Bell	UH-1B Iroquois	2	1966–1969	VIP transportation
Bell	UH-1H Iroquois	1051	1969–1975	765 delivered between 1969 and March 1972. 286 received with Projects Enhance and Enhance Plus in the last weeks before the ceasefire
Boeing	CH-47A Chinook	70	1970–1975	Equipped four squadrons in 1975
Cessna	A-37A/B Dragonfly	248	1969–1975	Equipped eight squadrons in 1975
Cessna	O-1A Bird Dog	146	1955–1975	Including dual-control variant
Cessna	O-1E Bird Dog	55		
Cessna	O-1G Bird Dog	211		
Cessna	O-2A Skymaster	35	1973–1974	Equipped two squadrons. Puted into storage in October 1974
Cessna	T-37C	24	1973–1975C	Put into storage in October 1974
Cessna	T-41D Mescalero	24	1970–1974	Put into storage in October 1974
Cessna	U-17A Skywagon	68	1962–1975	
Cessna	U-17B Skywagon	26	1962–1975	
Dassault	M.D.315 Flamant	39	1954–1955	Liaison and light attack operations
Douglas	A-1E Skyraider	36	1965–1975	Including 5 former EA-1Es
Douglas	A-1H Skyraider	233	1960–1975	
Douglas	A-1J Skyraider	14	1968–1975	8 from USN, 6 from USAF
Douglas	A-1G Skyraider	46	1965–1975	
Douglas	B-26K Invader	5	1970–1975	Instructional airframes only
Douglas	C-47 Skytrain	76	1954–1975	Equipped up to three transport squadrons
Douglas	AC-47D 'Spooky'	22	1969–1974	Disarmed in October 1974
Douglas	EC-47D	14		Including 12 C-47Ds converted in early 1972. Enemy radio post direction finding and location
Douglas	EC-47P	36	1973–1975	ELINT operations
Douglas	RC-47D	3		Photo and infra-red reconnaissance
Douglas	VC-47	6		VIP transportation
Douglas	DC-6B	1	1966–1975	Presidential aircraft

Manufacturer	Aircraft Type	No. Delivered	In Service from/to	Remarks
de Havilland Canada	C-7A Caribou	56	1972–1975	STOL transport operations carried out by three squadrons
de Havilland Canada	U-1 Otter	7	1970–1971	Seven U-1s were transferred from the US Army. Saw limited service due to a lack of logistical support
de Havilland Canada	U-6 Beaver	15	1958–1975	Liaison and Psy Ops operations
de Havilland Canada	RU-6	2		Enemy radio post direction finding and location
Fairchild	AC-119G 'Shadow'	24	1971–1975	Equipped one squadron
Fairchild	AC-119K 'Stinger'	22	1972–1975	Equipped one squadron
Fairchild	C-119G Flying Boxcar	35	1968–1975	Including 13 C-119Gs intended to be modified as RC-119Ls delivered at the end of 1972
Fairchild	C-123K Provider	51	1971–1973	Equipped three squadrons
Grumman	F8F Bearcat	49	1955–1960	Equipped the first VNAF fighter squadron
Lockheed	C-130A Hercules	32	1972–1975	Equipped two squadrons
Martin	B-57B	4		'On loan' from USAF, under American control
Morane-Saulnier	M.S.500 Criquet	122	1953–1955	Many aircraft received at the end of 1954 were immediately discharged. Equipped the Air Training Center as well as two observation squadrons
North American	T-6G Texan	55	1957–1965	
North American	T-28B/D Trojan	70	1962–1966	Including 18 RT-28Cs
Northrop	F-5A Freedom Fighter	137	1967–1975	7 F-5As received in 1970, and 5 F-5As in Project Enhance in early 1972 from United States; 36 from South Korea, 48 from Taiwan, 32 from Iran and 9 from USAF in Project Enhance Plus at the end of 1972
Northrop	F-5B Freedom Fighter	8	1967–1975	
Northrop	F-5C Freedom Fighter	17	1967–1975	Inherited from 10th ACS, USAF
Northrop	F-5E Tiger II	54	1974–1975	Equipped three squadrons
Northrop	RF-A Freedom Fighter	10	1970–1975	
Pazmany	PL-2	1	1971–1972	Intended to be assembled locally under licence
Republic	RC-3 Seabee	3	1953–1954	Liaison and maritime reconnaissance operations
Sikorsky	H-19 Chickasaw	10	1958–1964	
Sikorsky	CH-34C Choctaw	94	1960–1970	
Sikorsky	UH-34D Choctaw	56	1960–1970	
Sikorsky	UH-34G Choctaw	81	1960–1970	
Sud Aviation	SA.318 Alouette II	2	1961–1967	VIP transportation
Sud Aviation	SA.3160 Alouette III	2	1962–1966	VIP transportation

APPENDIX IV: ARTWORKS

This O-1G from the 124th OS (Bien Hoa AB) was successfully landed on USS *Midway* by Maj Ly Bung on 30 April 1975. The aircraft is today preserved at the National Naval Aviation Museum in Pensacola, Florida.

An A-1H from the 23rd Wing (probably the 514th FS) based at Bien Hoa AB in 1975. Like most VNAF Skyraiders it had been equipped with the Stanley 'Yankee' ejection seat by this time. It is shown armed with Mk 81 bombs and SUU-14 submunition dispensers. This A-1 was evacuated to Thailand.

This A-1E from the 23rd Wing (probably the 514th FS) was also evacuated to Thailand. The inset shows the fashion in which the Modex was applied on the forward doors of the main undercarriage bays on all VNAF Skyraiders. Noteworthy is the fact that the serial number actually consisted of a combination of the FY number (as used by the USAF) and the BuAerNo (as used by the US Navy): 52-133919.

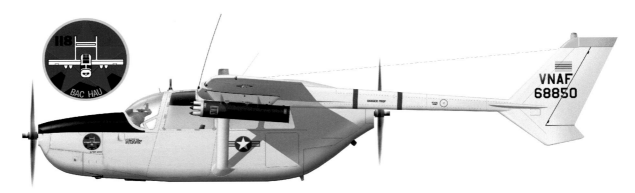

An O-2A of the 118th OS, as operated from Pleiku AB in 1974, and the fate of which remains unknown. Notable is the unusual, 'high' window over the pilot's seat, which was usually only half as high. The aircraft is shown armed with a seven-tube LAU-7H rocket pod, usually used to mark targets for faster fighter-bombers.

An AC-47D of the 817th AS, coded KF 503, depicted as it appeared around 1972. The final fate of the aircraft is unknown. Sadly, there is no precise reference concerning the markings of these aircraft in the 1973-75 period, by which time they should have received three-letter tailfin codes. Notable is the deletion of the SUU-11A Minigun pod from the main cargo doors on VNAF AC-47Ds.

This AC-119K of the 821st Attack Squadron was seen at Tan Son Nhut AB in April 1975. Of interest is the application of the 'tailfin code' on the forward fuselage.

A 'gunship' UH-1H of the 217th HS from Can Tho AB, armed with the XM93 weapons system (including the GAU-2B/A 7.62mm Minigun and the LAU-7H rocket pod), as seen in 1974. Notable are a number of upgrades that had been applied to most VNAF 'Hueys' by 1973, including an armour plate on the side of the engine and an exhaust suppressor to counter the SA-7 threat.

VNAF CH-47As were generally left in olive drab colours overall, but received box-like flare dispensers on the rear fuselage to counter the SA-7 threat. The main artwork and insets show the minimal differences in the usual application of serial numbers in the 1973-75 period: only a few CH-47s received full tailfin codes. '160' (probably from the 237th HS) was evacuated to USS *Midway*.

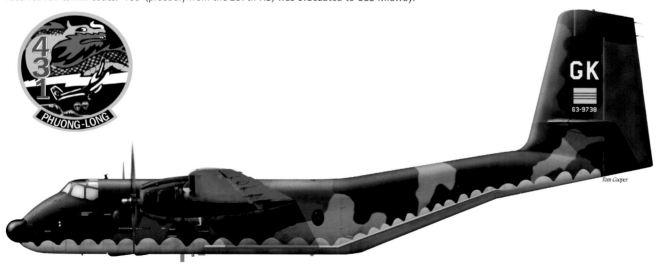

This C-7A Caribou was operated by the 431st TS from Tan Son Nhut AB in 1973, though its subsequent fate is unknown. The transport received the standard 'Southeast Asia' camouflage pattern, but with the coat of light grey (FS36622) on the lower surfaces applied in a rather unusual wavy pattern. Notable is the absence of national markings on the rear fuselage and large sections of the upper wing surfaces painted in 'US yellow'.

This C-130A of the 437th TS (GZJ/60-489) was knocked out by Communist artillery while preparing for a bombing mission at Tan Son Nhut AB on 29 April 1975. Within the VNAF administration as of 1973-75, each aircraft received a set of individual tailfin codes, which were considered more important than serial numbers. The first letter of the tailfin code identified the unit.

An A-37B from the 516th FS (61st Wing), as operated from Da Nang AB in 1974. The aircraft is shown armed with an LAU-7H rocket pod and carrying two drop tanks on the inboard underwing pylon. However, it did not wear the typical 'bleu' (blue) fuselage band with white stripes, as usually associated with this unit.

An A-37B from the 520th FS (74th Wing) as operated from Binh Thuy AB in 1974. It is shown armed with LAU-61 rocket pods for 19 2.75in (70mm) unguided rockets.

Another A-37B from the 520th FS, shown armed with BLU-27 napalm tanks. Aircraft from this unit usually had their rudders painted in blue, red or yellow, with white or black stars, indicating each of three flights that operated them.

An A-37B from the 524th FS (92nd Wing) at Phan Rang AB, as of 1973. This Dragonfly is shown armed with a mix of CBU-55 FAE bombs and Mk 81s. The inset shows the 92nd Wing insignia as usually applied on the starboard side of the tailfin. The same practice was followed by several other VNAF wings.

An A-37B from the 526th FS (74th Wing) at Binh Thuy AB, as of 1975, shown armed with Mk 82 bombs on the outboard underwing pylons. As in the case of A-37Bs from the 520th FS, each of this unit's three flights painted the rudders of its Dragonflies in either blue, red or yellow.

Another A-37B from the 526th FS (74th Wing), this time shown armed with Mk 81 (outboard) and Mk 82 bombs. Aircraft of this unit had their rudders and wingtip fuel tanks decorated with polka dots instead of stars: either red with white dots, blue with white dots, or yellow with black dots.

An A-37B from the 528th FS (61st Wing), as operated from Da Nang AB in 1973. This sister unit of the 516th FS decorated its aircraft with a blue fuselage band with white stars. This marking was usually associated with the 61st Wing, the crest of which was applied on the starboard side of the tailplane. This aircraft is shown armed with Mk 82 bombs and SUU-14 submunition dispensers.

An A-37B from the 548th FS (92nd Wing). This aircraft received the rare tailfin code, applied on relatively few Dragonflies towards the end of the war, and is shown carrying a maximum war load for attacks on the Communists that surrounded Phan Rang AB, including M117, Mk 82 and Mk 81 bombs. The aircraft was later involved in the attack on Tan Son Nhut AB on 28 April 1975, while in North Vietnamese hands.

An A-37B from the 550th FS (61st Wing), as operated from Da Nang AB in 1975. This was the third Dragonfly squadron raised at this base and most of its aircraft never received fuselage bands. This example, shown armed with Mk 82 bombs, was evacuated to Thailand.

F-5B HZA/65-10586 from the 522nd FS (63rd Wing), as operated from Bien Hoa AB in 1974. This was one of two F-5Bs originally delivered to the VNAF in 1967. Its final fate remains unknown, but the aircraft was likely taken over by the North Vietnamese.

This RF-5A (full FY serial number 69-7163) was probably among the last four examples operated by the 522nd FS (63rd Wing) from Bien Hoa as of early 1975. Its final fate remains unknown.

This F-5A (HJK/65-10544) was one of the few ex-Iranian Freedom Fighters over-painted in the SEA camouflage pattern by 1975. It was operated by the 536th FS (63rd Wing) when damaged by an SA-7 in January of the same year, and is shown armed with a BLU-27 napalm tank. Its final fate remains unknown.

This un-coded ex-Iranian F-5A (full FY serial number 65-10482) was sighted at Bien Hoa AB in early 1973, apparently while operated by the 536th FS. It is shown armed with SUU-14 submunition dispensers, usually used to launch small cluster ammunition in rear direction.

This F-5A (full FY serial number 71-10268) was originally destined for Libya, but was embargoed and instead delivered to the VNAF on 21 June 1972, where it served with the 536th FS before being evacuated to Thailand. It was left in its original colour of aluminium-silver overall, although the engine covers and wingtip tanks were replaced with those from a camouflaged example after it suffered some type of combat damage. It is shown with LAU-61 pods for unguided rockets.

This F-5E of the 538th FS (61st Wing), based at Da Nang until February 1975, was captured by the Communists at Tan Son Nhut AB on 30 April 1975, while still armed with four LAU-61 unguided rocket pods. The jet was later pressed into service with the Communist air arm and was last seen in 1989.

This F-5A (full FY serial number 71-1075) was also originally destined for Libya, but was delivered to the VNAF on 20 June 1972. It served with the 540th FS (63rd Wing) from Bien Hoa AB as of January 1975, but its eventual fate remains unknown. The aircraft is shown with a US-made M117 bomb.

Also serving with the 540th FS at Bien Hoa AB as of March 1975 was this ex-Iranian F-5A, coded FUE/64-13358. It is shown with the relatively rarely used Mk 82SE bombs (equipped with Mk 15 Snakeye retarding fins), used for low-level attacks. Its eventual fate remains unknown.

Another mount of the 540th FS was this F-5A coded FUK/63-8383, sighted at Bien Hoa AB in 1974. Only the 13th F-5A ever manufactured, it served with the IIAF before being delivered to South Vietnam under Project Enhance, and was eventually evacuated to Thailand. The aircraft is shown in another unusual configuration, with six Mk 82 bombs installed on the multiple ejector rack under the centreline.

This ex-USAF F-5C, coded HBG/65-10557, was handed over to the VNAF on 22 January 1969 and served with the 542nd FS (63rd Wing). It is shown in alert/CAP configuration, armed with two AIM-9B Sidewinders. Its final fate remains unknown.

This F-5E of the 544th FS (63rd Wing) was flown by Lt Nguyen Thanh Trung when he defected and bombed the Presidential Palace on 8 April 1975. Trung subsequently recovered at Phuoc Long airfield, already occupied by the North Vietnamese. For illustration purposes, the aircraft is shown with an AIM-9E Sidewinder on the wingtip pylon and a single Mk 82 bomb, which was a very rare combination during VNAF times.

BIBLIOGRAPHY

ANG CHEN GUAN, *Ending the Vietnam War, the Vietnamese Communists' Perspective* (Routledge Curzon, NY, 2004)

BERGER, C., *The United States Air Forces in Southeast Asia, 1961–1973* (Office of the US Air Forces History, Washington, DC 1977)

BUTLER, D., *The Fall of Saigon* (Sphere Books Ltd, London, 1986)

CAO VAN VIEN, 'Leadership', *Indochina Monographs*, Centre of Military History, United States Army, US Government Printing office, Washington, DC, 1981.

CAO VAN VIEN, 'The Final Collapse', *Indochina Monographs*, Centre of Military History, United States Army, US Government Printing office, Washington, DC, 1983.

CLARKE, J. J., *Advice and Support: The Final years, 1965–1973* (Centre of Military History, United States Army, US Government printing Office, Washington, DC, 1988)

DARCOURT, P., *Vietnam, Qu'as-tu Fait de tes Fils* (Editions Albatros, Paris, 1975)

DRENDEL, L., *Air War over Southeast Asia, Volumes 1, 2 & 3* (Squadron Signal Publication, Carrolton, TX, 1982)

DUY HINH NGUYEN, 'Vietnamization and the Ceasefire', *Indochina Monographs*, Centre of Military History, United States Army, US Government Printing office, Washington, DC, 1980

FRANCILLON, R. J., *Vietnam Air War* (Aerospace Publishing Ltd, London, 1987)

FUTRELL, R. F., *The United States Air Forces in Southeast Asia, the advisory years to 1965* (Office of the US Air Forces History, Washington, DC 1981)

GURNEY, G., *Vietnam; The war in the air* (Sidgwick and Jackson Limited, 1985)

HERRINGTON, S. A., *Peace With Honor? An American Reports on Vietnam, 1973–1975* (Presidio Press, CA, 1983)

HOEHN, J. P., *USAF et SVNAF au Sud Vietnam* (Collection Docavia, Editions Larivière, Paris, 2004)

HOI B. TRAN, *A Vietnamese Fighter Pilot in an American War* (Xlibris Corporation, Breinigsville, PA, 2011)

HOSMER, S. T.; KELLEN, K.; JENKINS, B. M., *The Fall of South Vietnam: Statements by Vietnamese Military and Civilian leaders* (Crane, Russack & Company, Inc, NY 1980)

HQ PACAF, 'Organisation, Mission and Growth of the Vietnamese Air Force 1949–1968', 1 January 1968, Project CHECO

HQ PACAF, 'VNAF Improvement and Modernisation Programme', 5 February 1970 Report, Project CHECO

HQ PACAF, 'VNAF Improvement and Modernisation Programme, July 1971 – December 1973', 1 January 1975 Report, Project CHECO.

KARNOW, S., *Vietnam – A History* (Penguin Books, Middlesex, 1984)

LANE, J. J., *Command and Control and Communication Structures in Southeast Asia* (Air University, AL, 1981)

'Last Flight from Saigon', *USAF Southeast Asia Monograph Series*, Volume IV, Monographs 6, Office of the US Air Forces History, Washington, DC 1977

LAVALLE, A. J. C., 'The Vietnamese Air Force, 1951–1975, An analysis of its role in combat and fourteen hours at Koh Tang', *USAF Southeast Asia Monograph Series*, Volume III, Monographs 4 and 5, Office of the US Air Forces History, Washington, DC 1975

LEEKER, Dr J. F., *The History of Air America; From Vietnamization to the end 1969–1975* (E-book, University of Texas, McDermott Library)

LE GRO, W. E., 'Vietnam from Ceasefire to Capitulation', *Indochina Monographs*, Centre of Military History, United States Army, US Government printing Office, Washington, DC, 1985

Lich Su Khong Quan Nhan Dan Viet Nam (1955–1977) (Nha Xuat Ban Quan Doi Nhan Dan, Hanoi 1993)

Lich Su Quan Chung Phong Khong, Tap 3 (1972–1977) (Nha Xuat Ban Quan Doi Nhan Dan, Hanoi 1994)

LIPSMAN, S.; Weiss, S., *The Vietnam Experience – The False Peace – 1972–1974* (Boston Publishing Company, Boston, 1985)

MESKO, J., *South Vietnamese Air Force* (Squadron Signal Publication, Carrolton, TX, 1987)

MIKESH, R. C., *Canberra at War 1964–1972* (Ian Allan Ltd, London 1980)

MIKESH, R. C., *Flying Dragons; the South Vietnamese Air Force* (Schiffer Publishing Ltd. Atglen, USA, 2005)

MUTZA, W., *A-1 Skyraider in Vietnam* (Schiffer Publishing Ltd, Atglen, PA, 2003)

NGO QUANG TRUONG, 'The Easter Offensive of 1972', *Indochina Monographs*, Centre of Military History, United States Army, US Government Printing office, Washington, DC, 1980

NGUYEN CAO KY, *Twenty years and Twenty Days* (Stein and Day Publishers, NY, 1976)

NGUYEN DUC PHUONG, *Chien Tranh Viet Nam, Toan Tap, Tu Tran Dau (Ap Bac – 1963) den Tran Cuoi (Sai Gon – 1975)* (Lang Van, Ontario, Canada, 2001)

PIKE, D., *PAVN: People's Army of Vietnam* (Presidio Press, CA, 1986)

RAUSA, R., *Skyraider, the Douglas A-1 'Flying Dump Truck'* (The Nautical & Aviation Publishing Company of America, Annapolis, MD, 1982)

ROBBINS, C., *Air America* (Avon Books, 1985)

SNEPP, F., *Decent Interval: The American Debacle in Vietnam and the Fall of Saigon* (Penguin Books Ltd, 1980)

TAMBINI, A. J., *F-5 Tigers over Vietnam* (Branden Publishing Company, 2000)

TODD, O., *Cruel April – The Fall of Saigon* (W. W. Norton and Company, NY, 1990)

TRAN VAN HOANG, *How South Vietnam Was Liberated* (The Gio Publsihers, Hanoi, 1992)

Van Tien Dung, *Dai Thang Mua Xuan. Nha Xuat Ban Quan Doi Nhan Dan* (Ha Noi, 1977)

'Victory in Vietnam; The official history of the Pople's Army of Vietnam, 1954–1975', *The Military History Institute of Vietnam*, translated from the Vietnamese by PRIBBENOW, M. L. (Kansas University Press, 2002)

Various issues of the following magazines: Air Combat, Air et Cosmos, Air Enthusiast, Air Force Magazine, Aircraft Illustrated, Air Pictorial, Aviation Week and Space Technology, Koku Fan, Le Fana de l'Aviation, Lich Su Quan Su, Life Magazine, Parameters, Quan Doi Nhan Dan Viet Nam, Newsweek, Paris Match, Vietnam Magazine.

INDEX

ADS (Air Defence Sector) 86, 152
Ai Nu 143
AIM-9B/E Sidewinder 86, 87, 166
Air America 69, 70, 107, 142, 153, 166, 196, 200, 202, 217
ALC (Air Logistic Command) 29
ALCC (Airlift Control Centre) 43
ALO (Air Liaison Officer) 77–79
AN/FPS-20 86, 96
An Khe 143
AN/ALE-20 83
AN/MSQ-77 43, 97
AN/TPB-1A 97
ANAN/TPS-6, 67, 86, 96
An Loc 31, 43, 49, 50, 90, 100, 170
Ap Bac 116
A Shau Valley 89, 122
Aulnat 17
Avord 17

Ba To 45
Banmethout 86, 96, 119, 135–137, 139, 146, 147, 150, 161
Bao Dai 15, 20
Bao Loc 81
Bay Hien 210
Ben Vanh 122
Bien Hoa 24, 62, 77, 87, 91, 97, 98, 100, 109, 110, 119, 124, 125, 128, 129, 154, 166, 170, 172, 173, 179–181, 199, 209, 219, 220
Binh Dinh 89, 118
Binh Long 71, 91
Binh Thuy 24, 35, 40, 52; 77, 81, 86, 88, 91, 98, 100, 115, 131, 147, 177, 179, 180, 198, 201, 209–212, 220
Binh Xuyen 21
Bird Air 142, 180
BOBS (Beacon-Only Bombing System) 6, 7, 97, 111, 118, 119, 122, 125, 126, 142, 152, 156, 187
Bo Duc 91
BLU-82 134, 163, 173, 174, 187
Bristol 170 178
Bui Huu 112
Buon Ho 137

CBU-24A/B 123
CBU-55 81, 134, 173
Ca Lu 85
Cai Cai 21
Cai Vuong 21
Cam Lo 89
Cam Ranh Bay 44, 96, 139, 148, 150, 152
Camp Holloway 142
Can Tho 114–116, 171, 177, 182, 209, 212
Cao Dai 21
Cao Van Li 215
Cao Van Vien 75
Chan Van Yen 143
Cheo Reo 143
China Airlines 70, 131
Chon Thanh 170
Chu Lai 96, 152, 155
Chu Pao Pass 143

CIA (Central Intelligence Agency) 69, 70, 107, 131, 142, 166, 180
Co Son 196, 201, 206, 211
Cu Chi 209
Cu Le Re 155
Cua Viet 80
Cung Thang An 44

DAO (Defence Attaché Office) 9, 69, 90, 104, 105, 107, 113, 114, 118, 131, 179, 187, 191, 195, 211
Da Lat 166
Da Nang 20, 24, 26, 35, 40, 44, 45, 52, 54, 55, 77, 86, 87, 89, 92, 97, 98, 101, 102, 109, 117, 119, 123, 124, 139, 149–155, 184, 220
Dai Viet 18
Dak Pek 102
Dak To 85, 143
Dan Cau Hai Bay 151
Dao Dinh Luyen 183
DASC (Direct Air Support Centre) 77, 86, 163
Darlac Plateau 119
Dien Bien Phu 17
Dinh Quan 174
Dinh Tuong 88
DMZ (Demilitarized Zone) 30
Do Huu Vi 15
Dong Ha 34, 85, 122
Duc Co 89
Duc Duc 101
Duc Hue 98
Duc Pho 101
Duc Phong 128
Dung Dinh Linh 102
Duong Quoc Lam 35
Duong Van Minh 177
Duyen Binh 118
Dynalectron 62

ECM (Electronic Countermeasure Equipment) 40, 85

Fai Foo Peninsula 123
Fort Rucker 49
Fort Wolters 49
Frederick C. Weyand 161

Gau Den 36
Gau Do Ha 169
Geneva Accords 17, 22
General Electric 62
Gi Plateau 118
Gia Nghia 45
Gia Vuc 120
Graham A. Martin 191

HALO (High Altitude, Low Opening – Parachute Drop) 43, 90, 100, 125
Ha Hau Sinh 46
Ha Thanh 45
Ha Van Hoa 44
Hai Van Pass 119, 150, 151, 154
Hainan Island 92
Hanoi 26, 31, 85, 95, 98, 117, 126, 159, 177, 184
HAWK (SAM) 86
Heinie Aderholt 216
Hieu Thanh Binh 35
Ho Chi Minh Trail 22, 34, 41, 159
Hoa Cong 125
Hoa Hao 21
Hoa Loi 125
Hoai Duc 127
Hoang Dieu 21
Honolulu Conference 37
Ho Vang Dang 35
Hong Nhu 81
Hue 28, 30, 85, 89, 96, 98, 117, 119, 139, 145, 148–151, 153, 159
Huynh Ba Tinh 168
Huynh Duy Anh 166

Huynh My Phuong   145
Huynh Thu Thoai   210

ICCS (International Commission for Control and Supervision)   72, 80, 85, 107

JGS (Joint General Staff)   75, 78, 90, 100, 139, 150, 191, 199, 203
Jones, David C.   131, 133

KA-77   54
KA-95   54
Ken Rice   186
Khanh Duong   139
Khanh Hoa   163
Khe Sanh   85, 89
Khiem Hanh   181
KhunVan Phat   205
Kontum   43, 88, 89, 117, 118, 135, 139
KS-92A   54

La Son   151
Lai Khe   129
Le Hung   194, 221
Le Thuan Loi 164
Le Van Hoac   15
Lam Van Phieu   111
Le Vang   35
Lechère   17
Lear Seigler   62
Le Van Thao   164
Le Xuan Lan   86, 152
Loc Ninh   85, 111, 112
Long Binh   172, 174
Long Khanh   127, 172
LORAN (Long Range Navigation)   153

Mac Huu Loc   163, 229
Marbod, Eric von   179
M'Drak Pass   138
Midway (Island)   32
Minh Long   120
Moc Hoa   116
MSQ-77   43, 97

Nakhon Phanom   71, 90
Nelson, James T.   61, 62
Nha Be   167, 168, 198
Nha Trang   16–20, 41, 44, 57, 58, 62, 63, 96, 99, 108, 126, 131, 134, 140, 143, 146–148, 163, 221, 225, 230
Nhon Co   45, 89
Nghia Dai   35
Ngo Dinh Diem   21, 23, 24
Ngo Hoang   166
Ngo Quang Truong   101, 154, 246
Ngo Xuan   47, 134
Nguyen Anh Tuan   122
Nguyen Ba Dam   44, 101
Nguyen Binh Tra   101
Nguyen Cao Ky   22, 24, 76, 198, 203, 213, 222
Nguyen Duc Khanh   45, 150, 223
Nguyen Gioang   155, 158
Nguyen Hong Tuyen   44
Nguyen Huu Canh   181
Nguyen Huu Tan   100, 227
Nguyen Khoa Nam   210
Nguyen Manh Dung   212
Nguyen Quang Tri   86
Nguyen Que Son   163
Nguyen Tan Minh   174
Nguyen Tan Ming   134
Nguyen Thanh Trung   167, 168, 184–187, 221, 244
Nguyen Tien Hung   139, 158
Nguyen Tien Xuong   143
Nguyen Van Chuan   153
Nguyen Van Hinh   15–19, 22

Nguyen Van Luom 167
Nguyen Van Thi 35, 42, 64, 225, 230
Nguyen Van Thieu 7, 31, 75
Nguyen Van Vuong 45
Nguyen Viet Xuong 44
Nixon, Richard 31, 32, 38, 84, 95, 159
Northrop Company 26, 34, 36, 58, 62, 63, 97, 108, 110, 132, 153, 189, 234
Nui Ba Den 127

Operation Babylift 177
Operation Frequent Wind 190, 191, 199, 200
Operation Commando Gopher 96

Pazmany PL-2 58, 234
Pham Huu Loc 179
Pham Ngoc Sang 140, 164, 170, 230
Pham Quang Khiem 8, 96, 181
Pham Vang 143
Pham Van Can 44–45, 101, 116
Pham Van Phu 146
Phan Rang 35, 40, 42, 44, 45, 58, 59, 74,81, 102, 108, 117–120, 136, 141, 143, 147, 164–172, 180, 181, 185, 187, 205, 215, 220, 225, 230, 231, 239, 240
Phan Thiet 81, 166, 187
Phan Vu Dien 112
Phu Bai 68, 96, 97, 119, 120, 220
Phu Cat 35, 44, 45, 69, 87, 114, 118, 119, 136, 141, 143, 147, 148, 155, 184, 220, 230, 231
Phu Quoc 161, 222
Phung Duc 131, 135–137
Phung Truong 189
Phuoc An 137–139
Phuoc Binh 127
Phuoc Long 78, 89–93, 112, 127–131, 163, 168, 244,
Ping Tung 92
Plei Djereng 89
Plei Me 102
Pleiku ("Plei Cu") 24, 27, 54, 74, 77, 86, 88, 89, 97, 102, 106–107, 115–119, 125, 135–144, 163, 164, 220, 230, 231, 236
Project Credible Chase 41, 64
Project Enhance 31, 34–35, 41, 42, 50, 56–61, 101, 189, 232, 233, 234, 244
Project Enhance Plus 34, 37, 40–42, 46, 50–52, 54–61, 189, 232, 233, 234
Project Peace Basket 92

Quang Duc 89, 115
Quang Nga i 45, 101, 120, 150
Quang Tien 101
Quang Tri 28, 66, 70, 85, 92, 122, 113, 114, 150
Que Son 102
Qui Nhon 147

RC-3 (Sikorsky) 234
RF-4C (McDonnell) 71, 122, 176
RF-5A (Northrop) 26, 29, 34, 35, 38, 54, 107, 110, 111, 122, 129, 141, 150, 156, 166, 216, 227, 241
RF-5E (Northrop) 108
Ruong Ruong, 92

S-2 65, 73, 85, 123, 163, 165, 173, 174, 178, 199
SA-7 50, 51, 66, 76, 80–83, 91, 92, 97, 98, 104, 106, 110, 112, 116, 121, 124, 131, 132, 138, 146, 188–191, 237, 242
Saigon 6–9, 20–24, 31, 32, 34, 38, 39, 44–48, 61, 78, 84, 86, 89–92, 95, 98–102, 107, 113, 117, 127–131, 140, 145–151, 154, 155, 159, 161–184, 189–196, 199–215
Salon de Provence 17
Se San 89
Singapore 104, 162, 181, 195, 220
Song Ba 144
Song Be 100, 112, 128, 168–169
Song Bo 133, 149
Son Cha (Island) 97
Soui Da 90
SR-71 (Lockheed) 122
Svay Rieng 99

TACAN (Tactical Air Navigation)   96, 139
TACC (Tactical Air Control Centre)   77, 86, 118, 132, 162
TACS (Tactical Air Control System)   76
T-54 (main battle tank)   66, 88, 118, 128, 129, 149, 173
T-55 (main battle tank)   210
Tam Ky   148–149
Tambini, Anthony J.,   62, 110, 153
Tan Son Nhut   6–8, 20, 24, 42–48, 51–55, 61, 70, 71, 77–79, 86, 89, 100, 112, 115, 116, 122, 129, 135, 147, 154,
       161, 162, 174, 178–180, 185–201, 206–213, 219–222, 229–231, 237–243
Tay Ninh   78, 90, 91, 98, 127, 128, 169, 181
Thai Ba De   45, 223
Thai Duong   36
Thailand, Bases
Korat RTAFB   71
Takhli RTAFB   71
      Udorn RTAFB   71
U Tapao RTAFB   71, 192, 194–197, 210, 211, 215–217, 222
Thien Loi   36
Tho Xuan   183
Thong Binh   21
Thu Bon   149
Thu Duc   6, 35, 172
Thuong Duc   101
Thua Thien   90
Tinh Bien   88
Ton Le Chon   79, 90, 100
Tran Dinh Giao   130, 136, 158
Tran The Vinh   30, 34
Tran Man Khoi   35
Tran Van Hien   187, 188, 229
Tran Van Huong   177
Tran Van Minh   32, 44, 131, 140, 152, 168, 177, 192–194, 223
Tri Tran   88
TRIM (Training Relation and Instruction Mission)   20, 108
Trung Nhia   88, 118
Tu De   185–186
Tu Thanh   111
Tuy Hoa 145–146

US bases in CONUS
Keesler AFB   59
Maxwell AFB   86
Randolph AFB   59
Shaw AFB   59
Sheppard AFB   59–61
Williams AFB   35, 50, 82
US bases in the Philippines
      Clark AFB   166, 184
USS Blue Ridge (LCC-19, command ship)   202
USS Coral Sea (CV-43, aircraft carrier)   199
USS Enterprise (CVN-65, aircraft carrier)   199, 200
USS Hancock (CV-19, aircraft carrier)   199, 200
USS Midway (CV-43, aircraft carrier)   198–204, 211, 216–218, 235, 237
USS Okinawa (LPH-3, helicopter carrier)   199, 200

Vampire (de Havilland)   17
Van Tieng Dung   183
Vinh   88, 183
Vinh Pho   154
Vo Van Si   166
Vo Xuan Lanh   141, 152, 226
Volpar   69, 72, 107, 166, 196, 217
Vu Phi Ho   35

Xuan Loc,   130–132

Young, Kendall   28
Youngblood, Roger   211

ZSU-23-4   178

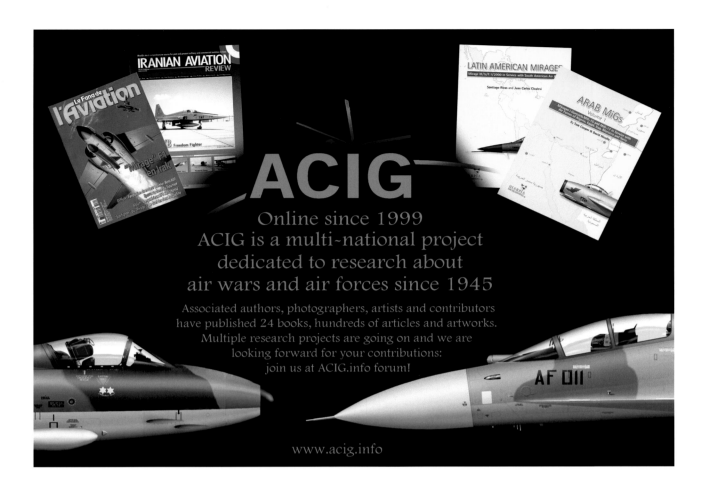

Dutch Aviation Society

P.O.Box 75545
1118 ZN Schiphol
The Netherlands
Fax: +31 (0) 84 - 738 3905
E-mail: info@scramble.nl
www.scramble.nl

The **Dutch Aviation Society** is a non-profit organisation run totally by volunteers. For those of you who have never heard of us, we will briefly explain our activities.

The main activities of the **Dutch Aviation Society** are:

– The publication of the monthly magazine **'Scramble'**.
– Maintaining the aviation website www.scramble.nl.
– To organise spotter conventions.
– Maintaining an aviation information database.
– Publishing from an aviation information database.

The production of the magazine, **Scramble**, is our core business. The magazine averages around 144 pages and more than 100 photographs from all over the world. It is published in the English language. It covers all aspects of civil and military aviation worldwide in many separate sections:

– Extensive civil airport and military airbase movements from the Netherlands;
– Civil and military movements from many European airports and airbases;
– Civil aviation news word wide (general news, jetliners, propliners, commuters, bizjets, bizprops, helicopters, extensive Soviet coverage, vintage aircraft, wrecks & relics);
– Dustpan & Brush (Stoffer & Blik), in depth reports about accidents and incidents worldwide;
– Military aviation news world wide (general news, procurement plans, unit changes, updates, orders of battle, vintage aircraft, wrecks & relics);
– Timetables and other information on shows, deployments, exchanges and other aviation events;
– Radio Activity (new frequencies, call signs);
– Show reports (full reports in all major aviation events);
– Fokker news (all about Fokker aircraft, including the Fairchild F-27 and FH-227);
– Full coverage of the Dutch Civil Aircraft Register;
– Trip reports from all over the world;
– A mix of large and small, civil and military articles.

If you would like a subscription, or more info on our magazine, please check out www.scramble.nl/subscribe.htm or send an E-mail to subscribe@scramble.nl

You are welcome to visit the official website. The website is in English and free for everybody. You can find more information about **Scramble** in the "Magazine" section of the Internet site. As **Scramble** Magazine covers both civil and military aviation, we have created sections for every interest. For a growing number of countries you will find an extensive Order of Battle on the site with unit-badges, database, base-overview, maps, pictures and links. For a considerable and growing number of countries you can access our database for your own reference. Scramble-subscribers even have more privileges and can get more information out of our databases. We hope you will enjoy our site. The pages are updated on a regular basis, so come back often to our website!

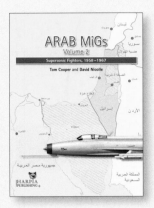

ARAB MiGs Volume 2, Supersonic Fighters, 1958–1967
Tom Cooper and David Nicolle
256 pages, 28x21cm, softcover
35.95 Euro   ISBN 978-0-9825539-6-1

Largely based on original, previously unavailable documentation from official archives, as well as interviews with participants and eyewitnesses, the second volume is an unprecedented study of the developments of six air forces during the late 1950s and 1960s. The authors present the main topic – the introduction of supersonic fighters such as the MiG-19 and MiG-21 – against the geopolitical backdrop. For the first time, the authors explain how and why specific air forces developed in the way they did, why they received specific aircraft types, and also why they suffered a defeat with such dramatic consequences during the June 1967 War with Israel. The volume is completed by an in-depth study of the application of early MiG-21 variants in combat, development of tactical combat methods in Syria during the mid-1960s, and finally an order of battle for the Egyptian Air Force as of 4 June 1967.

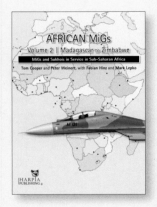

African MiGs Volume 2 | Madagascar–Zimbabwe, MiGs and Sukhois in Service in Sub-Saharan Africa
Tom Cooper and Peter Weinert, with Fabian Hinz and Mark Lepko
256 pages, 28x21cm, softcover
35.95 Euro   ISBN 978-0-9825539-8-5

Completing an in-depth history of the deployment and operations of MiG and Sukhoi fighters (as well as their Chinese-built Chengdu and Shenyang variants) in sub-Saharan Africa, Volume 2 covers 10 additional air forces, from Madagascar to Zimbabwe. This encyclopaedic account is so far the only one of its kind to provide detailed analysis of aerial conflicts including those waged between Ethiopia and Somalia, Tanzania and Uganda, and in Sudan. This book also provides a detailed, contemporary order of battle for 23 air forces described in both volumes, and a chapter about Antonov bomber operations in Sudan.

Latin American Mirages – Mirage III/5/F.1/2000 in Service with South American Air Arms
Santiago Rivas and Juan Carlos Cicalesi
256 pages, 28x21cm, softcover
35.95 Euro   ISBN 978-0-9825539-4-7

For more than four decades, different versions of the classic Dassault Mirage fighter have served as one of the most potent combat aircraft in Latin America. Equipping seven South American air forces in significant quantities, the delta-winged jets have seen action in various different wars and internal conflicts, and they continue to fulfil their mission with a number of operators. This book tells the story of all the members of the Mirage family in service with Latin American air arms, with individual histories of the air arms and their constituent units that have operated the Dassault-designed fighter, as well as its Israeli and South African derivatives. The volume provides a comprehensive collection of colour photographs and profile artworks that cover all the variants, plus maps, and tables that illustrate the individual stories of all the aircraft, their units and their various weapons.

THE AVIATION BOOKS OF A DIFFERENT KIND
UNIQUE TOPICS I IN-DEPTH RESEARCH I RARE PICTURES I HIGH PRINTING QUALITY